Do African Children Have an Equal Chance?

DIRECTIONS IN DEVELOPMENT
Poverty

Do African Children Have an Equal Chance?

A Human Opportunity Report for Sub-Saharan Africa

Andrew Dabalen, Ambar Narayan, Jaime Saavedra-Chanduvi, and Alejandro Hoyos Suarez, with Ana Abras and Sailesh Tiwari

WORLD BANK GROUP

ISBN (paper): 978-1-4648-0332-1
ISBN (electronic): 978-1-4648-0334-5
DOI: 10.1596/978-1-4648-0332-1

Cover photo: Schoolchildren in uniform walk long distances to and from school in rural Kwa Zulu Natal (South Africa). © Trevor Samson / The World Bank. Used with permission. Further permission required for reuse.
Cover design: Debra Naylor, Naylor Design

Library of Congress Cataloging-in-Publication Data has been requested.

Contents

Boxes

Figures

Maps

Tables

Foreword

Africa is now entering its twentieth year of unprecedented high economic growth. In our latest World Bank macroeconomic outlook for the continent, we estimate that average growth for Africa will rise from 4.7 percent in 2013 to 5.2 percent in 2014. Economies across the region are being turned around, political and social freedoms are expanding, and hopes are rising that Africa's families will endure significantly less poverty while enjoying the rewards of greater prosperity over the coming years.

As Africa rightly celebrates this performance, its citizens increasingly wonder whether these more hopeful economic times will translate into a better future for themselves and their families. We have long known that a person's chance of success in life is deeply influenced by early access to education, health services, safe water, and nutritious food. This, in turn, improves the likelihood that a child can live up to his or her human potential and pursue a rewarding life.

Therefore, we should never accept the view that circumstances alone should equal destiny and that chance factors such as gender, geography, and parental, social, and economic background automatically determine a child's access to opportunities.

Ensuring opportunity for all is front and center of the World Bank Group's twin goals of ending extreme poverty by 2030 and promoting shared prosperity. Achieving these goals across the generations will be difficult if people are systematically excluded from the development process. Shared prosperity will be possible only if countries nurture and develop people's individual potential by expanding opportunities right from early childhood.

This new report explores the landscape of opportunities for children in Sub-Saharan Africa (SSA) in the new millennium. It documents and analyzes how opportunities have changed over the past decade in 20 countries that are home to at least 7 in 10 African children. A major finding of this report is that positive, measurable progress has been achieved in improving opportunities for children in SSA.

We find that most African countries included in this study have made improvements. In most cases where progress has been rapid, the expansion has raised up children whose circumstances would have historically consigned them to lives of poverty and blunted opportunity.

One marker of this progress is the narrowing of gaps between better- and lower-performing African countries in securing children's access to health, education, and other key opportunities. We see this trend demonstrated in different ways—reductions over time in correlations between GDP and the human opportunity index (HOI) for key opportunities, average Francophone-Anglophone gaps in the HOI, and cross-country variation in HOIs. As a result, improving children's access to key services appears to be possible even in the poorest countries. It is important to note that policy initiatives have made a difference in these nations, bringing services to citizens and compensating for the inherent disadvantages they would otherwise have faced.

But more remains to be done. Almost a third of one-year-old children are still not vaccinated against measles, a quarter of all children of primary school age are not being educated, while another quarter lack access to clean drinking water. Moreover, many of Africa's children are also more likely to be born in poor rural households to parents with limited education, or may be orphaned. These factors, beyond their control, put them at a significant disadvantage compared to other children from better-off families.

Another issue that merits strong attention is early childhood opportunity. This study shows that almost all countries do better in access to services related to opportunities for older children (such as schooling) than for those in early childhood (such as immunization and nutrition at an early age). While countries that do well in opportunities for one age group also tend to do well for the other, exceptions remain, with significant gaps in access to basic services for children in various age groups.

Development research shows that better opportunities in early childhood enhance those later in life, such as attending and staying in school and learning achievements, and that early disadvantages are the hardest to reverse. Better health and nutrition in early childhood, therefore, is essential not just for its own sake but also for enhancing the impact of educational services later in the life of a child.

The findings in this report remind us of the significant progress Sub-Saharan African countries have made in the last several decades, as well as the challenges that remain in our historic mission to end extreme poverty and lay the foundations for shared prosperity. Identifying the range of solutions to expand opportunities for the next generation, especially in Africa where most of the world's poor reside, is *the* development goal of the World Bank Group.

Makhtar Diop
Vice President for Africa
The World Bank

Acknowledgments

This study was conducted as a joint effort between the Poverty Reduction & Equity (PRMPR) unit of the Poverty Reduction & Economic Management (PREM) Network and PREM in Africa Region (AFTPM). The report is authored by Andrew Dabalen and Ambar Narayan (Lead Economists, Poverty Global Practice); Jaime Saavedra-Chanduvi (former Director, PRMPR); and Alejandro Hoyos Suarez (Research Analyst, PRMPR), with significant contributions from Ana Abras (consultant) and Sailesh Tiwari (Senior Economist, Poverty Global Practice). The report benefited from overall guidance and advice at all stages from Marcelo Giugale (Sector Director, AFTPM). The authors acknowledge Bilal Habib, Noorulain Masood, and Shabana Mitra (consultants) for research assistance; Adam Broadfoot for coordination of the editing; Stephen Pazdan for production; and Maura Leary and Jeeyeon Seo for support on website and communications. The report also benefited from helpful suggestions from numerous individuals at workshops in and outside the World Bank, where early results were shared, and participants at the decision review meeting chaired by Makhtar Diop (Vice President, Africa Region of the World Bank). In particular, acknowledgments are due to Markus Goldstein, Luis-Felipe Lopez-Calva, and Ritva Reinikka for their extensive comments as peer reviewers; Claus Pram Astrup, Jose Cuesta Levia, Francisco Ferreira, Deon Filmer, M. Louise Fox, Jeni Klugman, Maureen Lewis, Jose Molinas Vega, John Newman, Josefina Posadas, and Joao Pedro Wagner de Azevedo from the World Bank; and external researchers Ricardo Paes de Barros, Javier Escobal, and James Foster. Finally, the authors are grateful for support and guidance from Ana Revenga (Senior Director, Poverty Global Practice) and Christina Malmberg-Calvo and Pablo Fajnzylber (Practice Managers, Poverty Global Practice).

This report is a part of the global work program on "Opportunities for All: Measuring and Analyzing Access to and Equality of Opportunity" that started in the Poverty Reduction & Equity unit in November 2010. The team is grateful to Luis-Felipe Lopez-Calva and Tara Vishwanath for their constructive comments at the concept stage of the work program. The work program, including this study, has been partly financed by a grant from the Nordic Trust Fund on "Equality of Opportunity and Economic and Social Rights."

About the Authors

Andrew Dabalen focuses on policy analysis and research in micro development issues, such as poverty and social impact analysis, inequality of opportunity, program evaluation, risk and vulnerability, labor markets, and conflict and welfare outcomes. He has published a number of scholarly articles and working papers on poverty measurement, conflict and welfare outcomes, and wage inequality. He has a PhD in agricultural and resource economics from the University of California, Berkeley, and an MS in international development from the University of California, Davis.

Ambar Narayan focuses on policy analysis and research on micro development issues, on topics such as inequality of opportunity, poverty reduction, policy and program evaluation, and the impact of economic shocks. In the past, he has worked in the South Asia region of the World Bank on poverty analysis, public expenditures, social safety nets, impact assessment of natural disasters, and lending operations in five countries. Among a number of studies for which he has been a lead author, some notable ones are the World Bank Poverty Assessment reports for Bangladesh and Sri Lanka, the edited volumes *Breaking Down Poverty in Bangladesh* and *Knowing When You Do Not Know...*, and "South Africa Economic Update, Focus on Inequality of Opportunity." He has also authored a number of scholarly articles and working papers, which reflect the eclectic mix of topics he has worked on over the years. He has a PhD in economics from Brown University and an MA in economics from Delhi University.

Jaime Saavedra-Chanduvi is currently Minister of Education of Peru. He spent 10 years at the World Bank, where the last positions he held were Director for Poverty Reduction and Equity and Acting Vice President of the PREM Network. At the Bank, Saavedra-Chanduvi oversaw operational and analytical work in poverty and inequality, labor markets, economics of education, and monitoring and evaluation systems. He has conducted extensive research and policy dialogue in these topics, co-authored many publications, and co-led the technical and institutional process toward the establishment of the World Bank Group goals of sustainably ending extreme poverty and promoting shared prosperity. Earlier, Saavedra-Chanduvi was Executive Director and Principal Researcher at Grupo de Análisis para el Desarollo, a nonpartisan think tank based in Lima, and a Principal Advisor to the Minister of Labor in Peru. He has been a consultant for institutions such as the World Bank, the Inter-American Development Bank (IDB), and the International Labour Organization, and served as President of the Executive Committee of the Network on Inequality and Poverty of the IADB, World Bank, and Latin American and Caribbean Economic Association (LACEA). He has a PhD in economics from Columbia University in New York.

Alejandro Hoyos Suarez has worked as a consultant for the World Bank and the Inter-American Development Bank. His research has focused on topics in labor economics and education, such as gender wage disparities, informality, and inequality of opportunities. Past works include various studies on gender wage gaps in Latin America, recently published in a book by the IDB, and a paper on the effects of social programs on informal labor markets in Colombia, among others. He is currently pursuing a PhD in economics at the University of Chicago and has an MA in economics from the Universidad de Los Andes.

Ana Abras conducts research on labor economics and macroeconomics. The main topics of interest are wage inequality and instability, information and labor contracts, and worker and job flows. She worked on several World Bank projects involving research and applied policy issues, including the book *Sewing Success* and studies on inequality of opportunity for African and Eastern European countries. She recently joined the University of São Paulo, continuing her work on labor issues in developing countries. She has a PhD in economics from the University of Maryland College Park and an MA in economics from the University of São Paulo.

Sailesh Tiwari is a senior economist in the Middle East and North Africa region of the World Bank. His current work focuses on diagnostic and policy work at the nexus between growth, poverty, and inequality, particularly inequality of opportunity. During his time at the Bank, he has led and participated in several analytical products on areas of food security, child nutrition, climate change, and vulnerability in several parts of the world. He has a PhD and an MA, both in economics, from Brown University and an MSc in finance and economics from the London School of Economics and Political Science.

Abbreviations

ACRWC   African Charter on the Rights and Welfare of the Child
AU   African Union
BIA   Benefit Impact Analysis
CRC   Convention on the Rights of the Child
CV   coefficient of variation
CWIQ   Core Welfare Indicator Questionnaire
DHS   Demographic and Health Surveys
D-Index dissimilarity index
GDP   gross domestic product
GHOI   Geometric HOI
HOI   Human Opportunity Index
IHDI   Inequality-adjusted Human Development Index
LAC   Latin America and the Caribbean
LSMS   Living Standard Measurement Surveys
MDGs   Millennium Development Goals
Opp-BIA Opportunity Benefit Impact Analysis
PASEC   Programme for the Analysis of Education Systems
PPP   purchasing power parity
SACMEQ   Southern and Eastern Africa Consortium for Monitoring
         Educational Quality
SSA   Sub-Saharan Africa

Overview

If the 1980s is remembered as the "lost decade" in Africa, the current consensus about the continent could not be more starkly different. Increasingly, a growing literature has settled on a narrative of an emerging continent.[1] This is hardly surprising. In the last two decades, Africa has been growing, so that for the first time in nearly two decades, the share of the population in sub-Saharan Africa (SSA) living in extreme poverty fell from 57 percent in 1990 to 48 percent in 2008, although the number of poor people in the region still increased from 290 million to 386 million.[2] Even more impressive progress has been achieved in human development, especially in health and education. As we approach 2015, the finish line agreed to by the international community to achieve specific development targets—dubbed the Millennium Development Goals (MDGs)—many Africans would no doubt be wondering whether these goals have been achieved, and if these hopeful signs mean better futures for them. In particular, they would want to know whether opportunities for their children are improving or not?

This study explores the changing opportunities for children in Africa. While the definition of "opportunities" can be subjective and depend on the societal context, this report focuses on efforts to build future human capital, directly (through education and health investments) and indirectly (through complementary infrastructure such as safe water, adequate sanitation, electricity, and so on). It follows the practice of earlier studies conducted for the Latin America and the Caribbean (LAC) region (Barros et al. 2009, 2012) where "opportunities" are basic goods and services that constitute investments in children. Although several opportunities are relevant at different stages of an individual's life, our focus on children's access to education, health services, safe water, and adequate nutrition is due to the well-known fact that an individual's chance of success in life is deeply influenced by access to these goods and services early in life. Children's access to these basic services improves the likelihood of a child being able to maximize his/her human potential and pursue a life of dignity. The guiding principle is one of equality of opportunity (see, for example, Roemer 1998), which states that the "circumstances" a person is born into, such as gender, location, and parental, social, and economic background, should not determine access to opportunities, so that the individual's outcomes and achievements in life depend only on her effort and innate ability. The World Bank's *World Development Report 2006: Equity and Development*, argues that inequality of opportunity, both within and among nations, results in wasted human potential and weakens prospects for overall prosperity. Selecting a minimalist notion of basic opportunities also allows most societies to agree on equality of opportunities being a worthy goal to aspire to, and this fact may have been a key factor in guiding international agreements such as the MDGs.

However, in many African countries these minimal goals remain distant—a person's circumstances still matter a great deal in determining her access to basic goods and services. We still find almost a third of one-year-old children without measles vaccination, a fourth of children of primary school age not attending school, and a fourth not able to access any form of safe water for consumption. Underlying the regional trends are vast differences between countries, and between socioeconomic groups within countries. For example, Ghana, Mali, and Zambia were among the SSA countries that made substantial progress in school attendance of children in the 6- to 11-year age group between the late-1990s and mid-2000s. However, both the level and rate of progress vary widely across countries. Also, in all three countries, the gap between children in the richest and poorest wealth quintiles (20 percent) is substantial and has narrowed only slightly over time in two of the three countries. To cite another example, in 2007 a one-year-old child in the richest 20 percent of the population (quintile) in Namibia was almost 20 percentage points more likely to be fully immunized than a child in the poorest 20 percent. Uneven progress in human development over time, across countries and between different groups within countries is a common feature in SSA.

To track the twin desires of making progress toward the ideal of universal access to opportunities while ensuring that available opportunities are distributed according to a principle of equality of opportunities, we use the Human Opportunity Index (HOI), which was created in 2008 by researchers in and outside the World Bank (see Barros et al. 2009). The HOI is simple, practical, intuitive, and built on a sound economic foundation. The measure fundamentally looks at whether the playing field for individuals is level rather than the equality of outcome for those individuals. The HOI synthesizes in a single indicator how *close a society is to universal coverage* for a given opportunity, along with *how equitably coverage of that opportunity is distributed* among groups with different circumstances. The HOI may be thought of as an inequality-sensitive coverage rate, which "penalizes" the extent to which different circumstance groups have different coverage rates. The HOI improves when inequality decreases with a fixed number of opportunities in a society, or when the number of opportunities increases and inequality stays constant.

We use recent data from Demographic and Health Surveys (DHS) from 20 SSA countries that represent more than 70 percent of the region's population: Cameroon, the Democratic Republic of Congo, Ethiopia, Ghana, Kenya, Liberia, Madagascar, Malawi, Mali, Mozambique, Namibia, Niger, Nigeria, Rwanda,

Senegal, Sierra Leone, Tanzania, Uganda, Zambia, and Zimbabwe. The study covers the roughly eight-year period between the late 1990s (circa 1998) and the mid- to late 2000s (circa 2008), with the exact years for each country depending on the timing of the DHS surveys. For 17 of these countries, comparison between the two periods is possible[3]; for the remaining 3, the results for only the latest period are reported.

Which Opportunities and Circumstances?

The *opportunities* included in this study are restricted to the information available in the DHS and are classified as education, basic infrastructure, and health. Unlike a country-specific analysis where a more thorough and contextual treatment of opportunities could be explored, a multicountry analysis demands a consistent list and definition of opportunities across countries. For education, we use *school attendance* since it is a decent proxy for access to education, and measure it for *children of age 6–11 years* and *12–15 years* separately. Achievement indicators are a proxy for both school quality and a child's ability to use her education to attain a basic level of learning. Lacking any information on direct measures of achievement, we use indicators for *starting primary school on time* (among children of age 6–7 years) and *finishing primary school* (among 12- to 15-year-olds), which, in part, reflect the quality of the education system.

For basic infrastructure facilities, the opportunities selected are access to a *safe source of drinking water*, appropriate *sanitation* facilities, and *electricity* for children between 0 and 16 years old. Water and sanitation are primary drivers of public health. Improvements in access to safe water and sanitation have been shown to reduce incidence of diarrhea among children and its serious long-term consequences such as malnutrition, pneumonia, and physical or mental stunting. Access to electricity is an important contributor to quality of life and increases productivity, as it facilitates studying, improves access to information, and reduces the time spent on physical chores. For health, we select two opportunities: *full immunization* among children of age one year, and *not being stunted* for children of age three years and under. The first is an indicator of the opportunity of being protected against deadly but preventable diseases. The second is an indicator of being adequately nourished—a key measure of health status in childhood, with implications for human potential and lifelong earnings.

Circumstances are characteristics that a child is born with, such as gender, location, or socioeconomic attributes of parents. In order to *satisfy the principle of equality of opportunity* in a society, circumstances should not be correlated with access to a basic good or service. For the purposes of this study, a set of circumstances common across all countries is selected to allow for cross-country comparisons. The choice is guided by the principle that these characteristics are accepted by most societies as those that *should not* matter for a child's access to basic goods and services (but *may in fact* matter). The list of circumstances is also informed by the choices made for previous work on the HOI in the LAC region by Barros et al. (2009, 2012), albeit with some changes reflecting differences in the regional contexts of Africa and Latin America and the nature of data available for each region.

The selected circumstances can be categorized into five main groups: *characteristics of the child, household composition, location, characteristics of the household head* (or mother), and *socioeconomic status* of the household. We keep these categories the same for all opportunities when analyzing the links between circumstances and opportunities. However, within each category there are some differences in the definitions of circumstances used for education and infrastructure with those used for health opportunities.[4] These differences arise due to data availability and the relevance of a particular circumstance for an opportunity.

What Is the State of Opportunities for Children in the Late 2000s?

The most recent year for which data are available (circa 2008) offers a mixed picture for the 20 SSA countries included in the study. Among education opportunities, school attendance in most countries is much higher—and with lower inequality of opportunity—than indicators of achievement like primary completion and on time start of primary school. The cross-country average HOI for school attendance for children of age 6–11 and age 12–15 is 63 and 72, respectively, compared to 27 for starting primary school on time and for finishing sixth grade. Even as school attendance remains a challenge in some countries—the HOI for attendance among 6- to 11-year-olds is below 30 in Liberia and Niger, compared to more than 80 in Zimbabwe, Kenya, Namibia, Malawi, Ghana, and Uganda—late entry into and noncompletion of primary school are pervasive challenges in all countries. Even in Malawi, the country with the highest HOI for timely start to primary school, 62 percent of 6- to 7-year-old children have started school on time and the "penalty" due to inequality results in an HOI of only 56. And the country with the highest HOI for completion of primary school among 12- to 15-year-olds (Zimbabwe) has an HOI of only 78.

The low and variable HOIs in starting primary school on time and finishing primary school suggest that quality of schooling, which these indicators reflect to a limited extent, is an important area of concern in SSA countries. Student achievement scores (from the SACMEQ-III project) in eight of the countries included in the study support this concern. The percentage of sixth graders who have basic skills in reading and mathematics varies widely across countries—ranging from 56 percent in Zambia to 97 percent in Tanzania for reading, and from 33 percent in Zambia to 89 percent in Kenya for numeracy. Large gaps in achievement are also seen between groups within countries—urban-rural gaps in Malawi, Uganda, and Zimbabwe in particular; and gaps between children of different socioeconomic status in Mozambique, Namibia, Zambia, and Zimbabwe.

Depending on the standard used to define "adequacy," access to safe water, sanitation, and electricity in SSA countries ranges from uneven to poor. Access to electricity is extremely low across the board and inequality is high—the HOI is below 10 for 14 out of 20 countries. The HOIs for access to safe water and sanitation are very low as well, when the more demanding standards for adequacy—piped water and flush toilet—are used. Using more liberal standards for water and sanitation—more appropriate for the level of income of SSA countries—the picture gets significantly better but remains highly uneven across countries. Safe water by these standards (piped-, well-, or rainwater) is more widely available and with lower inequality of opportunity than adequate sanitation (flush or pit toilet).

For both water and sanitation, inequality of opportunity (gap between HOI and coverage) is lower when the less demanding standards are used. In other words, as an opportunity is defined by a higher standard, the association between circumstances and the opportunity increases, which is quite intuitive. The two different sets of standards for water and sanitation also yield very different rankings of the countries by an HOI, suggesting that the capacity level of each country to provide different types of facilities varies widely, even within the same class of basic infrastructure.

Opportunities in health, as measured by full immunization and not being chronically malnourished (not being stunted), are well below universal in most countries, as illustrated by average HOI scores of 53 (full immunization) and 59 (not being stunted). Inequality of opportunity is higher for immunization than for nutrition in most countries. To put this in context, however, these two indicators provide a highly limited view of health opportunities among children. An HOI for immunization varies more than that for nutrition, and there is almost no correlation between the two opportunities. Niger, Nigeria, and Ethiopia have an HOI of lower than 27 for immunization, in contrast to an HOI of more than 75 for the top three (Ghana, Malawi, and Rwanda). Low correlation between the two HOIs suggests that the factors influencing a country's performance in immunization are quite different from those influencing nutrition. The former is more closely related to quality of child health services provided by the government, whereas the latter is a result of myriad and complex factors such as dietary practices.

For a few countries, an HOI for one or both health opportunities is so low as to merit special concern. Nigeria, Ethiopia, Niger, and the Democratic Republic of Congo have an HOI below 30 for full immunization; Niger is also the only country with an HOI of below 50 for not being stunted. In immunization, Nigeria, Liberia, Madagascar, and Mozambique are characterized by large gaps associated with circumstances (that is, they have particularly high penalties for inequality of opportunity). While inequality of opportunity tends to be low for nutrition, Tanzania, Uganda, and the Democratic Republic of Congo have higher penalties compared to other countries.

To compare countries using a combined index, we use a definition of opportunity that yields "composite HOIs," reflecting the extent to which children of a particular age group are covered by an age-relevant *bundle*. For children of 0–1 year, the opportunity consists of access to safe water, adequate sanitation, full immunization, and not being stunted; for children of 6–11 years, it consists of water, sanitation, and school attendance. One composite HOI is generated for each age group in every country. The composite HOIs reflect the idea that none

Figure O.1 Composite HOI and Coverage for Access to Basic Opportunities

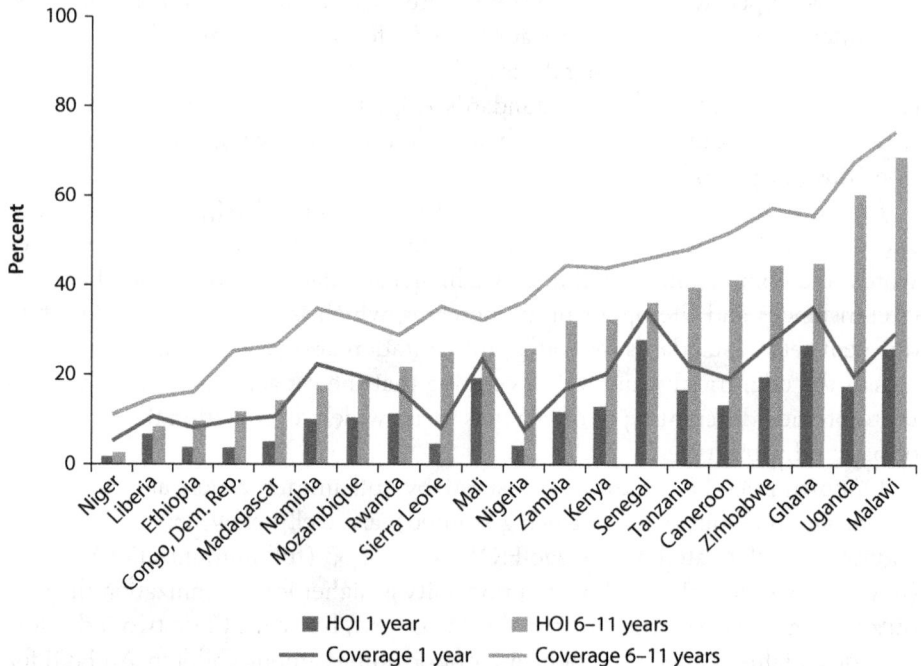

Source: Authors' calculations using Demographic and Health Surveys data, various years.
Note: (1) *Children 1 year*: opportunities included are access to water (piped-, well-, or rainwater), access to sanitation (pit or flush toilet), full immunization, and no stunting. (2) *Children 6–11 years*: opportunities included are school attendance, access to water (same as above), and access to sanitation (same as above). (3) A child has access to a bundle of opportunities assuming coverage by all the opportunities defined above, by age group. (4) Countries are sorted in increasing order by the HOI for 6–11 years. HOI = Human Opportunity Index.

of the basic goods and services is a substitute for another, and the absence of any one of them is an inadequacy in human opportunities that society must care about. Figure O.1 shows the two composite HOIs and corresponding coverage rates for all 20 countries (circa 2008).

All countries do better in an HOI for the older children than that for younger children. High correlation between the two measures indicates that countries that do relatively well in terms of access to opportunities for young children tend to do so for older children as well, with some exceptions. Ghana, Malawi, Zimbabwe, and Uganda, all of which are ranked in the top six by either HOI measure, are the relative success stories. Niger, the Democratic Republic of Congo, Ethiopia, and Madagascar are ranked among the bottom six by either HOI. Mali and Senegal rank much better by an HOI for younger children than that for older children, and the converse is true for Nigeria.

Inequality of opportunity within countries is higher, on average, for the composite bundle of younger children than that of the older children. Niger, the Democratic Republic of Congo, and Namibia have the highest inequality of opportunity for the composite bundles relative to what would be expected given their coverage rates. Conversely, Uganda and Mali have the lowest inequality of opportunity given their coverage rates for the younger and older children, respectively. Among single opportunities, inequality of opportunity is high for access to electricity and sanitation and for finishing primary school; and low for not being stunted, immunization, and school attendance. The countries with significantly higher than expected inequality of opportunity include Nigeria for school attendance and full immunization, and the Democratic Republic of Congo for starting primary school on time and access to safe water.

Four implications of these findings on the current state of opportunities in 20 SSA countries are important to highlight. *First*, if the concerns embedded in the HOI are consistent with the implicit social welfare function of policy makers, improving welfare would require a combination of expanding coverage and enhancing equity in coverage. An explicit focus on equity, along with coverage, is likely to yield the best results for opportunities with relatively high inequality in most countries: access to electricity and sanitation and finishing primary school. *Second*, lack of access to basic opportunities in infrastructure and health is a source of serious concern in most SSA countries. Safe water, adequate sanitation, and vaccination are perhaps the most important predictors of a child's health status and even school attendance and performance. *Third*, and related to the previous point, improving opportunities early in a child's life should be a high priority for most countries. Opportunities for children younger than one year are invariably worse than for older children. *Fourth*, as education opportunities among children in SSA countries improve, policy makers are likely to focus more and more on the quality of learning imparted in schools. The variation in SACMEQ-III test scores of sixth graders across eight countries, and among children with different circumstances within countries, hints at significant inequality of opportunity in learning.

How Have Opportunities Changed over the Decade?

How have HOIs evolved for each country and every opportunity considered so far, over the roughly 10-year period between the late-1990s and late-2000s? The evidence presented points to reasons for both optimism and caution. In the short period from the late 1990s (circa 1998) to the mid- to late-2000s (circa 2008), one can observe statistically significant increases in an HOI measured as annual average increase in several indicators of access to services and goods.

Trends in a composite HOI indicate how much progress countries have made in providing an age-relevant bundle of opportunities to children of certain age groups (figure O.2). The progress tends to be larger and more consistent across countries for the older children compared to the younger children. All countries other than Namibia show statistically significant improvement in a composite HOI for children of age 6–11 years. In the case of children of age 1, the composite HOI has increased for only 10 out of 16 countries and actually declines for 1 country (Zambia). Uganda, Cameroon, and Malawi make up the top three countries in improvements in the composite HOI for both age groups, with an annual average increase of nearly one percentage point for 1-year-olds and two or more

Figure O.2 Progress in Access to Bundle of Opportunities between circa 1998 and circa 2008

Average annual change in composite HOI for each age group[a]

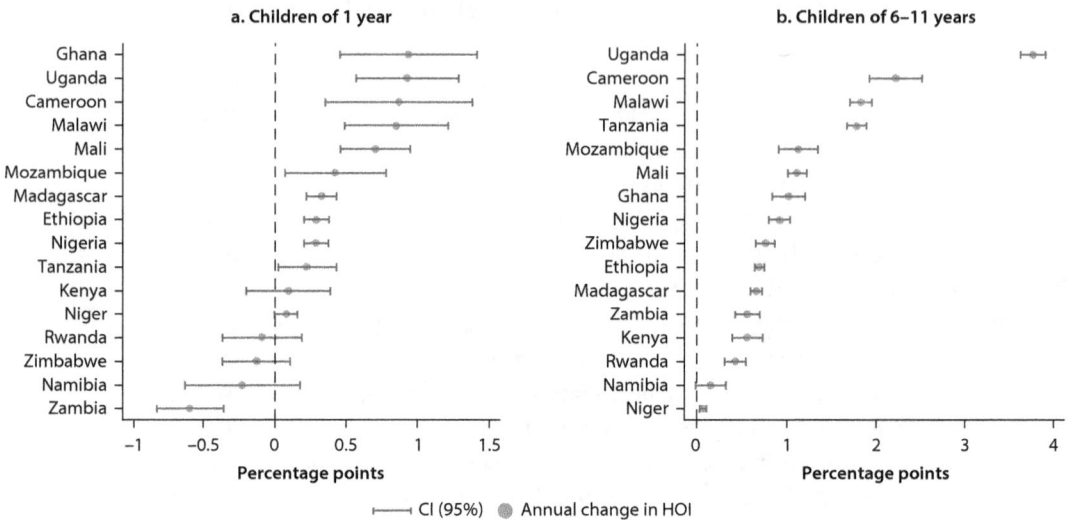

a. Children of 1 year

b. Children of 6–11 years

CI (95%)   ● Annual change in HOI

Source: Authors' calculations using Demographic and Health Surveys data, various years.

Note: (1) CI (95%) refers to 95% confidence intervals of the point estimate of the annual change. (2) Children 1 year: opportunities included are access to *water* (piped-, well-, or rainwater), access to *sanitation* (pit or flush toilet), full immunization, and no stunting. (3) Children 6–11 years: opportunities included are school *attendance*, access to *water* (same as above), and access to *sanitation* (same as above). (4) A child has access to bundle of opportunities if meeting the standard (of coverage) for *all the* opportunities. (5) The sample includes only 16 countries for which information on all the opportunities used here is available. HOI = Human Opportunity Index.

a. Annual change in any HOI is computed as the average annual change in the period between two survey years.

percentage points for 6- to 11-year-olds. Uganda stands out for achieving rapid progress in the composite HOI for 6- to 11-year-olds in particular, far outpacing any other country in this age group.

Another indicator of overall progress is a count of the number of opportunities for which a country has experienced a statistically significant increase in an HOI (figure O.3). Three countries—Ethiopia, Madagascar, and Malawi—lead by this measure, showing improvements in at least eight out of the total of nine opportunities. At the other end of the spectrum are Nigeria and Ghana with improvements in only five out of nine opportunities.

Looking at opportunities one at a time provides a more detailed view of trends. Thirteen countries show a statistically significant annual average increase in HOIs for school attendance among children of age 12–15, and all 16 countries show a statistically significant annual average increase in the same HOIs among children of age 6–11 years. Eight countries show statistically significant improvements in any HOI for *all four* education opportunities: Ethiopia, Madagascar, Malawi, Mali, Namibia, Rwanda, Uganda, and Zambia.

Improvements in education achievement appear to have lagged behind that in attendance: progress has been uneven across countries in the HOIs for primary school completion among 12- to 15-year-olds and timely entry into school, and even more anemic in reading and mathematics test scores of sixth graders between 2000 and 2007 (SACMEQ-III data for seven countries). The two

Figure O.3 Number of Opportunities with Statistically Significant Increase in an HOI

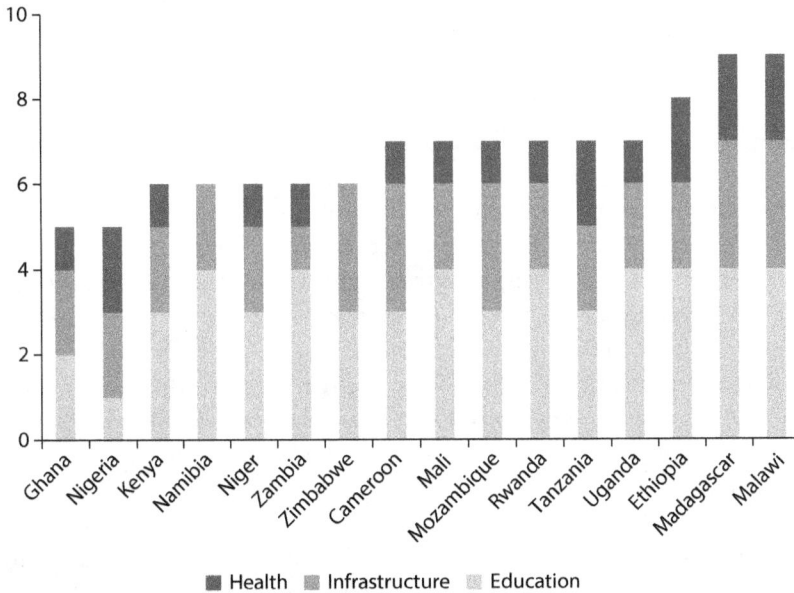

■ Health   ▓ Infrastructure   ▒ Education

Source: Authors' calculations using Demographic and Health Surveys data, various years.
Note: (1) Total no. of opportunities: four in education, three in infrastructure, and two in health. (2) Does not take into account the *size* of the improvement. HOI = Human Opportunity Index.

Figure O.4 Change in Student (Sixth Grade) Test Scores in Select SSA Countries

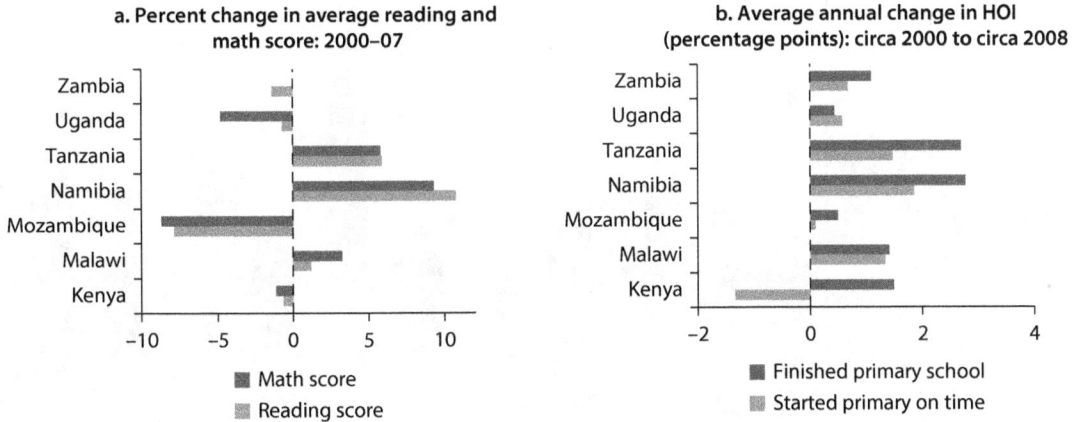

a. Percent change in average reading and math score: 2000–07

■ Math score
▒ Reading score

b. Average annual change in HOI (percentage points): circa 2000 to circa 2008

■ Finished primary school
▒ Started primary on time

Source: Makuwa 2010; and authors' calculations using Demographic and Health Surveys data, various years.
Note: HOI = Human Opportunity Index; SSA = Sub-Saharan Africa.

countries with significant progress in average test scores (Tanzania and Namibia) also had the largest improvement in HOIs for completion of and timely start to primary school (see figure O.4), suggesting that rising opportunities in completing and timely start to primary school have occurred with improved learning among students in these countries.

Trends in access to safe water, adequate sanitation, and electricity are more mixed than those for education. Using the more liberal standards, 11 and 12 out of 17 countries experienced a statistically significant increase in the HOI for water and sanitation, respectively. Even though no country experienced a fall in the HOI for *both* water and sanitation, only six (Cameroon, Madagascar, Malawi, Mozambique, Uganda, and Zimbabwe) showed improvements in both—illustrating the low correlation between improvements in water and sanitation. In access to electricity, the story is that of stagnation: only 3 out of 17 countries show an average annual increase in the HOI of more than 0.5 percentage point and none exceeds an annual increase of 2 percentage points.

Twelve and seven (out of 16) countries show a statistically significant increase in the HOI for immunization and not being stunted, respectively. Mozambique and Nigeria show the highest rate of improvement in the HOI for immunization and nutrition, respectively, by a large margin relative to other countries. Zambia and Zimbabwe experienced significant decreases in the HOI for immunization and Niger and Namibia did so in the HOI for nutrition.

How have gaps *between countries* in opportunities for children evolved between the late-1990s and late-2000s? *First*, as figure O.5 shows, coefficient of variation (CV)—which measures the extent of variability relative to the mean—has declined over time for all the HOIs, including those for individual

Figure O.5 Cross-Country Variation (CV) of HOIs in Each Period
Measured by the coefficient of variation

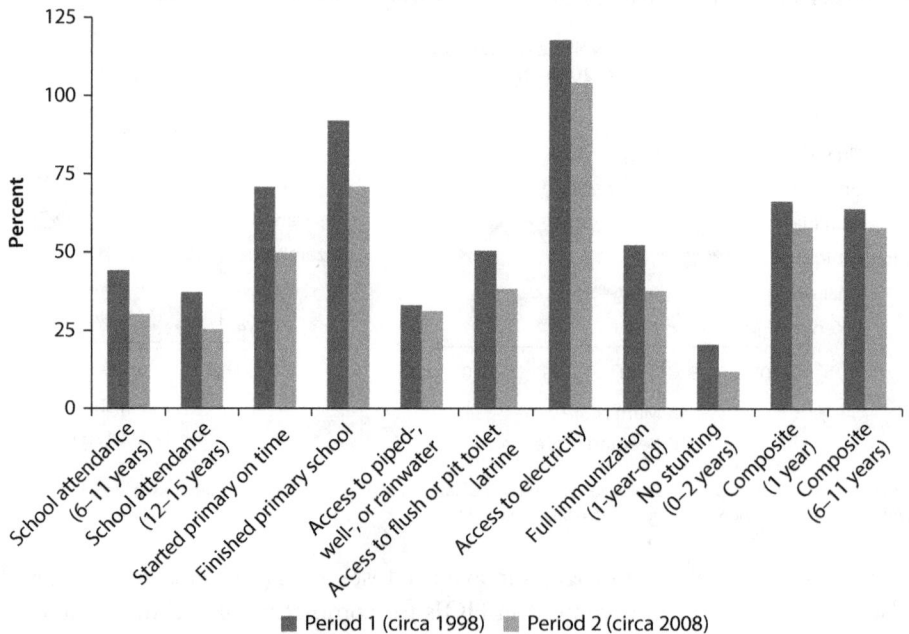

■ Period 1 (circa 1998)   ■ Period 2 (circa 2008)

Source: Authors' calculations using Demographic and Health Surveys data, various years.
Note: CVs are calculated using the sample of countries for which an HOI is available for *both* years (17 for water, sanitation, and electricity, 16 for others). HOI = Human Opportunity Index.

Do African Children Have an Equal Chance? • http://dx.doi.org/10.1596/978-1-4648-0332-1

and composite opportunities, with the extent of decline being quite similar (as a proportion of the initial CV) across all opportunities. *Second*, there are significant differences in the extent of cross-country variation across opportunities in both periods. Access to electricity, finishing primary school, and starting primary school on time have the highest CV in both periods, whereas school attendance and health opportunities have the lowest. The decline in cross-country variation over time for all HOIs indicates some degree of convergence in access to opportunities between countries. For six out of nine opportunities, the cross-country *standard deviation* actually fell between the two periods, indicating that differences between countries have indeed narrowed.

What Explains Changes in Opportunities over Time?

What does the change in an HOI for an opportunity in a country tell us about the underlying changes in coverage, inequality, and child characteristics, which may in turn be linked to policy initiatives? Scale effect (increase in access proportionally for all circumstance groups) has contributed the most toward the improvements in the HOIs for most opportunities and countries. Equalization effect (reallocation of opportunities among groups, holding the overall coverage constant) has been less important but significant when progress in the HOI has been substantial. In education, for example, equalization effect is particularly significant in three countries (Ethiopia, Mali, and Madagascar) that have shown improvements in all education opportunities. In water and sanitation, equalization effect is more important for the top five HOI-improving countries. For health opportunities, even as scale effect predominates, equalization has contributed substantially in countries with the highest rate of improvement in HOI—Mozambique for immunization and Nigeria for nutrition. That said, equalization effect tends to be weaker for nutrition than immunization. And equalization and composition effects are much more important for access to electricity than other opportunities—equalization is the dominant force in 5 of the top 10 improvers in the HOI for access to electricity.

SSA countries that have made rapid progress toward universalization of basic opportunities for children have achieved this through expansion of services to all groups and, to a lesser extent, by improving equity in access to services among groups. The dominance of scale effect—seen in almost every instance where there is a substantial improvement in an HOI—suggests that progress almost always comes with expansion of services to all groups in the population. In some cases, notably for Mali (in education), Ethiopia (education and sanitation), Mozambique (water and immunization), Nigeria (nutrition), and Senegal (electricity), the expansion has favored underserved groups. The trend toward higher equity, wherever it has occurred, probably reflects policy successes and/ or changes in behaviors and attitudes in society. In contrast to scale and equalization effects that are likely to reflect policy initiatives in service delivery, composition effects—reflecting demographic or socioeconomic shifts that are less likely to be influenced by public policies in the short run—play a negligible role in explaining changes in an HOI. This carries a positive implication—circumstances are not destiny, and improvement in children's opportunities can occur in spite of persistent differences in circumstances of children at birth.

If scale effects indicate the likely effects of broad-based policy initiatives to expand access, the lack of scale effects for access to electricity in most countries points to a serious lack of policy focus in that sector. Given the extremely low HOI of electricity in the late-1990s, tangible gains would have required improving coverage across all groups, which clearly did not occur in the period up to the late-2000s. Consequently during this period, the HOI for electricity improved to some extent in only two countries—Ghana and Senegal—due to a combination of scale and equalization effects.

How Do Circumstances Matter for Inequality?

Given that access to most basic services in SSA countries is not universal and equitable, it is important to understand better how different socioeconomic characteristics influence a child's likelihood of access to a particular opportunity. In other words, what is the "contribution" of a specific circumstance (or a group of related circumstances) to inequality of opportunities (the dissimilarity or D-Index), among the key set of circumstances included in the analysis? This question is addressed by decomposing the D-Index according to the Shapley value concept, which allows us to quantify the role of each circumstance in explaining inequality, as its marginal contribution to the inequality of opportunity index or D-Index.

Figure O.6 shows the results of these decompositions for every opportunity, in terms of the average contribution of each group of circumstances to the D-Index, where the average is calculated for the 10 countries that have the highest D-Index for a particular opportunity. Focusing on the top 10 countries by inequality makes sense, since the contribution of a circumstance to inequality does not mean much if a country has low inequality in the opportunity in the first place.

In interpreting figure O.6, it is important to consider the differences in inequality not just across countries but also across opportunities. As figure O.7 shows, average inequality (D-Index) is much higher for some opportunities than others—for instance, access to electricity compared to not being stunted—with other opportunities somewhere in between. Comparisons across opportunities can be misleading without taking into account the total inequality of a particular opportunity. For example, a circumstance that accounts for a significant share of inequality in nutrition can be much less "unequalizing" than one that contributes a smaller share of the inequality in access to electricity, for which the D-Index tends to be much higher.

Figure O.6 shows that a child's socioeconomic background is crucial in explaining her/his chances of accessing basic services and goods. Wealth and education of the head of the household that the child belongs to (or mother's education in the case of health opportunities) have the largest contributions to inequality across most countries and opportunities, followed by the

Figure O.6 Contribution of Each Circumstance to Inequality of Opportunity

Averages for high inequality countries (top 10 by D-Index)

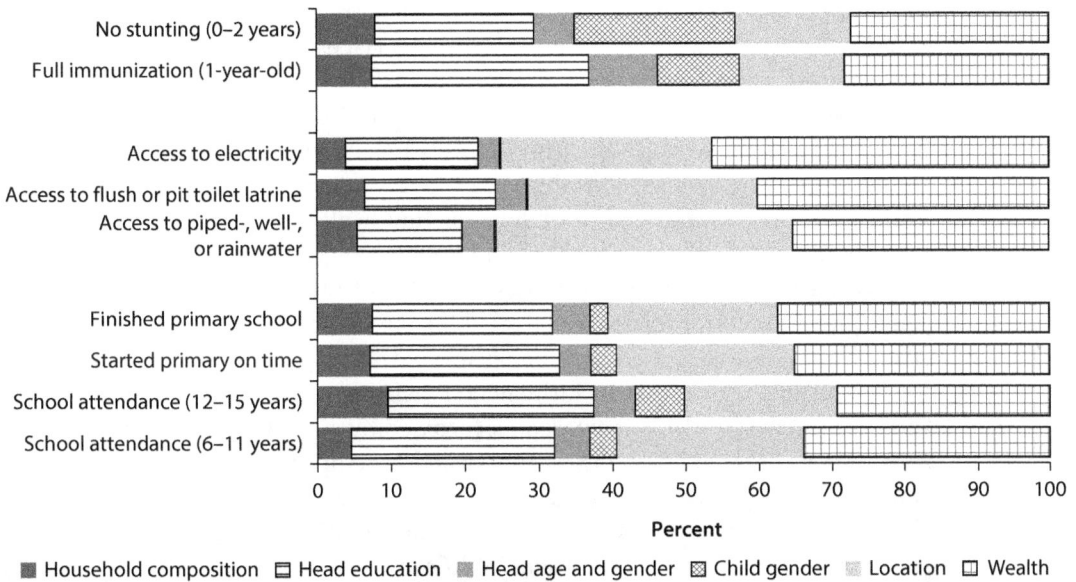

Source: Authors' calculations using Demographic and Health Surveys data, various years.
Note: (1) High inequality for each opportunity refers to the top 10 countries by D-Index for that opportunity. (2) The average contribution of a circumstance to inequality of opportunity for a group of countries is calculated as the unweighted or simple average (across all countries) of Shapley decompositions of the D-Index for that opportunity. (3) The list of circumstances is slightly different for immunization and not being stunted from that for the other opportunities. D-Index = dissimilarity index.

Figure O.7 Inequality and Coverage by Opportunity

Averages for all countries and high inequality countries

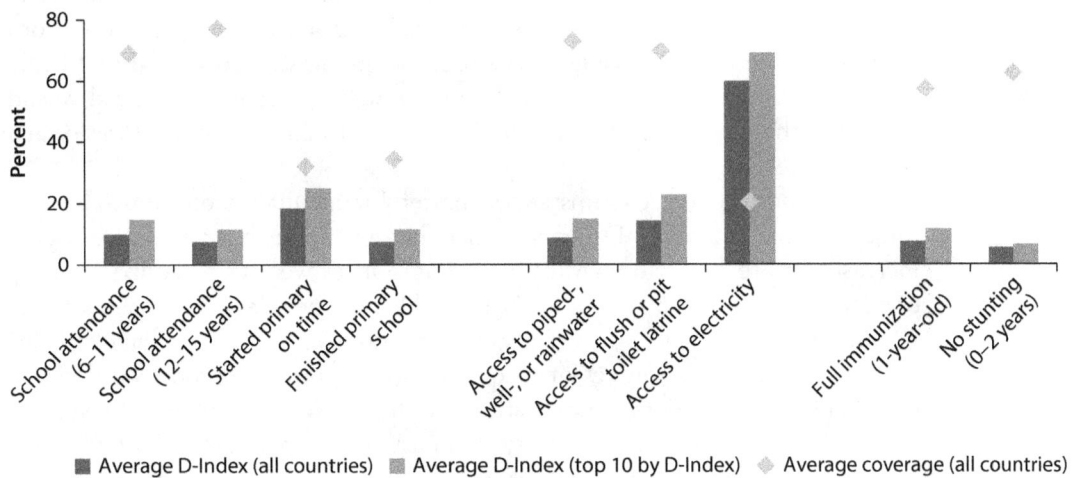

Source: Authors' calculations using Demographic and Health Surveys data, various years.
Note: Average D-Index and coverage for each opportunity is calculated as the simple unweighted average of D-Index and coverage across all countries. Top-10 countries by D-Index for each opportunity are the same group of countries considered as "high inequality" countries in figure O.4. D-Index = dissimilarity index.

Do African Children Have an Equal Chance? • http://dx.doi.org/10.1596/978-1-4648-0332-1

location (rural or urban) of the household. Belonging to a household that is richer and with more education, and being located in an urban area are favorable circumstances for access to almost all opportunities. When "opportunity" refers to a bundle of basic goods and services appropriate for a child of a certain age, the same three circumstances are again the most important contributors.

Underlying the averages are important variations across countries and types of opportunity. The average contribution of location is more pronounced for infrastructure opportunities than for education and health opportunities; and education of the head of the household has, on average, a higher contribution to inequality of education opportunities than that of other opportunities. Mother's education matters significantly in explaining inequality of opportunities in health (being fully immunized and not being stunted).

Access to opportunities is influenced by circumstances that go beyond poverty, remoteness, or lack of awareness (proxied by education of household head or mother)—depending on the country and type of opportunity. In such cases, inequality of opportunities is partly attributable to factors such as gender and household composition, which may be symptomatic of social barriers that are more resistant to policy initiatives. While circumstances traditionally associated with discrimination, such as gender of the child or the household head, appear to be less prominent, on average, there are important exceptions. In the case of education, for example, gender differences between the most and least vulnerable groups are stark in Liberia and Niger for the very same opportunities in which these countries rank as the most unequal among all countries. The gender difference in nutrition (not being stunted) seen in some countries turns out to be a disadvantage for boys, consistent with some of the literature on this issue.

Like gender, household demographics play a small role in the decomposition, on average, but again with a few exceptions. For example, being an earlier-born child of the family and having fewer siblings improves the opportunity of being immunized and not being stunted in a few countries; and parents being alive and present in the household are associated with better education opportunities in a few countries.

In considering how circumstances matter for inequality, one must bear in mind that the estimated D-Index is in effect an "upper bound" that can only increase if more, hitherto unavailable, circumstances were to be added. One set of circumstances missing in our analysis but likely to be relevant in many settings would be some measure of ethnicity, including religious, tribal, or linguistic differences. While these sources of inequality are important to consider, they are better suited for in-depth country studies rather than in a multicountry setting, where the need for a cross-country comparison compels the use of identical circumstances across all countries. If inequalities exist due to any of these social factors, our measures of inequality (D-Index) and inequality-adjusted coverage of an opportunity (HOI) can go in only one direction, namely, that of a higher D-Index that in turn implies a lower HOI.

How Do Circumstances Matter: The Tale of Two (Hypothetical) Children

To illustrate how circumstances matter for opportunities, consider an example of two hypothetical children between age 6 and 11 years with starkly different profiles: child A (and B), a girl (boy) child in the lowest (highest) quintile of household wealth, living in a rural (urban) area and in a household headed by a woman (man) with no (10 years or more of) education.

Figure O.8 shows that if the more vulnerable child (child A) lives in Malawi, her likelihood of being covered by the bundle of basic services relevant for her age (school attendance, safe water, and sanitation) would be higher than that of a similar child in *any other country*, but 40 percentage points lower than that of *child B of the same age in Malawi*. Thus, even in a country where child A has better access to certain opportunities than in any other country, she suffers from a huge disadvantage when compared to child B. And in countries where the opportunities of child A are low, the gap can be much larger. In Namibia, Niger, Mozambique, and Madagascar, the probability of having the composite bundle of opportunities is 85 percent or higher for child B, compared to nearly 0 percent for child A.

Figure O.8 Probability of Accessing Basic Goods or Services: Two Children of Different Profiles

Composite bundle (6–11 years)

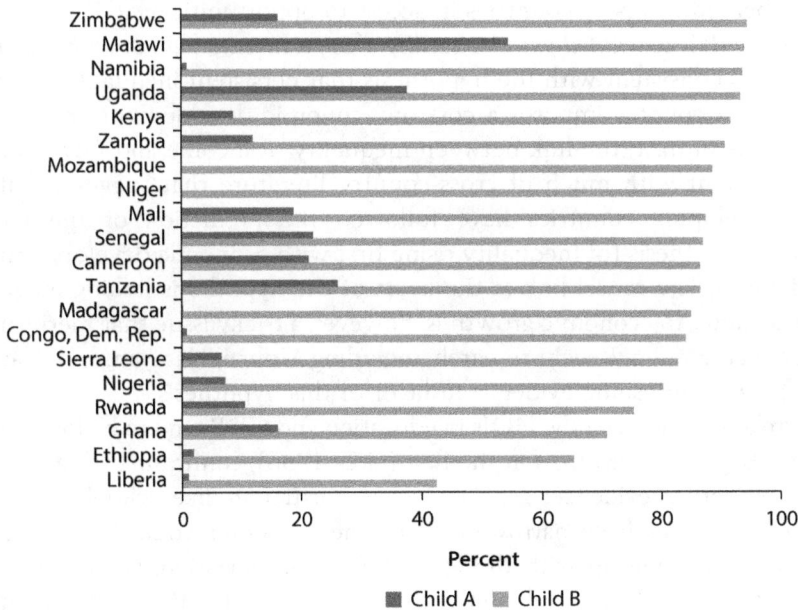

Source: Authors' calculations using Demographic and Health Surveys data, various years.
Note: **Child A:** a girl of between age 6 and 11 years, living in a rural household belonging to the bottom quintile of wealth and headed by a woman with zero years of education. **Child B:** a boy of between age 6 and 11 years, living in an urban household belonging to the top quintile of wealth and headed by a man with 10 or more years of education.

Do African Children Have an Equal Chance? • http://dx.doi.org/10.1596/978-1-4648-0332-1

Cross-Country Comparisons of Opportunities

While the focus so far has been on access to opportunities among children and the factors that matter for access, it is also useful to take a more aggregated approach that relies on cross-country correlations. This involves, first, comparing access to opportunities with indicators of economic development, such as gross domestic product (GDP) per capita and inequality of income. Second, it involves comparing access to opportunities between children in Francophone and Anglophone countries included in our sample, recognizing that countries in each group share some common historical and institutional characteristics. The third comparison will be between our sample of 20 SSA countries and countries in the LAC region. Limited and superficial as such comparisons are in scope, they can indicate the areas of relative success and challenges for SSA countries against the benchmark of a different region.

The HOI and the composite index of inequality of opportunity (for 1-year-olds) are correlated with GDP per capita across SSA countries (figures O.9a and O.9b). The correlation with GDP is stronger for an HOI of some opportunities (e.g., education) than for others (e.g., immunization), and significant for a composite HOI that combine multiple opportunities. At the same time, inequality of opportunity is uncorrelated with inequality of income (figure O.9c), and inequality of income is uncorrelated with per capita GDP (figure O.9d). Consistent with the correlation between an HOI and GDP, consumption poverty and a composite HOI are negatively correlated, with poorer countries lagging behind less poor countries in access to opportunities.

That *GDP is correlated with inequality of opportunities but not with inequality of income* is consistent with the hypothesis that persistent inequality of opportunities in a country imposes a cost on economic development and reduces growth. In contrast, the link between inequality of income and GDP is tenuous, consistent with much of cross-country literature that suggests that not many developing countries have followed the prediction of the famous Kuznets Hypothesis (of inequality rising first with economic development and then falling). The causal link at the heart of the hypothesis linking inequality of opportunity to economic growth is, however, a tricky issue that merits much deeper examination. Recent research, including Molina, Narayan, and Saavedra (2013), has found some evidence in favor of this hypothesis.

Correlations between the HOIs in education and GDP tend to be lower in the late-2000s (circa 2008) than in the first (circa 1998), confirming what was suggested by earlier evidence: gaps in key opportunities like school attendance between countries have narrowed over time as poorer countries have made progress in catching up with the leaders. For immunization, where the cross-country gaps have low correlation with differences in GDP, evidence points to the narrowing of gaps between leading and lagging performers.

Factoring in the level of economic development can be important for a cross-country comparison of opportunities. Figure O.10 provides an example of how this can be done. Countries are ranked here by the composite HOI (for

Figure O.9 GDP, Income Inequality, and Composite HOI (1-Year-Old)

Cross-country correlations in period 2 (circa 2008)

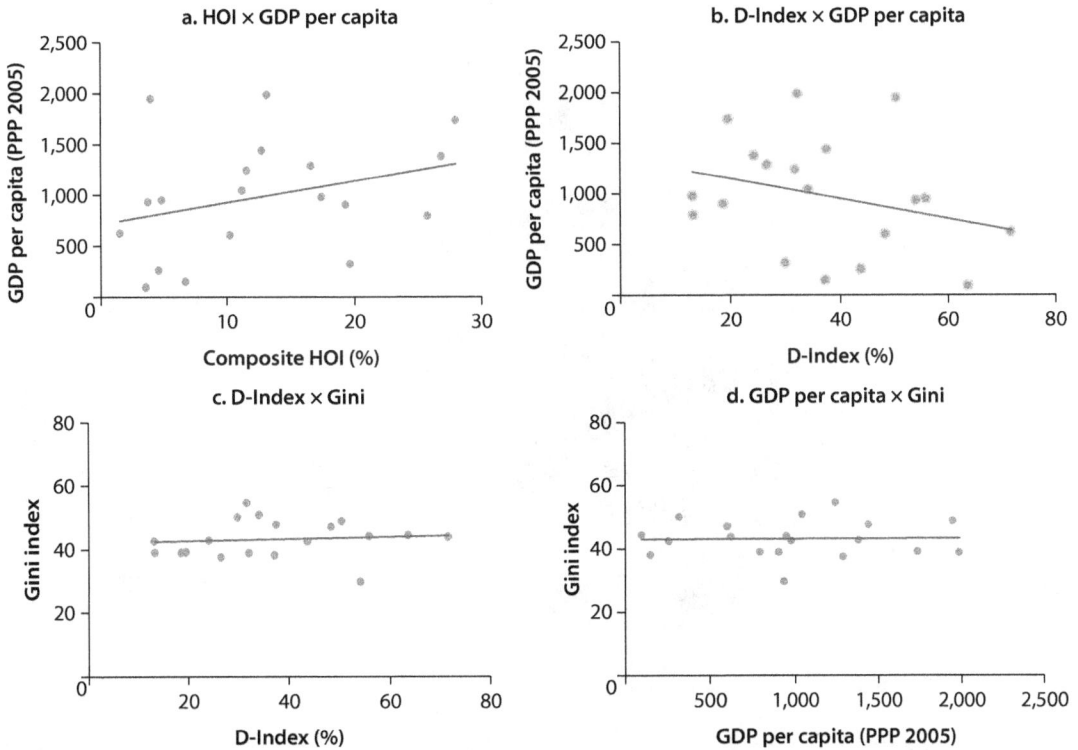

a. HOI × GDP per capita

b. D-Index × GDP per capita

c. D-Index × Gini

d. GDP per capita × Gini

Source: Authors' calculations using World Development Indicators (2011) and Demographic and Health Surveys data, various years.
Note: D-Index = dissimilarity index; GDP = gross domestic product; HOI = Human Opportunity Index; PPP = purchasing power parity.

Figure O.10 Opportunities Relative to Income Levels

Rank by composite HOI, unweighted and weighted by GDP/capita

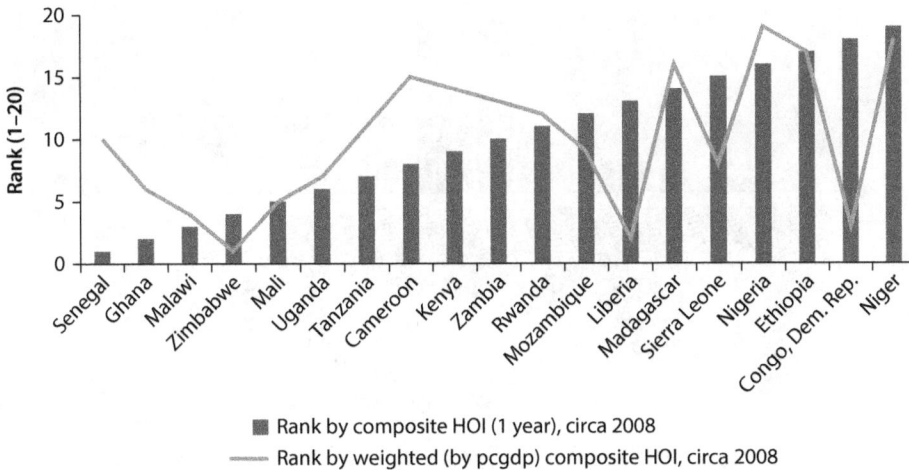

■ Rank by composite HOI (1 year), circa 2008
— Rank by weighted (by pcgdp) composite HOI, circa 2008

Source: Authors' calculations using Demographic and Health Surveys data, various years.
Note: Lower number denotes higher rank. Countries are sorted by descending order of rank by composite HOI. GDP = gross domestic product; HOI = Human Opportunity Index; pcgdp = per capita gross domestic product.

Do African Children Have an Equal Chance? • http://dx.doi.org/10.1596/978-1-4648-0332-1

Figure O.11 Comparing HOI in Education in LAC and SSA Countries

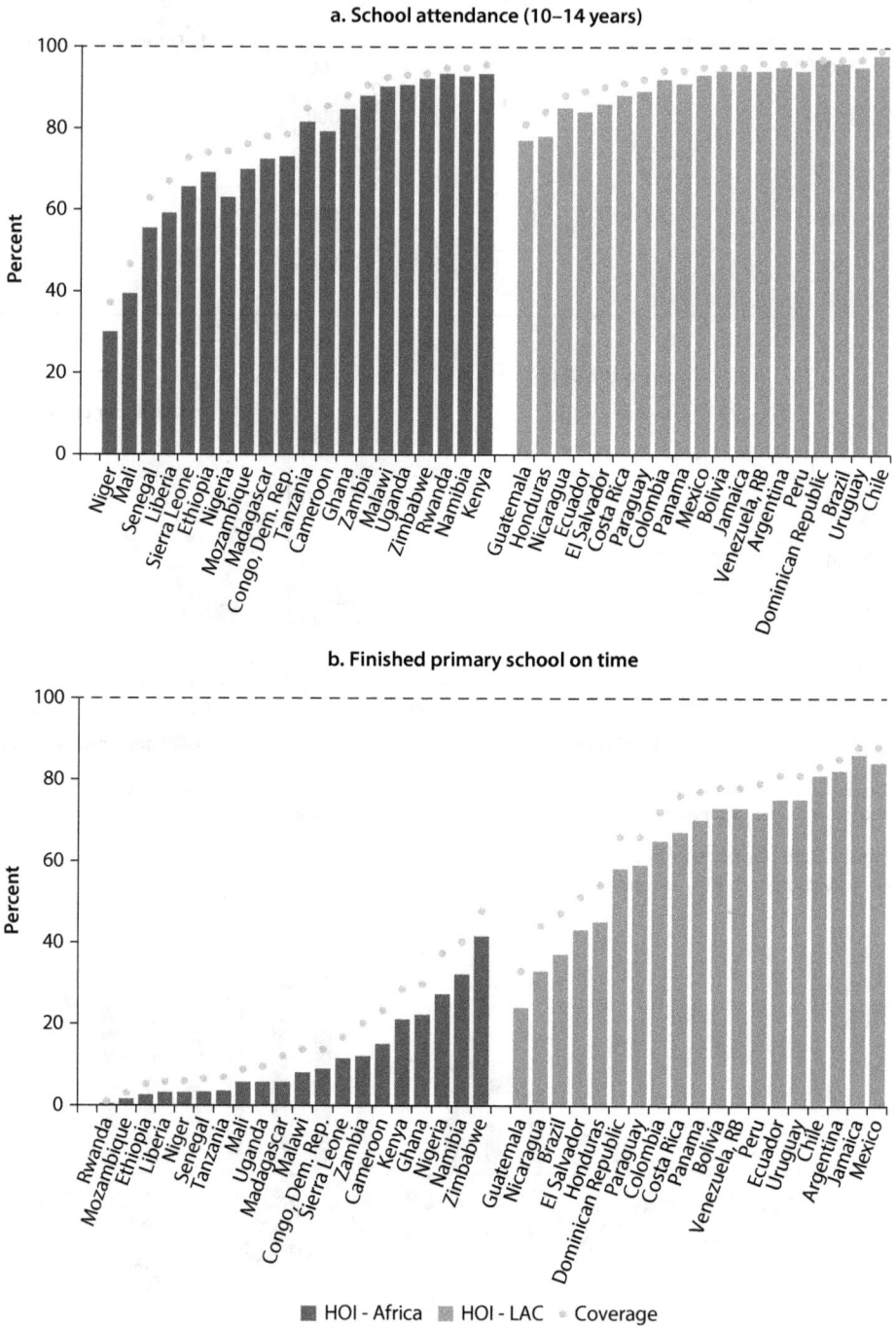

a. School attendance (10–14 years)

b. Finished primary school on time

■ HOI - Africa   ■ HOI - LAC   ● Coverage

Source: Barros et al. (2012); and authors' calculations using Demographic and Health Surveys data, various years.
Note: (1) Finishing primary school *on time* refers to completing sixth grade by age 12. (2) Percentage point change refers to
annual average change in an HOI and coverage. HOI = Human Opportunity Index; LAC = Latin America and the Caribbean;
SSA = Sub-Saharan Africa.

1-year-olds), unweighted and weighted by per capita GDP. Based on the weighted HOI, some countries (e.g., Zimbabwe, Mozambique, Malawi, Liberia, Sierra Leone, and the Democratic Republic of Congo) improve their cross-country ranking significantly, relative to their rank by the (unweighted) composite HOI. And for some countries, like Senegal, Cameroon, and Kenya, it is the opposite, indicating that they underperform relative to their income levels.

As a group, Anglophone countries do better, on average, than Francophone countries in terms of the HOI in both periods. Most of the gaps between the two groups are attributable to differences in coverage rate. The gap has narrowed over time—between circa 1998 and circa 2008—for immunization, starting primary school on time, and school attendance of both age groups. Wide variation within each group implies that country-specific factors matter much more for access to opportunities than systematic institutional or historical differences between the two groups.

SSA countries lag far behind LAC countries on access to basic infrastructure, with the gaps being narrower but still present if per capita GDP of the countries is taken into account. In education, SSA countries compare quite well with LAC countries for an HOI in school attendance among 10- to 14-year-olds (figure O.11a), after the gaps have narrowed considerably between the late-1990s and late-2000s. SSA countries, however, lag far behind LAC countries in completing sixth grade *on time* (by age 12) (figure O.11b). Most of the SSA countries, with the exception of Namibia and Zimbabwe, have also lagged behind LAC countries in terms of average annual progress in the HOI for finishing primary school between 1998 and 2008.

Concluding Remarks

Some of the key implications from the findings in this study are worth revisiting. *First*, it is important to note that some positive, measurable progress has been achieved in improving opportunities for children in Africa. Whether we measure progress on single opportunity, bundle of services, or for young or older children, we notice that most African countries in the study have made improvements. And in almost all cases where progress has been rapid, improvement in coverage has been accompanied by a reduction in inequality of opportunity, which implies that the expansion has favored children whose circumstances have made them less likely to have the opportunity in the first place. *Second*, we find that the evidence overall suggests an important trend of convergence: gaps between better-performing and lagging SSA countries in terms of a few key opportunities for children (particularly in education and health) have narrowed over time. This trend is manifested in different ways—reductions over time in correlations between GDP and the HOIs for key opportunities, average Francophone-Anglophone gaps in the HOI, and a cross-country variation in the HOIs. Thus, improving access to some basic services among children appears to be possible, even for the poorest countries. *Third*, the rapid strides made in improving these opportunities support the view that *policy initiatives* can make a difference, even in resource-constrained environments, in bringing services to citizens *and* compensate for the inherent disadvantages faced by groups whose circumstances are not favorable. The results from decomposition of changes in opportunities show that the main drivers of the changes have been scale effects, the type of policy actions that increases access proportionally to all groups.

Fourth, most SSA countries have achieved impressive progress in school attendance that have closed the gap substantially with many countries in the LAC region, but less so in "second-generation" education opportunities like completing and starting primary school on time, which are likely to influence the quality of education a child receives. Available evidence on student learning achievements from seven countries also seems to suggest that progress on quality has been insufficient. Average reading and mathematics test scores for five out of these seven countries covered by the SACMEQ-III project have shown little or no improvement between 2000 and 2007. The fact that improvement in school attendance would precede improvements in second-generation opportunities that are influenced by a complex combination of factors is understandable by itself. But for the very same reason, the former will not inevitably lead to the latter. Rather, achieving gains in these would depend on the extent to which countries can invest in improving the quality of education, and preschool and early childhood learning.

Fifth, the rapid improvements in some dimensions should not distract policy makers from the challenges posed by the relative lack of progress in others. In addition to the second-generation education opportunities mentioned above, one area where such policy action calls for more effort is in expanding opportunities in infrastructure. Considerable challenges remain in access to critical services such as safe water, adequate sanitation, and electricity, where even the best performers among SSA countries lag behind the lowest performers in the LAC region. Improving coverage and reducing inequality of opportunity in these services, as well as in immunization and nutrition, will require as concerted an effort as has been seen in many of the SSA countries for improving the coverage of primary education.

Sixth, and finally, an additional area where significant policy action can lead to substantial payoffs is focusing on providing opportunities for children early in life. As the study has shown, all countries do better in providing opportunities for the older children than that for younger children. While there is a strong correlation between the levels of opportunities for younger and older children— meaning that countries that do well in providing opportunities for younger children also tend to do well in providing opportunities for older children— exceptions remain, and the gap between the younger and the older children remains large across all opportunities.

Notes

1. Some prominent publications include *The Economist*'s "The Hopeful Continent," *Time Magazine*'s "Africa Rising," and the McKinsey Global Institute's "Lions on the Move."
2. This refers to the number of people living below a poverty line of $1.25 per person per day at 2005 purchasing power parity (PPP) prices. The number of poor was higher in 2008 because the SSA population in 2008 was much higher than it was in 1990.
3. For Senegal, only a partial comparison between the two periods is possible—excluding education and health, information on which are unavailable for the initial period for Senegal.
4. While the categories are the same for all types of opportunities, three of the individual circumstances—gender of the child, presence of an elderly person (65 years and older) in the household, and location (urban or rural) of the household—are identical across all opportunities. For the rest, there are some differences in the definition of the circumstances used for education and infrastructure opportunities versus those used for health opportunities.

References

Barros, R., F. Ferreira, J. Molinas Vega, and J. Saavedra. 2009. *Measuring Inequality of Opportunities in Latin America and the Caribbean*. Washington, DC: World Bank.

Barros, R., J. Molinas Vega, J. Saavedra, and M. Giugale. 2012. *Do Our Children Have a Chance? A Human Opportunity Report for Latin America and the Caribbean*. Washington, DC: World Bank.

Demographic and Health Surveys. Various years. USAID. http://www.dhsprogram.com.

Makuwa, D. 2010. "What Are the Levels and Trends in Reading and Mathematics Achievement?" SACMEQ Policy Issues Series, No. 2, September. http://www.sacmeq.org/sites/default/files/sacmeq/reports/sacmeq-iii/policy-issue-series/002-sacmeqpolicyissuesseries-pupilachievement.pdf.

Molina, E., A. Narayan, and J. Saavedra. 2013. "Outcomes, Opportunity and Development: Why Unequal Opportunities and Not Outcomes Hinder Economic Development." Policy Research Working Paper 6735, World Bank, Washington, DC.

Roemer, J. 1998. *Equality of Opportunity*. Cambridge, MA: Harvard University Press.

World Bank. 2007. *World Development Report 2006: Equity and Development*. Washington, DC: World Bank.

World Bank. 2011. *World Development Indicators*. http://data.worldbank.org/data-catalog/world-development-indicators/wdi-2011.

CHAPTER 1

Introduction

Opportunities for Children in Africa: Setting the Stage

Inequality in society has been an important concern for citizens, governments, and social researchers alike through the ages. Recently there has been a heightened sense of urgency because rapid gains in reducing income poverty in many countries have not always translated into a consensus that society is doing better for all its citizens. While the apparent divergence between perception and reality depends on myriad factors, the inequality of how "opportunities" are distributed among the population appears to be an important one. To see why this is important, consider that in most developing countries, including those in sub-Saharan Africa (SSA), an individual's chance of success in life is deeply influenced by characteristics he or she is born into, such as ethnic group, skin color, gender, the location of birth, or the wealth of the family. Personal circumstances over which an individual has no influence remain strongly relevant to his or her opportunities in life, even when such opportunities are defined in the minimalist sense of access to the most basic set of goods and services in the absence of which an individual cannot have a fair chance to achieve her human potential. Differences in opportunities materialize at all stages in an individual's life: not all young children have access to basic health care or primary education of minimal quality, not all youth have access to professional or technical education, and not all adults have the same level of access to land, credit, or job opportunities. And despite recent improvements, not all African children have the same opportunities in life that allow them to attain their human potential—a concern that is the central focus of this study.

Most societies agree on a set of basic opportunities that should be available to all children. Few will disagree that all children should have access to sanitation and clean water, to electricity, and to decent basic education. At least for basic services like these, universality is a valid and feasible objective. But most SSA countries are far from this target, in spite of significant progress in recent years. Moreover, available opportunities are often distributed unequally, depending on the circumstances that children are born into.

Achieving progress toward the ideal of universal access to basic goods and services, while ensuring that such progress is also inclusive of all groups in society, requires an analytical tool to guide policy makers. Such an analytical tool, built around a metric known as the Human Opportunity Index (HOI), was created in 2008 by a consortium of researchers sponsored by the World Bank (see Barros et al. 2009).[1]

The HOI calculates how personal circumstances (e.g., birthplace, wealth, race, or gender) influence the probability of a child to access the services that are necessary to succeed in life (e.g., timely education, basic health, or access to safe water and sanitation). The measure is fundamentally about equity and not equality, and evaluates whether the playing field for individuals is level at an early stage of life, rather than the equality of outcomes for those individuals. Importantly, the analytical approach offers a way out of the politically polarizing debate over inequality seen in many countries. Consensus on questions such as whether governments should try to redistribute wealth, protect private property rights, or enforce social justice or legal contracts is hard to achieve. But people across the political spectrum, regardless of how they feel about the role of government, markets, and individual responsibility, can agree on the appealing principle of providing people with equal chances of success early in life, independent of the socioeconomic background and other circumstances they are born into. To some, equality of opportunity in a society is about creating a level field for everyone, which would eventually lead to a more equitable distribution of income; to others, it is about creating a society where individual effort and talent, as opposed to circumstances one is born into, determine outcomes in life. Whatever ideology is used to justify it, the principle of equality of opportunity appears to be one that most societies can agree on as an ideal to strive toward.

This chapter briefly introduces the principle of equality of opportunity and the HOI as a metric for measuring it, and discusses the relevance and use of these concepts in the context of SSA. Subsequently, chapter 2 will discuss in more detail the conceptual and empirical issues in measuring equality of opportunity, outline the definition and salient properties of an HOI, and discuss how it can be useful in a policy context. Chapter 2 also sets the stage for applying these concepts to a group of 20 SSA countries, by examining the choice of data and surveys, countries, and opportunities for the rest of the volume. The selected countries are Cameroon, the Democratic Republic of Congo, Ethiopia, Ghana, Kenya, Liberia, Madagascar, Malawi, Mali, Mozambique, Namibia, Niger, Nigeria, Rwanda, Senegal, Sierra Leone, Tanzania, Uganda, Zambia, and Zimbabwe, which represent more than 70 percent of the population of SSA. Opportunities that are analyzed relate to children's access to education (e.g., school attendance), health (e.g. immunization) and infrastructure (e.g., water and sanitation). Chapters 3 to 6 present the results from the analysis, highlighting key patterns and determinants of inequality across countries and drawing implications for policy wherever appropriate. For 17 out of 20 countries, the analysis includes assessing how access to opportunities has evolved between two points of time—late-1990s (approximately/circa 1998) and late-2000s (circa 2008).

Motivation for a Human Opportunity Index[2]

The World Bank's *World Development Report 2006: Equity and Development* uses the term "opportunities" to describe access to basic goods and services, such as basic education and health services, safe water, adequate sanitation and nutrition. The report argues that inequality of opportunity, both within and among nations, propagates deprivation, and weakens prospects for overall prosperity and economic growth (see the second section of chapter 2). Lack of opportunities results in wasted human potential, since these opportunities are considered essential to determining whether a person will be able to live a life of her choosing. The ideal of equal opportunity—first formalized as a concept by the economist John Roemer (1993, 1998)—requires that an individual's opportunities are independent of her circumstances: characteristics that an individual is born into and has no influence over, such as race, religion, gender, place of birth, or the wealth and education of one's parents. Most societies agree that policy should work to ensure this independence, so that an individual's outcomes and achievements in life depend only on her effort and innate ability.

How does the concept of equality of opportunity as proposed by Roemer and others translate to measurable objectives for countries? *First*, while defining and measuring "opportunities" can be subjective and depend on the societal context, most societies can agree on a basic set of goods and services, such as (but not limited to) safe water, adequate sanitation, nutrition, and primary schooling that conform with a minimalist notion of "opportunities" available to citizens. *Second*, in most societies there is a broad consensus around the notion that granting access to a basic set of goods and services (e.g., clean water, sanitation, or primary education) to every individual, regardless of the circumstances he or she was born into, is fundamental to building a just society and fostering economic and social development. Accordingly, the provision of universal access to such goods and services is a major objective of social policy for most countries and a key consideration in setting national constitutions and international agreements such as the Millennium Development Goals (MDGs) and the Universal Declaration of Human Rights.

However, in most developing countries the goal of universal and equal access to basic goods and services remains distant—a person's circumstances still matter a great deal in determining her access to some or all basic goods and services. For example, in 2006, a child of age 6–7 years from an urban household in Niger was nearly three times more likely to start primary school on time (at the correct age) than a child in a rural household; and in 2008 a one-year-old child in the richest 20 percent of the population (quintile) in Nigeria was almost eight times more likely to be fully immunized than a child in the poorest 20 percent.[3]

Do African Children Have an Equal Chance? • http://dx.doi.org/10.1596/978-1-4648-0332-1

As a country develops and increases its capacity to deliver access to basic goods and services to its citizens, additional access can be allocated in many different ways. Unfortunately, the allocation pattern is almost always influenced, by accident or design, by the circumstances of the beneficiaries, which is inconsistent with the principle of equality of opportunity. For example, as full immunization (among one-year-old children) increased substantially in Madagascar during 1997–2009, the gap between urban and rural children also widened. And while the percentage of children who start primary school on time almost doubled in Niger over the same period, the gaps between urban and rural children and between children in the richest and poorest quintiles expanded. In other words, children with more favorable circumstances have benefited more from the additional opportunities, with the result that an overall (or average) increase in opportunities has not necessarily led to a reduction in inequality of opportunity. These examples convey a larger point: as the focus of the global community has been on MDGs and other national targets to track progress, these averages in many cases mask persistent and even rising inequality in opportunities among groups within a country.

A metric to measure the extent of equality of opportunity in a society needs to be intuitive, taking into account the extent to which opportunities are universal in the country *and* whether opportunities that do exist are distributed equitably among individuals of different circumstances. The metric also needs to be computable from existing socioeconomic data in most countries in order to inform public policy, whether by tracking aggregate changes over time, evaluating programs, or improving the targeting of social policy. The index known as the HOI, which was developed by the World Bank with external researchers and first presented in the 2009 publication *Measuring Inequality of Opportunities in Latin America and the Caribbean* (Barros et al. 2009), combines most of these qualities.[4] This report uses an analytical framework centered on the HOI to examine children's access to a set of basic goods and services—access to clean water, sanitation, and electricity; completing sixth grade on time; and attending school from age 10 to 14—in 19 Latin American countries. For a child, not being covered by a good or service can be considered as being deprived of that particular opportunity. Unlike what one may argue for adults, lack of access to a good or service cannot be explained away as lack of effort by the child: most societies are committed to making these services available for all children rather than designate them as "rewards" for a child's effort.

The HOI is a synthetic measure that considers (a) how far a country is from the goal of providing universal access to a set of goods and services and (b) the degree to which there is equality of opportunity to access the goods and services. This is done by measuring the extent to which coverage is correlated with particular circumstances (e.g., of a certain gender, race, place of birth, or socioeconomic background) that should not matter for access, which is to say if these basic goods and services are allocated according to a principle of equality of opportunities. Intuitively, the HOI is an inequality of opportunity discounted coverage rate. The higher the correlation between access and circumstances, the larger is the discount or "penalty" to the coverage rate in computing the HOI. A more detailed discussion of the motivation of and concepts underlying the HOI can be found in chapter 2 of this study.

Poverty and Inequality in Africa

Over the past decade, there has been some progress in SSA countries toward meeting the MDGs, which measure the different dimensions of welfare including monetary poverty, and access to basic goods and services such as sanitation, primary education, and nutrition. This progress has been fueled mainly by economic growth—as countries become better-off, more resources are available and access to goods and services can be increased. But even as social indicators have improved in many countries, SSA continues to lag behind the rest of the world. For example, the share of the population in SSA living below the $1.25 per person per day poverty line (purchasing power parity, or PPP, at 2005 prices) was 47 percent in 2008—not much lower than in 1981, when the poverty rate was 51 percent, but showing substantial progress since 1990, when the poverty rate was 58 percent. In contrast, the East Asia and the Pacific Region (led by China) made dramatic progress, with poverty incidence dropping from 78 percent to 17 percent from 1981 to 2005; the poverty rate fell in South Asia, Latin America and the Caribbean and Middle East and North Africa as well, although the number of the poor has remained static in these regions.

In other dimensions of welfare, the trends for SSA are positive but the pace of improvement has been slow. Despite growth in net primary enrollment rate in the last two decades, it remained low at 73 percent in 2007. With 32 million children (nearly one-quarter) of primary school age being out of school, moving toward universal access to primary education remains a daunting challenge for the region as a whole.[5] The region also has a long way to go in terms of gender parity in enrollment, access to improved sources of drinking water, and access to improved sanitation facilities, which rose from 28 percent in 1990 to just 31 percent in 2008.[6] Overall, progress in SSA countries toward many of the year 2015 targets defined as MDGs lags behind that in other regions.[7] Progress has been especially slow toward health-related MDGs, such as in reducing infant mortality, largely due to the uncontrolled spread of HIV and the persistence of tuberculosis. For example, the absolute numbers of under-five mortality have increased in SSA since the early-1990s, so that the region currently has 20 percent of the world's children under age five but 50 percent of all child deaths; maternal mortality remains stubbornly high; and the region accounts for more than 80 percent of the world's AIDS-related orphanhood. The goals of universal education and equality are also distant for many SSA countries.[8] Table 1.1 shows the progress in three key MDG indicators between the early-1990s and late-2000s for SSA and other regions.

Progress also remains uneven across different indicators of human development and across countries. Using three countries as examples, figure 1.1 shows changes in school attendance of children of age 6–11 and the percentage of children (of age 1 year) who have been fully immunized, between the late-1990s

Table 1.1 Progress in Key MDG Indicators, by Region

Region	Prevalence of underweight (children < 5 years)		Net primary enrollment ratio		Percent of immunized against measles (1-year-olds)	
	1990	2009	1991	2009	1990	2009
Developing regions	30	23	81	89	71	80
Northern Africa	10	6	80	94	85	94
Sub-Saharan Africa	27	22	54	76	56	68
Latin America and the Caribbean	10	4	86	95	76	93
Eastern Asia	15	6	97	96	98	94
Eastern Asia excluding China	11	5	97	98	95	95
Southern Asia	52	43	77	91	57	75
Southern Asia excluding India	59	39	68	77	60	85
South-Eastern Asia	30	18	94	95	70	88
Western Asia	11	7	82	88	77	82
Caucasus and Central Asia	7	5	–	93	81	94

Source: United Nations 2011.
Note: MDG = Millennium Development Goals.

and late-2000s. Both the level and the rate of progress in school attendance (in Ghana, Mali, and Zambia) and full immunization (in Ethiopia, Mali, and Namibia) vary widely across countries.

But averages are only part of the story. In addition to the low level of average welfare reflected by social indicators, inequality within countries poses a challenge. Existing economic literature provides some evidence on inequality of outcomes in SSA. Efforts to compile and analyze information on income inequality in the region date from the mid-1990s (see Deininger and Squire, 1996). The studies since then have generally found the region to be highly unequal, with levels of income inequality comparable to Latin American countries. Deininger and Squire provide evidence that the Gini coefficient at the regional level was stable in the period of the 1960s to 1990 with Latin America showing the highest inequality with an income Gini of almost 0.50, followed closely by SSA with an income Gini of 0.46. They also find that heterogeneity in Gini across countries was large among African countries, ranging from 0.29 in Rwanda to 0.62 in South Africa. By the decade of 2000 African countries still had not shown much progress in reducing inequality and Gini coefficients were as high as 0.47 in Rwanda, 0.58 in South Africa, and 0.50 in Zimbabwe (UN *Human Development Report 2010*).[9]

Beyond the income dimension, there is evidence to suggest large inequalities in education and health within SSA countries. The Inequality-adjusted Human Development Index (IHDI) developed for the *Human Development Report* indicates that the loss in potential human development due to inequality is higher in SSA than in regions with comparable income inequality such as Latin America.[10] Assessing the trends in non-income inequality is an elusive task, but recent work constructing Gini coefficients for preschool age stunting and female educational attainment also suggests high levels of inequality and slow progress over time in African countries (Sahn and Younger 2007).

Figure 1.1 Progress in Human Development in Selected African Countries

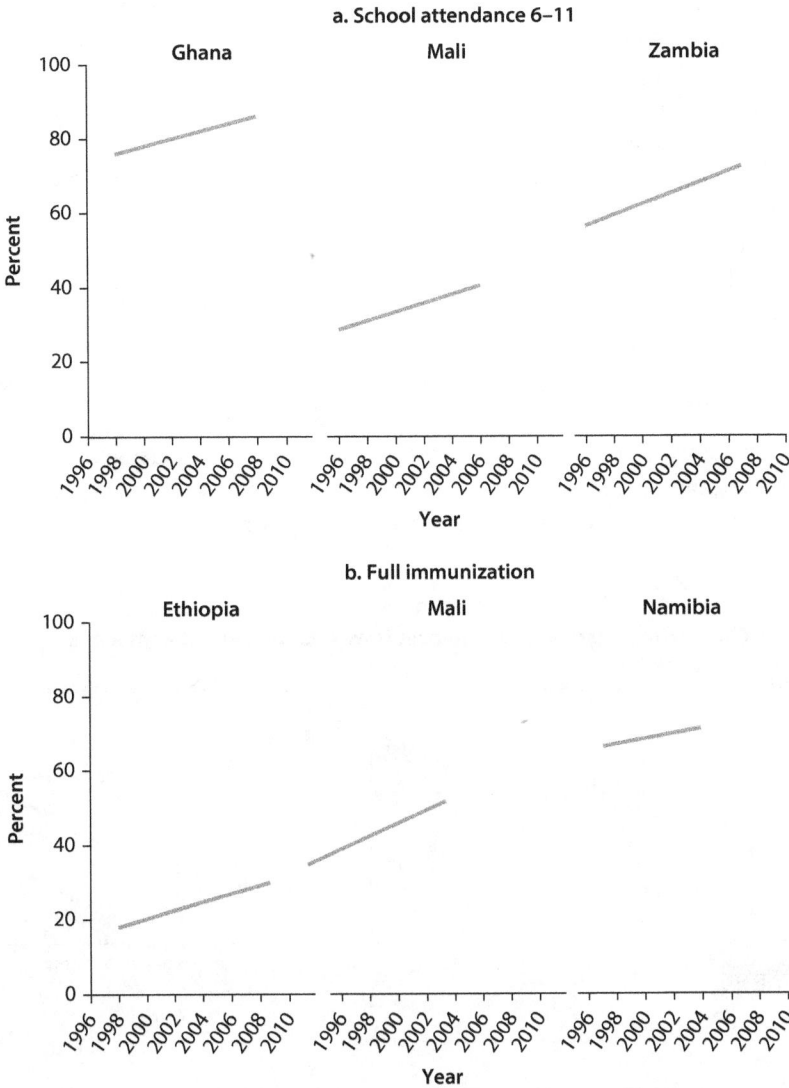

a. School attendance 6–11

b. Full immunization

Source: DHS various countries, various years.

Inequality of Opportunities in Africa

Within African countries, access to opportunities among children from varying socioeconomic backgrounds is uneven, with sharp differences (in levels and changes over time) across countries and opportunities. Consider the examples of countries included in figure 1.1, which have had some success in improving average school attendance and full immunization among children between the late-1990s and late-2000s. Even as average access to these opportunities has improved, gaps between the richest and poorest 20 percent of the population (i.e., top and bottom quintiles) have changed at very different rates across countries (figure 1.2). For example, the rich-poor gap in school attendance has narrowed slightly in two out of the three countries shown in the graph, while remaining unchanged for the third; and the rich-poor gap in immunization has narrowed only for one country, while widening significantly for two. In countries where the rich-poor gaps in school attendance have closed slightly, the gaps still remain large enough to indicate that a child's economic background matters a lot for his or her access to education opportunities.

The same country examples also illustrate that the gaps between rural and urban children, and the change in these gaps over time, differ widely across countries and opportunities as well (figure 1.2). Between the late-1990s and late-2000s, the rural-urban gap in school attendance has shrunk slightly for two out of the three countries, increased slightly for the third, and remained significant in all three countries. The rural-urban gap in full immunization (children of age one) has narrowed in two out of three countries and was unchanged in the third.

The few examples in figures 1.1 and 1.2 illustrate what is likely true for many SSA countries: access to even the most basic opportunities—such as primary

Figure 1.2 Gaps between Children of Different Circumstances Have Changed at Different Rates

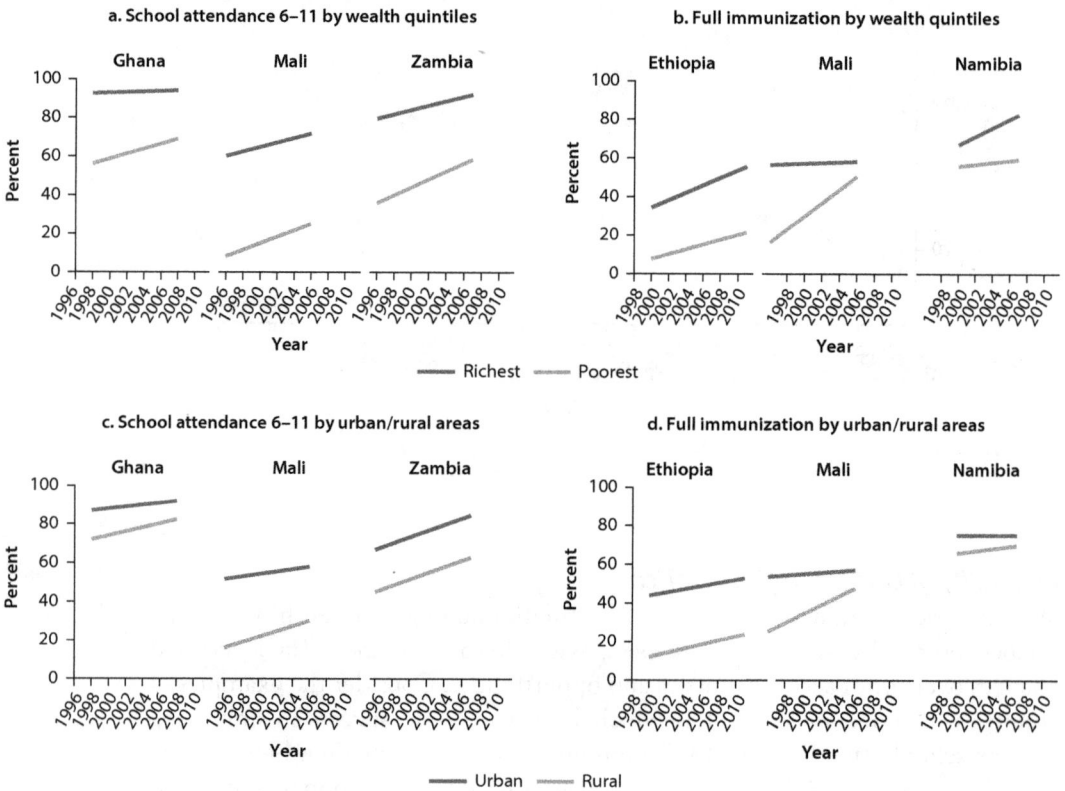

a. School attendance 6–11 by wealth quintiles

b. Full immunization by wealth quintiles

c. School attendance 6–11 by urban/rural areas

d. Full immunization by urban/rural areas

Source: DHS various countries, various years.

education, nutrition, immunization and access to safe water and adequate sanitation—is well below universal and strongly correlated with circumstances children are born into, like household wealth and geographic location. The gaps between groups with different circumstances vary widely across countries and opportunities, and over time these gaps have persisted or widened in some countries even as those countries have made progress in improving the average indicators of basic services among children.

The literature on inequality of opportunity in Africa is at an early stage, with just a few studies that have analyzed income and labor market, education and health outcomes in an inequality of opportunity framework (Bossuroy and Cogneau 2008, Cogneau et al. 2006, Cogneau and Mesplé-Somps 2008, and Pasquier-Doumer 2010). These studies focus on specific Western African countries with detailed household data, given the paucity of surveys that contain information on both individuals and parents (see box 1.1). They find evidence that in the countries studied, education opportunities in particular are strongly associated with the socioeconomic background of a child, such as gender of the child, parental education and occupation, and location. A different strand of literature, concerned mainly with questions of intergenerational transmission of opportunities, finds the income and occupation of adults are strongly influenced by the parental characteristics. Taken together, for the countries studied, the evidence suggests a low degree of social mobility and high inequality in access to opportunities among groups defined by social and parental characteristics.

The evidence highlighted so far is patchy in terms of coverage of countries and opportunities. That said, concerns about inequality, particularly in service delivery, have been reflected in work done by the Bank's research group and the Human Development network over the years, using a variety of statistical tools and methods. Some of this work was presented in the World Development Report of 2004 as symptoms of service delivery failures.[11] An intuitive, scalar measure like the HOI can complement such work by introducing a unifying framework that combines averages with distributional concerns, and allows systematic comparison across countries and over time.

As a scalar measure that incorporates inequality of opportunity, the HOI is a particularly useful metric for policy makers to track progress in service delivery at the country level. It offers a way to measure access to opportunities in countries—as defined by access to basic services—taking into account how far away a country is from universal coverage of a service, *as well as* how available services are distributed among children of different circumstances. In other words, an indicator like the HOI allows countries to go beyond averages and assess whether progress in a certain dimension is inclusive of different groups in the population. The HOI would improve *less* than the average coverage rate for a service, for example, in a country where an increase in coverage has been accompanied by a widening of the rich-poor or urban-rural gap. Conversely, an HOI may increase much more than the coverage rate in a country where underserved groups have had a disproportionate share of the increase in coverage of a service. In either case, the use of an HOI can help in informing policy makers about whether their policy

---

Box 1.1 Inequality of Opportunities in Africa: Evidence from Economic Literature

In examining the case of inequality of opportunity in education, the available literature for Africa suggests low intergenerational mobility. In Cotonou (Benin), Dakar (Senegal), and Lome' (Togo), individuals whose fathers have access to at least lower secondary school are about seven times more likely to complete lower secondary school than individuals whose fathers never completed primary school (Pasquier-Doumer 2010). Cogneau et al. (2006) studied inequalities in nutrition and primary schooling among children of preschool and school age, respectively, in Côte d'Ivoire, Ghana, Guinea, Madagascar, and Uganda. They found that at least 20 percent of children of age 9–11 years had never attended school, with the likelihood of attendance varying by the child's gender, parental background, and place of residence. A child whose father is a farmer has a 40–60 percent lower chance of attending school, and a girl has half the chance of attending school compared to a boy. In the case of nutrition, the authors found that inequality in consumption and food consumption for children 0–5 years old was similar to that for the household as a whole. But while consumption inequality is usually associated with socio-economic background, the relationship is weaker for nutrition indicators. There seems to be little variation, for instance, between girls and boys in the incidence of stunting, wasting, and underweight, and the correlation between stunting and consumption or parent's education tends to be low as well.

The approaches used to analyze inequalities in income and labor market opportunities differ from the one used in this volume, as they focus largely on questions of social mobility or intergenerational transmission of opportunities, such as whether income, education, or occupation of the father affects income and occupation of the son. The main statistics constructed are odds ratios which express the relative probability for two individuals of different social origins to reach a specific destination or outcome. The authors found evidence of low social mobility. For instance, in the city of Bamako in Mali, an individual whose father worked in the public sector, which is usually a better paying and more stable and prestigious job, is six times more likely to end up in the public sector than an individual whose father worked in the informal sector (Pasquier-Doumer 2010). Social origins such as ethnicity and parents' education are found to affect an individual's chances of success directly through the accumulation of social capital in the family or indirectly by influencing educational outcomes of children.

---

initiatives have had a positive impact on equality of opportunity in their country. The analysis also has something to tell policy makers about *how* equality of opportunity can be enhanced: given limited resources and capacity, which groups (in terms of the circumstances of children) should perhaps be the priority of public policy to improve equality of opportunity in a given society?

Notes

1. Also see Barros et al. (2010, 2012).
2. This section draws extensively from the discussion in Barros, Vega, and Saavedra (2010) and Barros et al. (2012).

3. Demographic and Health Survey or DHS (2006–07).

4. A subsequent World Bank report for the LAC region, *Do Our Children Have a Chance* (Barros et al. 2012) uses the same framework to update the results from the earlier report and complement those with new results.

5. Education for All Global Monitoring Report 2010. Regional fact sheet—"Sub-Saharan Africa (SSA)." United Nations Educational, Scientific and Cultural Organization (UNESCO).

6. The Millennium Development Goals Report 2011. United Nations.

7. *Children and the Millennium Development Goals: Progress towards a World Fit for Children.* Ban Ki-Moon, Secretary General of the United Nations. UNICEF (2007). An adapted version of the Secretary-General's report "Follow-up to the Special Session of the General Assembly on children" of 15 August 2007, considered by the General Assembly at its 62nd session in September 2007.

8. The daunting challenge is illustrated by one figure: it is estimated that double the current number of teachers would be needed in SSA in order to meet the primary education target by 2015.

9. That said, the analysis of inequality trends in the region is not without controversy. Some recent work suggests that poverty and income inequality have been falling steadily in Africa as a whole over the last decade (Sala-i-Martin and Pinkovskiy 2010), although concerns about the data used for this study cast some doubt over their findings.

10. In 2010, the loss in the inequality-adjusted life expectancy at birth index and the inequality-adjusted education index were 44 percent and 34 percent respectively, in SSA, compared to 15 percent and 22 percent, respectively, in Latin America (United Nations 2010).

11. *World Development Report 2004: Making Services Work for Poor People* (World Bank 2003).

References

Barros, R., F. Ferreira, J. Molinas Vega, and J. Saavedra. 2009. *Measuring Inequality of Opportunities in Latin America and the Caribbean.* Washington, DC: World Bank.

Barros, R., J. Molinas Vega, and J. Saavedra. 2010. "Measuring Progress Toward Basic Opportunities for All." *Brazilian Review of Econometrics* 30 (2): 335–67.

Barros, R., J. Molinas Vega, J. Saavedra, and M. Giugale. 2012. *Do Our Children Have a Chance? A Human Opportunity Report for Latin America and the Caribbean.* Washington, DC: World Bank.

Bossuroy, T., and D. Cogneau. 2008. "Social Mobility and Colonial Legacy in Five African Countries." Working Papers DT/2008/10, DIAL (Développement, Institutions et Mondialisation). http://ideas.repec.org/p/dia/wpaper/dt200810.html.

Cogneau, D., T. Bossuroy, P. De Vreyer, C. Guenard, V. Hiller, P. Leite, S. Mesplé-Somps, L. Pasquier-Doumer, and C. Torelli. 2006. "Inequalities and Equity in Africa." Working Papers DT/2006/11, DIAL (Développement, Institutions et Mondialisation). http://ideas.repec.org/p/dia/wpaper/dt200611.html.

Cogneau, D., and S. Mesplé-Somps. 2008. "Inequality of Opportunity for Income in Five Countries of Africa." *Research on Economic Inequality* 16: 99–128.

Deininger, K., and L. Squire. 1996. "A New Data Set Measuring Income Inequality." *World Bank Economic Review* 10 (3): 565–91.

Demographic and Health Surveys. Various years. USAID. http://www.dhsprogram.com.

Pasquier-Doumer, L. 2010. "Inequality of Opportunity on the Urban Labour Market in West Africa." Working Papers DT/2010/09, DIAL (Développement, Institutions et Mondialisation). http://ideas.repec.org/p/dia/wpaper/dt201009.html.

Roemer, J. 1993. "A Pragmatic Theory of Responsibility for the Egalitarian Planner." *Philosophy & Public Affairs* 22 (2): 146–66.

———. 1998. *Equality of Opportunity*. Cambridge, MA: Harvard University Press.

Sahn, D., and S. Younger. 2007. "Inequality and Poverty in Africa in an Era of Globalization: Looking Beyond Income to Health and Education." Mimeo, Cornell University.

Sala-i-Martin, X., and M. Pinkovskiy. 2010. "African Poverty Is Falling … Much Faster Than You Think!" NBER Working Paper 15775, National Bureau of Economic Research, Cambridge, MA.

UNICEF. 2007. *Children and the Millennium Development Goals: Progress towards a World Fit for Children*. New York: UNICEF.

United Nations. 2010. *Human Development Report 2010: The Real Wealth of Nations: Pathways to Human Development*. New York: United Nations.

———. 2011. *The Millennium Development Report 2011*. New York: United Nations.

World Bank. 2003. *World Development Report 2004: Making Services Work for Poor People*. Washington, DC: World Bank.

CHAPTER 2

Measuring Inequality of Opportunities: The Human Opportunity Index

Before applying the concept of equality of opportunity—specifically the idea that a person's access to basic goods and services is independent of her circumstances—to empirical analysis for African countries, it is useful to revisit the definitions embedded in the concept in more detail and logical sequence. This chapter examines the requirements for a metric that helps to track progress toward universal availability of basic goods and services for children and evaluate progress through the lens of equality of opportunity; how the Human Opportunity Index (HOI) addresses these requirements, and how analysis of opportunities using the HOI framework will be conducted for sub-Saharan African countries.

Concepts and Measurement of Inequality of Opportunities[1]

Equality of Opportunity, Not Outcome

While social scientists and philosophers before the 1970s dealt mostly with the fairness of outcomes, the work by Rawls (1971) and Nozick (1974) brought to the forefront the question of fairness of process. Dworkin (1981a, 1981b) and Arneson (1989, 1990) built on this work, dealing, respectively, with equality of resources and equality of opportunity for welfare. Cohen (1989) proposed equality in "access to advantage." Sen (1979, 1985) argued for an equitable distribution of "capabilities," which refer to sets of functionings effectively available for people to choose from, so that they can pursue "life plans" they have reason to value.[2] Roemer characterizes these proposals as attempts "to equalize opportunities, rather than outcomes: for Rawls and Dworkin, primary goods and resources, respectively, are the wherewithal with which people carry out projects that lead to outcomes that have value to them; for Sen, the capabilities to function in various ways are the prerequisites for what individuals make of themselves; and Cohen's 'access' is similar to Arneson's straightforward 'opportunity'" (Roemer 1993).

In his work published in 1993 and 1998, Roemer formalized an equality of opportunity principle, arguing that policy should work to equalize opportunities independent of circumstances and outcomes should depend only on effort.

Although the focus of development debate is often on inequality of outcomes such as income, measuring inequality of opportunities has an intuitive appeal that transcends ideological differences. To see why, consider the example of two people who were born with the exact same set of opportunities. Most people would probably agree that differences between the two in, say, income are in part due to differences in life choices, innate abilities, or effort. But now consider two people with identical innate ability but vastly different sets of opportunities to begin with. In such a case, it is entirely possible that they end up with different outcomes *despite* exerting the same amount of effort or making similarly sound life choices. Most people would regard such a scenario as unfair. In other words, inequality of opportunities is fundamentally objectionable, whereas inequality of outcomes is objectionable *only to the extent that it is caused by inequality of opportunity*. This problem is exacerbated when the distribution of opportunities is linked to circumstances, such as ethnicity, birth, gender, or family background, because these can impede the upward mobility of an entire group of people.

Therefore, it makes sense to measure inequality of opportunities, since that is fundamentally what society cares about. Shifting the policy debate to focus on opportunities may also facilitate a political consensus that has proved to be elusive on policy choices related to redistribution of income or wealth. On the other hand, measuring opportunities tends to be more difficult than measuring outcomes, a problem that can be partly mitigated by a measure like an HOI.

Defining Opportunity as "Access"

Having decided on equality of opportunity as a worthwhile goal, the next step would be to develop a precise definition of "opportunity." For the purpose of this report, and following the footsteps of similar reports by the Bank (e.g., those produced for the LAC region), opportunities will be defined as access to basic goods and services in education, health, and basic infrastructure that are necessary for an individual to realize his/her human potential. While this definition is intuitive and empirically tractable, it is important to mention some important caveats and limitations to adopting such a definition.

Opportunities can be best understood as the possibility to effectively choose among available options in a set or "take advantage" of some combination of events to enhance a person's life achievement potential. Opportunities require the existence of "functionings" (see Sen 1979, 1985). *Access to goods and services is a necessary, but not sufficient, condition for these functionings to materialize.* Since functionings are hard to measure, "access" is considered synonymous with opportunities in this report.

Transforming such access into functionings and thus eventually taking advantage of opportunities, through a combination of individual choice and effort, depends to a large extent on the context in which this transformation takes place. Judgments about social states cannot be based just on access to goods and services (through a measure like the HOI), and should also take into account the processes through which equality of opportunity is achieved. This is because the different processes through which orthogonality between circumstances and outcomes can be achieved may not be ethically equivalent. For example, a totalitarian state can in theory achieve complete independence between circumstances and opportunities, at the cost of individual autonomy, agency, and rights. Conversely, processes that are associated with strong autonomy, agency, and rights to civil and political participation are desirable for a society.

Given the important caveat above, the diagnostics and ranking of countries by an HOI in this report are not intended to be a judgment of the state of a society, relative to that of other societies. A higher HOI in a society just implies greater access to a basic good or service, which provides only a limited and partial view of the state of that society.

Focus on Children

When opportunities are defined as above, the number of different opportunities affecting outcomes later in life can be infinite, from access to primary education and nutrition when very young to access to credit and employment opportunities as an adult. Although theorists frequently disagree on where to draw the line, there is widespread agreement that, at the very least, basic opportunities should be *affordable* (otherwise universal access would not be economically feasible) and completely *outside the control* of the individual. A reasonable interpretation of the first condition is that universalization of a good or service is technologically feasible, given the state of knowledge, and economically viable, at least in the medium term. The second condition necessarily limits the set of opportunities, because it excludes any good or service that is available to an individual as a result of effort or ability.

For the purpose of this report, we remove the ambiguity of this definition by *limiting the space of opportunities to those that are provided to an individual in childhood*, a stage of life during which the individual cannot be held responsible for his/her actions. Adults may make choices that inhibit their own opportunities, such as dropping out of school due to lack of effort. For a child, however, opportunities are exogenous, because family, society, geography, or the government should be responsible for ensuring whether or not he/she will have access to them.[3] While the outcomes in life also depend on genetic traits that a child inherits from parents, most would agree that the critical inputs necessary for the child's development should be provided to all children regardless of his/her genetic makeup.

Interventions to equalize opportunities earlier in life are also found to be significantly more cost-effective and successful than are those attempted later in life. Research shows that preschoolers with low levels of cognitive development have lower school achievement and earn lower wages in adulthood (Currie and Thomas 1999; Case and Paxson 2006). More recent studies suggest that early childhood education has substantial long-term impacts, ranging from adult earnings to retirement savings (Chetty et al. 2010). Moreover, lost opportunities during childhood cannot always be compensated for. Child malnutrition, for example, can generate life-long learning difficulties, poor health, and lower productivity and earnings over a lifetime (Alderman, Hoddinott, and Kinsey 2006; Hoddinott et al. 2008).

What Constitutes "Access"?

Finally, if we are to define opportunities as access to basic goods and services, such as basic education and health services, adequate nutrition, safe water, and sanitation, we must be clear about what "access" means. For example, does access to schooling mean merely having a school nearby or actually attending the school? And does the quality of the school matter?

Since we are dealing exclusively with children in this report, we treat access and utilization of a service to be equivalent. For example, if a child has a school close to her home, but does not attend school because her parents do not value education or cannot arrange an affordable means of transportation, for our effective purpose the child does not have access to schooling. For all services that society considers basic, it must provide the service *and* ensure that the child uses it. By this definition, access to primary schooling is synonymous with enrollment rate in primary schools and access to immunization is interchangeable with immunization rate among children of the appropriate age. In all these cases, the *society and the family are jointly responsible* for establishing all the necessary conditions for the child to actually benefit from the good or service. A child's lack of access to an opportunity, by this definition, may be due to the failure of the government, society, or the child's family, or any combination thereof, with the division of responsibility being immaterial to the way we measure. The extent to which a government should be held accountable for lack of access to a particular service is a judgment we would leave to our readers to make.

Another key consideration is quality. Basic goods and services are usually not homogeneous due to large variations in quality. Not all schools, for example, provide the same quality of instruction. In a study of equality of opportunity, it is important to assess what would be the minimum threshold of quality for each basic good or service. For example, sanitation may be considered a basic good, but a researcher must determine the level of sanitation that can be deemed a minimum standard within a particular cultural context. In the case of education, it would not be possible to take quality into consideration, except through imperfect proxies like completion of primary school on time (which may be related to learning outcomes or student achievement). The third section outlines our reasoning for selecting a set of opportunities for African countries.

From Concept to Measurement of Inequality of Opportunities

Traditionally, the opportunity indicator of choice for policy makers has been the coverage rate, i.e., the proportion of the population with access to a given opportunity, ignoring inequality among individuals with differing circumstances.

For example, if a quarter of the people in a country have access to clean water, the coverage rate is 25 percent, which ignores *how* opportunities are distributed among the population—the fact that a child's likelihood of access may depend on her circumstances, such as gender, ethnicity, or place of birth. When coverage of a basic good or service is 100 percent (or zero), the allocation of coverage across children with different circumstances is irrelevant. But when coverage is partial, the allocation mechanism—which child gets access and who does not—is important, and determines how equal a society is in terms of that opportunity.

The idea of combining coverage rate of a good or service with a measure of equality of opportunity is therefore appealing, with the condition that any comparative metric of equality of opportunity should reward more egalitarian allocation mechanisms. For complete equality of opportunity to prevail, all group-specific coverage rates must be the same. While coverage rates can be disaggregated by circumstance groups using incidence analysis, this approach does not provide a single synthetic scalar measure of how far a society is from both equality of opportunity and universal coverage. To track hundreds of coverage rates would be too cumbersome to be useful to both policy makers and other key stakeholders in society.

While the empirical literature on equality of opportunities is relatively recent, it has branched out in several directions that can be classified into two main categories: (a) studies with a clear sectoral and policy focus that explore causal links between circumstances and specific opportunities; and (b) diagnostic studies that include measuring the extent of equality of opportunities in a given country or region. Diagnostic studies also differ in terms of the circumstances and opportunities they consider (for a partial overview of this literature, see box 2.1). The literature provides a number of satisfactory measures of equality of opportunity—see, for example, Bourguignon, Ferreira, and Menendez (2007), Checchi and Peragine (2005), and Lefranc, Pistolesi, and Trannoy (2008, 2009); but none of these can be characterized as a simple *scalar measure* that is computable from the typical data available in developing countries.

The HOI is just such a measure, which synthesizes in a single indicator how close a society is to universal coverage in a given opportunity, along with how equitably coverage of that opportunity is distributed among groups with different circumstances. Opportunities are goods and services that constitute investments in children, thus increasing their human capital, such as primary education and adequate housing. Equality of opportunity would imply that a child's likelihood of accessing these key goods and services is not correlated with circumstances that are beyond his or her control, such as gender, parental background, or ethnicity. The HOI may be thought of as an inequality-sensitive coverage rate, which "penalizes" the extent to which different circumstance groups ("types" in Roemer's terminology, see box 2.1) have different coverage rates: the penalty is zero if coverage rates across different circumstance groups are equal and positive and increasing as differences in coverage among circumstance groups increase.

Box 2.1 Empirical Literature on Equality of Opportunities: An Overview

As a starting point, consider the five key concepts specified by Roemer (1998). *Objective* is the goal that equal opportunities are expected to achieve. *Circumstances* are the attributes of the environment of the individual (social, genetic, or biological) that affect the achievement of the objective, but that are beyond the control of the individual and for which society does not regard him or her responsible. *Effort* refers to individual behaviors and decisions that together with circumstances determine the level of objective accomplished. *Instrument* refers to the policy—typically the provision of resources—used to equalize opportunities. *Type* is the set of individuals, all of whom have the same circumstances (also referred to as "circumstance groups" in some literature). *Equality of opportunity* exists when an objective or opportunity is achieved across identical levels of effort across different circumstances groups or types. Roemer's work seeks the value of the instrument that equalizes the value of the objective across types at any given degree of effort (Roemer et al. 2003, 542). Examples of some empirical applications are Betts and Roemer (2007) and Bourguignon, Ferreira and Menendez (2007). Both of these papers analyze the effect that circumstances (father's and mother's education, father's schooling, race, and region of birth) and specific effort variables (such as own education, labor market status, and migration as opposed to an undefined residual) have on wage earnings differentials in Brazil.

Other strands of work—while remaining rooted in Roemer's concepts—have estimated inequality of opportunity in different ways. For example, Van der Gaer (1993), Ooghe, Schokkaert, and Van de Gaer (2007), Hild and Voorhoeve (2004), and Cogneau and Mesplé-Somps (2008) regard the dependence of the distribution of expected earnings on social origins to be a measure of inequality of opportunities. This body of work generally entails the estimation of the conditional expectations of earnings or consumption from the distribution of average income across several socioeconomic categories and performing tests of stochastic dominance. Opportunities are regarded to be more equally distributed if the distribution of earnings or income conditional on social origins cannot be ranked according to the stochastic dominance criteria (e.g., Lefranc, Pistolesi, and Trannoy 2008). Another method, used to measure inequality of opportunity in a number of countries in Latin America and Turkey, involves decomposing inequality of an outcome (consumption or income, or its proxy) into a between-component attributable to circumstances and a within-component attributable to effort or luck (Ferreira and Gignoux 2011; Ferreira, Gignoux, and Aran 2011).

Source: Summarized from Abras et al. (2013).

How Opportunities Matter for Economic Growth and Prosperity

The 2006 World Development Report argues that inequality of opportunity, within and among nations, weakens prospects for overall prosperity and economic growth. Extrapolating from the kind of micro-level evidence mentioned earlier, one would expect that increased opportunities in childhood in a country would have positive impacts on its growth prospects. The rich cross-country empirical literature linking economic growth with human capital has some relevance to this hypothesis. For example, Barro (2001) finds growth to be positively related to the average years of school attainment of adult males at the secondary and higher levels at the beginning of the period, in a panel of 100 countries observed from 1965 to 1995. While "quantity" of schooling is important, quality of schooling as measured by internationally comparable test scores is even more so. A number of studies in recent years have shown the effect of health on economic growth to be important (see Grimm 2011 for an overview).[4] Recent literature has also assessed the effect of *inequality in health* on economic growth. Grimm (2011) uses a cross-national panel data set of 62 low- and middle-income countries between 1985 and 2007 and finds a "substantial and relatively robust negative effect of health inequality on income levels and income growth."

While research establishing a causal link between *inequality of opportunity* and growth at the macro level is still at a nascent stage, the evidence so far seems to favor the hypothesis that inequality of opportunity has an adverse impact on growth and development. In a historical data set of nearly 100 countries, Molina, Narayan, and Saavedra (2013) find that inequality of opportunity (attributable to circumstances an individual is born into) in education among children has a negative impact on per capita income. Marrero and Rodriguez (2013), using data from states in the United States, find a negative relationship between the component of income inequality attributable to circumstances and economic growth (for a more detailed discussion of these papers, see box 2.2). Finally, in chapter 6 of this report, a measure of inequality of opportunity (which is a component

---

Box 2.2 Growth and Inequality of Opportunity: Recent Evidence

The relationship between inequality and economic development has been a subject of extensive research. Results are generally inconclusive due to the difficulties in measuring and testing competing hypotheses. More recently, new studies have taken a different route of measuring the impact of inequality of opportunity on development and gross domestic product (GDP) growth. The research starts with stressing the difference between two types of inequality: inequality due to differences in effort and innate ability, which can have a positive impact on economic growth by stimulating human capital accumulation; and inequality attributable to circumstances an individual is born into, which can have an opposite effect, by discouraging effort and education among the more talented individuals. Van der Gaer, Schokkaert, and Martinez (2001) have pointed out that inequality of opportunity reduces the role that talent plays in competing for a position by worsening intergenerational mobility.

The different types of inequality cannot be disentangled if one uses only aggregate measures such as the Gini coefficient of income. Molina, Narayan, and Saavedra (2013) estimate the relationship between a Human Opportunity Index (HOI) of education opportunities and per capita income of countries, on a historical data series of nearly 100 countries. The results

box continues next page

Box 2.2 Growth and Inequality of Opportunity: Recent Evidence *(continued)*

suggest that inequality of opportunity inhibits development. Moreover, the HOI and D-Index seem to proxy well for structural inequality that matters for growth: after controlling for equality of opportunity and instrumenting it with variables traditionally used in the literature, income inequality has no role in explaining average income levels. Another study using very different (income-based) measures of inequality of opportunity has pointed in the same direction. Marrero and Rodríguez (2013) test the hypothesis that inequality of opportunity and inequality of returns to effort affect economic growth in different directions, using the Panel Study of Income Dynamics (PSID) database for 23 states of the United States in 1980 and 1990. They find a negative relationship between inequality of opportunity and growth and a positive relationship between inequality of returns to effort and growth.

The literature has also found evidence to suggest that inequality in health matters for GDP. Grimm (2011) uses a cross-national panel data set of 62 low- and middle-income countries between 1985 and 2007. The gradient in child mortality over mothers' education groups is used as a proxy for disparity in health conditions to which different socioeconomic groups in a society are exposed. Even with such a narrow definition, the paper finds a significant negative effect of health inequality on economic growth, which is robust to different specifications, estimation methods, and time spells. A conservative estimate in the paper is that a reduction in health inequality caused by a reduction in the number of children—(born to mothers with a low education level)—who die before the age of five by about 4.25 per 1,000 children per year (a reduction of 5 percent) leads to an almost 8 percent increase in GDP per capita after a period of 10 years.

---

of the HOI) is found to be negatively correlated with per capita gross domestic product (GDP) of SSA countries. These correlations are *consistent* with the hypothesis that inequality of opportunity is harmful for economic prosperity in SSA, but do not provide conclusive evidence, which would require establishing a causal relationship.

Therefore, improving opportunities for children—by improving coverage and reducing inequality of opportunity—is not just about "fairness" and building a "just society," important as these principles are, but also about realizing a society's aspirations of economic prosperity. Notably, micro- and macrolevel evidence seems to suggest that the dividends of investing in opportunities among children are likely to accumulate over time and across generations.

Constructing the Human Opportunity Index[5]

The construction of the HOI involves aggregating circumstance-specific coverage rates in a scalar measure that increases with overall coverage and decreases with the differences in coverage among groups with different sets of circumstances. This implies that two societies that have identical coverage or an average access rate of a particular service may have a different HOI if the access to the service in one country is more concentrated among children of a certain set of circumstances. Specifically, the HOI (H) for a particular opportunity is the average coverage rate of access ($\bar{C}$) discounted by a penalty (P) due to inequality in coverage between children of different sets of circumstances:

$$H = \bar{C} - P. \tag{1}$$

The penalty is defined according to the set of circumstances considered.[6] It also implies that the maximum value of the HOI for a particular opportunity is the average coverage rate for that service, given by $\bar{C}$. It also implies that an HOI of 1 would be possible only when access is universal ($\bar{C}$ is equal to 1 and P is equal to 0). Alternatively, the HOI can be expressed as the coverage rate multiplied by a factor of equality:

$$H = \bar{C}\left(1 - \frac{P}{\bar{C}}\right) = \bar{C}(1 - D). \tag{2}$$

where $(1 - D)$ is the equality factor that is equal to 1 if access to the opportunity is independent of the circumstances, in which case the HOI is equal to the average coverage rate. D can be interpreted as share of the total number of opportunities that needs to be reallocated between circumstance groups[7] to ensure equality of opportunities, which we refer to as the dissimilarity index (henceforth, D-Index) or the inequality of opportunity index. With disjoint circumstance groups, one can compute D as follows:

$$D = \frac{1}{2\bar{C}} \sum_{k=1}^{m} \alpha_k \left| \bar{C} - C_k \right|. \tag{3}$$

Here k denotes a circumstance group (group of children with a specific set of circumstances); C_k the specific coverage rate of group k; α_k the share of group k in total population of children; and m the numbers of disjoint groups defined by circumstances. D is equal to zero when $C_k = \bar{C}$ for all k circumstance groups, in which case the HOI is equal to the coverage rate $\bar{C}$. It can be shown that D is equal to the *share* of total opportunities that are "misallocated" in favor of (against) circumstance groups that have coverage rates higher (lower) than $\bar{C}$. This also implies that any reallocation of opportunities to "vulnerable" groups (those with coverage less than $\bar{C}$) from "nonvulnerable" groups (with coverage more than $\bar{C}$) will reduce D and increase the HOI. Thus the HOI improves when inequality between circumstance groups decreases with a fixed number of opportunities in a society, or when the number of opportunities increases and inequality among circumstance groups stays constant.

Box 2.3 outlines a simple example of how the HOI is measured, in a hypothetical situation with two countries with identical populations of children and average coverage rates of primary school enrollment. The example demonstrates how the HOI is sensitive to inequality in coverage and how it would change in response to an increase in overall coverage or reallocation favoring the more disadvantaged group.

Box 2.3 A Stylized Example of an HOI

Consider two countries, A and B, each with a total population of 100 children, who can be divided into two groups, I and II, consisting of the top and bottom 50 percent by per capita income, respectively. Coverage rate of school enrollment (or the average enrollment rate) for both countries is 0.6, that is, 60 children attend school in each country. The table shows the number of children going to school in each group for each country.

Equality of opportunity will hold true for each country if each group has the same rate of coverage (30 children in school). But in reality group II has 20 enrollments in country A and 25 in country B. This suggests that, first, opportunities are unequally distributed, and second, inequality of opportunities is higher in country A. The D-Index is the share of total enrollments that is "misallocated," namely, 10/60 and 5/60 for A and B, respectively. Therefore, $HOI_A = 0.6 \times (1 - 10/60) = 0.50$; $HOI_B = 0.6 \times (1 - 5/60) = 0.55$. Thus, even though both countries have equal coverage rates, higher inequality of opportunity in country A leads to the D-Index being higher for A than for B, and the HOI being higher for B than for A. It is also easy to see that the HOI will increase in a country if (a) the number of enrollments in each group increases equally (in proportionate or absolute terms); (b) enrollment for any group increases without decreasing the coverage rates of the other group; and (c) enrollment for group II increases, keeping the total number of children enrolled unchanged. These three features relate to the "scale," "Pareto improvement," and "redistribution" properties of the HOI, respectively.

	No. of children enrolled in school	
Groups by circumstance (e.g., income)	Country A (100 children)	Country B (100 children)
I: top 50% by income	40	35
II: bottom 50% by income	20	25
Total	60	60

Note: HOI = Human Opportunity Index.

Properties and Limitations of the HOI

The important properties of the HOI are as follows: (a) *range:* the value of the HOI lies between $\bar{C}^2$ and $\bar{C}$; (b) *sensitivity to scale:* if coverage for all groups changes additively or multiplicatively by k, the HOI also changes (additively or multiplicatively) by the same factor k; (c) *sensitivity to Pareto improvements:* if coverage for one circumstance group increases without decreasing the coverage rates of the remaining groups, the HOI increases; and (d) *sensitivity to redistribution:* if the coverage rate of a vulnerable group increases holding the overall coverage rate constant, the HOI also increases. Properties (b), (c), and (d) are attractive properties for a measure like the HOI to have, as they ensure that improvements in overall coverage as well as a move toward greater equality in coverage among groups result in a higher HOI for a country.

Change in the HOI over time can be used to assess progress in access to opportunity in a society, taking into account both coverage and inequality in access among different circumstance groups. A decomposability property of an HOI is useful to understand the factors that contribute to the change. A change in an HOI can be decomposed into (a) the *composition* effect, which refers to changes in the distribution of circumstances (such as the distribution of wealth or urban/rural share of the population); (b) the *scale* effect, which refers to proportional change in the coverage rate of all groups; and (c) the *equalization* effect, which refers to change in the coverage of vulnerable groups (groups with coverage below the national average), with the average coverage rate held unchanged. The composition effect shows how the underlying circumstances that children are born into are changing over time, for example, because of demographic changes, economic growth, or social progress. The scale effect shows how opportunities are changing for all groups in the society, perhaps as a result of public policy or increased awareness among all households. The equalization effect indicates the trend in equity in a society, showing whether available opportunities are distributed more equitably among its members, so that the circumstances a child is born into begin to matter less for access to basic goods and services.

There are caveats to the measure as well, as would be the case for any measure, which are important to consider for interpreting the results. The first caveat is that by construction, the D-Index (and therefore the HOI) is a function of the set of circumstances and can change if a different set of circumstances is considered. This is a result of the HOI, by design, being sensitive only to inequality *between* circumstance groups. The problem that there is no *unique* D-Index or HOI for a particular opportunity in any population is mitigated somewhat by another property: the D-Index for a particular opportunity will not be lower (i.e., the HOI will not be higher) if more circumstances are added to an existing set of circumstances.[8] This is a useful property, given that it is impossible to consider *all* relevant circumstances for any population and opportunity; the selection of circumstances, which are exogenous to individuals, and relevant for society to consider, is a matter of subjective judgment *and* depends on what the data allow.

The second caveat relates to the *sensitivity* of the index to inequality. The D-Index does not change with redistribution of opportunities *among* vulnerable (or nonvulnerable) groups, namely, among groups that have below (or above) average coverage rate.[9] A third caveat is that the index is not *subgroup consistent*. This implies that the D-Index (and the HOI) for a population cannot be decomposed into similar measures for subgroups of the population, which means that the change in the HOI over time for the whole population may not be consistent with the change in the HOI for subgroups of the same population. The second and third caveats can be avoided by considering an alternative measure of the HOI, the "geometric HOI" (see annex). This measure is used in some country studies for disaggregated analysis of opportunities for subregions and subgroups within the country, but not in this report where such disaggregation is not attempted.[10]

Computing the HOI from Household Data

To compute the HOI for a particular opportunity for the children of a country, household survey data are essential. To allow computation of the HOI for specific opportunities, the survey must have a minimum set of information, at the individual (child) or household level as appropriate. Examples of these would be whether the child is attending school or not, grade level, last grade completed, and health indicators such as weight and height of the child and whether the child has been immunized or not. Computing the HOI for access to basic infrastructure, like safe water, electricity, and sanitation would require that household-level information on these indicators is available. With regard to circumstances, the minimum information needed to make the analysis meaningful would be gender, age, and location (urban/rural and/or regional) of the child; demographic characteristics of the household (size and composition); characteristics of the parents (gender, age, and education); and some measure of household income, consumption, or wealth.

In practical terms, computing the HOI for a particular opportunity when the number of circumstances is relatively large requires an econometric exercise,[11] which involves obtaining a prediction of the D-Index from observed access to opportunities and circumstances among children. In simple terms, the exercise consists of running a logistic regression model to estimate the relationship between access to a particular opportunity and circumstances of the child, on the full sample of children for whom the HOI measure will be constructed. The estimated coefficients of the regression are used to obtain for each child his/her predicted probability of access to the opportunity, which is then used to estimate the D-Index, the coverage rate, and eventually the HOI (see box 2.4).[12]

Examples of How the HOI Can Inform the Policy Debate

A society that attempts to provide equitable access to basic services would require progress toward two objectives: first, ensuring that as many people as possible get the opportunities; and second, allocating newly created opportunities first to those who are at a disadvantage due to their circumstances. An index like the HOI can be used to monitor progress toward these simultaneous objectives and help identify possible trade-offs between the two objectives. A common example of a trade-off would be one where improving coverage of a particular good or service among vulnerable (or underserved) groups costs more than that among the nonvulnerable groups in the country. In that scenario, a policy maker with a limited budget would face a trade-off between maximizing coverage (C), which will imply prioritizing in favor of children for whom the unit cost of expanding coverage is lower, and minimizing the penalty due to inequitable distribution among groups (P). Resolving this trade-off and deciding on policy choices will in effect depend on the social welfare function that the policy maker is trying to optimize.

If the definition of the HOI is consistent with the social welfare function of the policy maker, maximizing the HOI—subject to the budget constraint facing the policy maker—can be a possible objective to guide the decisions of the policy maker. In practical terms, this will come down to identifying the different groups (as defined by their circumstances), allocating appropriate amounts, and deciding on the strategy for improving coverage of the particular good or service

Box 2.4 Estimating the Human Opportunity Index from Household Survey Data

To obtain the conditional probabilities of access to an opportunity for each individual in the sample based on his/her circumstances, a logistic model is estimated, linear in the parameters β, where the event I corresponds to accessing the opportunity and x the set of circumstances:

$$\ln\left[\frac{Pr\{I=1|X=(x_1,\ldots,x_n)\}}{1-Pr\{I=1|X=(x_1,\ldots,x_n)\}}\right]=\sum_{k=1}^{n}x_k\beta_k, \tag{4}$$

where x_k denotes the row vector of variables representing n circumstances and β_k a corresponding column vector of parameters. From the estimation of regression (4) one obtains estimates of the parameters $\{\beta_k\}$, denoted as $\left\{\hat{\beta}_{k,m}\right\}$, where m denotes the sample size. Given the estimated coefficients, one can obtain for each individual in the sample his/her predicted probability of the opportunity in consideration:

$$\hat{p}_{i,m}=\frac{Exp\left(x_i\hat{\beta}_m\right)}{1+Exp\left(x_i\hat{\beta}_m\right)}. \tag{5}$$

Using the predicted probabilities ($\hat{p}$) and sample weights (w_i), we can find the predicted overall coverage rate ($\hat{\bar{C}}$) and D-Index ($\hat{D}$) as:

$$\hat{\bar{C}}=\sum_{i=1}^{m}w_i\hat{p}_{i,m} \tag{6}$$

$$\hat{D}=\frac{1}{2\hat{\bar{C}}}\sum_{i=1}^{m}w_i\left|\hat{p}_{i,m}-\bar{C}\right| \quad \text{(Note: } \hat{\bar{C}}=\bar{C}\text{)} \tag{7}$$

$$\hat{H}=\bar{C}\left(1-\hat{D}\right). \tag{8}$$

The list of regressors does not include any interaction terms between circumstances (e.g., between parental education and location). Given the number of circumstances we have (all dummy variables), limited sample sizes, and the large number of countries and opportunities for which these regressions have to be run, including interactions would lead to intractable problems in at least some of the cases. The interaction terms are thus omitted, even though translating the exact definition of the D-Index to the logistic regression model would require including these terms. If the interactions were included, it would result in a higher D-Index (and lower HOI), just as would happen if more circumstances were added. This in turn implies that the estimated D-Index for all countries and opportunities is the *lower bound* of inequality of opportunities (and the estimated HOI is the upper bound) for a given set of circumstances.

Source: Adapted from Barros, Molinas Vega, and Saavedra (2010).
Note: HOI = Human Opportunity Index.

among the targeted groups. That said, a social welfare function does not necessarily have to be consistent with the formulation of the HOI, in which case alternative ways of resolving such trade-offs would have to be found.

If a government prioritizes on improving certain services among underserved groups of children, an HOI analysis can provide guidance on which groups should be prioritized for what type of service. Chapter 5 of this report illustrates how the analysis can identify the circumstances that characterize the children with the least opportunity in a particular service. This can be useful for defining groups to target interventions, designing the *type* of interventions needed, and identifying overlaps in vulnerability (groups with deprivation along multiple dimensions), considering the cumulative impact of multiple deprivations on children. In all such cases, an HOI analysis must be seen as an important but small part of the full set of diagnostics needed to design and implement social policy interventions. It can provide broad guidance but would not substitute for more detailed analysis, which would include the modeling of behavior and learning from the implementation and evaluation of pilot interventions.

Toward an Empirical Analysis for African Countries

This analysis covers 20 countries from sub-Saharan Africa (SSA), which were selected by employing certain criteria. The first is that a Demographic and Health Survey (DHS) is available for each country for a recent year and, if possible, for an earlier year in the late 1990s or early 2000s.[13] Among the set of countries for which relevant DHS data are available, efforts were made to ensure that the selected set of countries together constitutes a large share of the population of SSA and has broad geographic coverage (in terms of regions within SSA).

Why is availability of a recent DHS the most important criterion for selecting a country for analysis? Although other surveys are available for these countries, the most important reason that a DHS is preferred over any other survey is that it is conducted using a (largely) similar methodology across countries and years, and is thus comparable across countries and over time. No other survey, including national household budget surveys and Living Standard Measurement Surveys (LSMS), offers this advantage for African countries. What makes the DHS special is also the extensive information it collects on health and education indicators for each individual child and access to basic infrastructure facilities for the household (see box 2.5).

The other two criteria are important as well. The 20 countries covered by the analysis—Cameroon, the Democratic Republic of Congo, Ethiopia, Ghana, Kenya, Liberia, Madagascar, Malawi, Mali, Mozambique, Namibia, Niger, Nigeria, Rwanda, Senegal, Sierra Leone, Tanzania, Uganda, Zambia, and Zimbabwe—represent 73 percent of the population of all of SSA.[14]

Map 2.1 shows the countries included in the study. For 17 countries, DHS data are available for two periods, where the "first" period corresponds to surveys collected in the late-1990s (circa 1998) and the "second" period to the late-2000s (circa 2008).[15] For the remaining three (the Democratic Republic of Congo,

Box 2.5 Demographic and Health Surveys as a Database for Analysis

For all countries and years, the Demographic and Health Survey (DHS) is a nationally representative household survey, which is usually representative at the level of urban/rural and some regions within a country as well. Every DHS includes information about the basic sociodemographic characteristics of all household members, household characteristics, and detailed nutritional and health information for women aged 15–49 years and their children. The DHS does not include an income or consumption module but does include information about household assets, housing, and infrastructure, which can be used to calculate a "wealth (or asset) index" for each household. There is compelling evidence that the wealth index is a good indicator for the economic status of a household and, according to some researchers, may even be better suited than the more commonly used consumption or income for explaining differences in education and health indicators (Rutstein and Johnston 2004; Filmer and Pritchett 2001). Another important feature of the DHS is its accessibility—the survey instruments and other documentation as well as the data are available freely on the Internet. This is a point in favor of its use for Human Opportunity Index (HOI) analysis as well; all computations in this volume can be replicated by anyone who adopts the methodology used here, which adds to the transparency of the analysis and its results.

Map 2.1 Countries Included in the Study

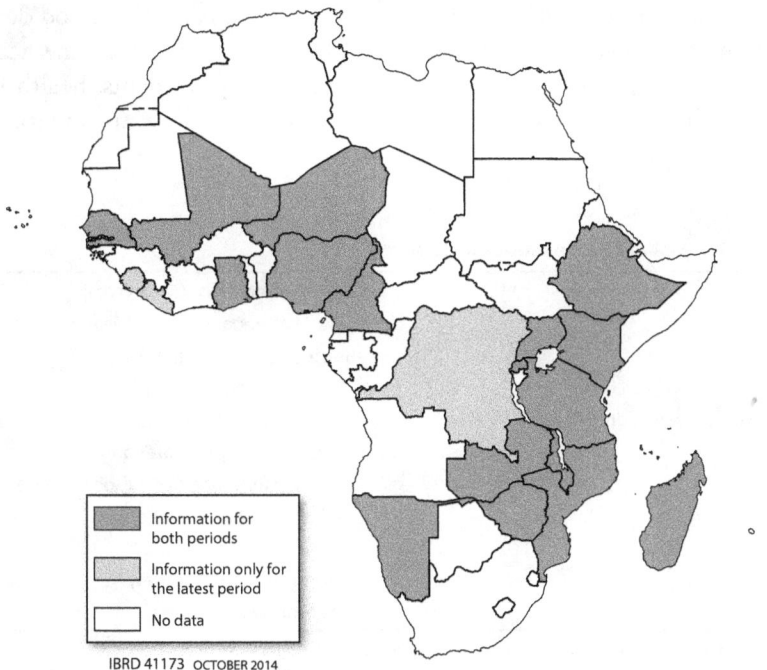

Information for both periods

Information only for the latest period

No data

IBRD 41173 OCTOBER 2014

Liberia, and Sierra Leone), data from only the more recent period are available (see annex 2A, table 2A.1 for a list of countries with survey years). Seven of these countries are in Western Africa, 10 are in Eastern Africa, 2 are in Central Africa, and 1 is in Southern Africa. Eleven of these countries can be classified as Anglophone and seven are Francophone, a distinction often used to classify countries in regional studies of SSA.[16] The map shows that there are large gaps in the coverage of countries by this study in the western part of SSA.

Selecting and Defining Opportunities for the Analysis

A useful starting point for selecting indicators that are proxies for opportunities is the medical literature, which suggests a set of basic prerequisites needed for childhood development. These include adequate nutrition and housing, a violence-free environment, and cognitive stimulation. Although adopting this ideal in practice is not easy when faced with data constraints, they do provide some guidance on the kind of opportunities that matter for a child to reach his or her potential.

Table 2.1 provides a list of indicators used as opportunities throughout the analysis for all countries and years. While these indicators are mostly about access to services and do not fully satisfy the definition of opportunities, they will be considered as representing opportunities in this study (see the discussion in the first section). The short list of indicators in this table is not in any way intended to represent all opportunities that should be available to a child to achieve his or her potential in life. A comprehensive list of key opportunities would cover a number of other indicators. These include indicators of early childhood development, learning achievement among children of different ages, children's access to preventive and curative health care and intake of key nutrients, health of the child at birth, access to key services for the mother at birth and pre- and

Table 2.1 List of Opportunities Included[a]

Education	School attendance (6–11 years)
	School attendance (12–15 years)
	Started primary on time[b]
	Finished primary school[c]
Infrastructure (children of age <16 years)	Access to piped-, well-, or rainwater
	Or Access to piped water only
	Access to flush toilet or pit toilet latrine
	Or Access to flush toilet only
	Access to electricity
Health	Full immunization (1 year)
	No stunting (0–2 years)

a. Education opportunities and health opportunities are not available for Senegal in period 1.
b. Defined for children 6–7 years old—attending primary school for 6-year-olds and having one or more years of education for those of age 7 years.
c. Defined for children 12–15 years old—attending sixth grade for 12-year-olds and completing six or more years of education for those of age 13–15 years.

postnatal care for mothers. All these basic goods or services (and others) would play some role in influencing the child's likelihood of achieving his or her potential in life and therefore the outcomes in adult life. Many of these would also be country- and context-specific; in other words, these would matter more for some countries and/or periods than for others.

Out of the long list of potential opportunities, the much shorter list in table 2.1 has been selected on the basis of two main criteria: first, that they represent key opportunities that are likely to be important for all 20 countries and second, that they are available from the DHS and can be defined similarly for all countries and years. In making the selection of opportunities and deciding on the standards for defining the opportunities, we have also been guided to some extent (but not fully) by MDGs. Given the large set of potential indicators and standards to choose from, MDGs provide a useful benchmark, as they reflect some degree of global consensus on priorities for developing countries. The MDG indicators are also consistent with what many, including African nations, regard as critical economic and social rights of children, with the implication that universality in these dimensions should be the goal for all countries to strive toward (see box 2.6).

Box 2.6 The Rights and Welfare of the Child and MDGs

Out of the eight Millennium Development Goals (MDGs) for 2015, six are directly linked to the well being of children and their rights to health, education, protection, and equality: poverty and hunger eradication, universality in primary education, gender equality and female empowerment, reducing child mortality, improving maternal health, and combating HIV/AIDS and other diseases. As mentioned earlier, Sub-Saharan Africa (SSA) progress toward those goals lags behind other regions.

The well-being of children has been a long-standing concern expressed by the Geneva Declaration of the Rights of the Child of 1924, the Declaration of the Rights of the Child adopted by the General Assembly on November 20, 1959, and the current Convention on the Rights of the Child (CRC) negotiated among United Nations Member States. The core values of the CRC are centered on the care for children in order to enable them to develop their full potential and live free of abuse or exploitation. The fundamental principles guiding those values concern nondiscrimination, a child's right to have a say in decisions affecting them, and a focus on the best interests of children, their survival, development, and protection. The African Union (AU, previously Organization of African Unity) adopted the African Charter on the Rights and Welfare of the Child (ACRWC), which was entered into force in 1999. The ACRWC was inspired in the CRC with regard to its principles, although originated by member states of the AU under the concern that the CRC missed some of the sociocultural and economic realities particular to Africa. As of March 2010, among the 20 countries included in this study, the Democratic Republic of Congo was the only country yet to ratify the ACRWC.

box continues next page

Box 2.6 The Rights and Welfare of the Child and MDGs *(continued)*

How is a right-based approach to provision of basic services to children consistent with the HOI-based approach used here? The answer is complex. The rights-based approach, which emphasizes universal coverage of basic services, satisfies the equality of opportunity principle trivially. But the two also diverge, since universal coverage is not *necessary* for equality of opportunity. The HOI, however, is a measure that *combines* universality with equality of opportunity, penalizing a society not just by its distance from universal coverage but also by the extent of inequity in coverage among different groups. The equity-sensitive coverage measured by the HOI is thus consistent with the principle of nondiscrimination embedded in a rights-based approach. One must, however, be cautious about how the HOI is interpreted: inequality of opportunity is by no means synonymous with discrimination; it can at best be a useful starting point into further inquiry about the causes of inequality, including the role of policy discrimination, if any. The HOI can also serve as a measure to track progress toward progressive realization of a particular economic, social, or cultural right, another key element of the rights-based framework.

Sources: UNICEF 2007; Official text of CRC and list of country signers available at http://www.africa-union.org.
Note: HOI = Human Opportunity Index.

The opportunities included in this report are restricted to the information available in the DHS and are classified into three dimensions: education, basic infrastructure, and health. Since we are conducting a multicountry analysis, the definition of all opportunities should be identical across countries. Although a country-specific analysis could employ a more thorough and contextual treatment of opportunities, having a uniform list and definition is necessary to compare across countries, which is a key objective of this volume. Therefore, we find that the negatives of being constrained to a set of opportunities that is uniform across countries are outweighed by the benefit of constructing an index that is comparable across countries.

For education, we use indicators for both attendance and achievement. Access to education would require, in addition to the availability of quality schools, a number of complementary inputs such as safe transportation, positive attitudes among parents toward education, and an intra-household division of labor that allows children to attend schooling. In the absence of direct information on such ancillary inputs to educational access, the school attendance measure provides a good proxy since it presupposes that these conditions have already been met. The indicators selected are attendance in school for children of age 6–11 years (primary school age) and children of age 12–15 years (post-primary school age). Finally, it is important to note that what is referred to here and throughout the study as "attendance" is synonymous with "enrollment." In other words, attendance refers to a child being enrolled in school, and does not take into account the number of days actually spent in school during a specified period of time.

Achievement indicators are a proxy for both school quality and a child's ability to use his or her education to attain a basic level of learning. Information on direct measures of achievement is not available for many of the countries included in this study. Standardized test scores of fifth or sixth graders are available from two separate projects—the Southern and Eastern Africa Consortium for Monitoring Educational Quality (SACMEQ) and the CONFEMEN Programme for the Analysis of Education Systems (PASEC). Even after pooling the two sources, test scores are unavailable for 5 out of 20 countries included in this study. Most important, it would not be appropriate to combine test score data from two different sources for a comparison of equality of opportunity across countries.[17] Therefore, in an HOI analysis, we use indicators for starting primary school on time (among children of age 6–7 years) and finishing primary school (among 12- to 15-year-olds), as partial and indirect proxies for quality of education. Starting primary school on time improves the likelihood that a child gets the necessary educational inputs at an early age. Children who complete primary school by a certain age are more likely to have achieved minimum learning and stayed in school continuously without dropping out, characteristics that may also bode well for their education beyond primary level, compared to those who do not.

For basic infrastructure facilities, the indicators selected as opportunities are access to a safe source of drinking water, appropriate sanitation facilities, and electricity for children between 0 and 16 years old. Water and sanitation are primary drivers of public health, improvement in which have been shown to reduce incidence of diarrhea and its serious long-term consequences such as malnutrition, pneumonia, and physical or mental stunting. Access to electricity is an important contributor to quality of life and facilitates access to other opportunities, as it facilitates studying, improves access to information, and reduces the time spent on physical chores (Barros et al. 2009).

Since information on these infrastructure facilities is available at the household level, we assume that all children living in the household enjoy identical access to these services. One challenge is to define appropriate standards for "safe" water and "adequate" sanitation that are comparable across countries and over time. Taking into account internationally accepted standards and the data source available to us (DHS), we decided to use two indicators for safe water for all countries: a restrictive standard of piped water being available in the household and a more lenient standard of the household having access to piped, well, or rainwater. There are two main reasons for adopting two alternative standards for safe water. *First*, access to piped water is considerably low for Africa (which limits the usefulness of the HOI as a metric) and may not be a realistic objective for poor and predominantly rural countries to attain in the medium term. *Second*, given the lack of a universal standard for what constitutes safe water, using both standards offers the choice to policy makers to focus on the results with the standard that is most relevant for their country. For similar reasons, we use two standards for sanitation as well: access to a flush toilet (restrictive) and access to a flush toilet or pit toilet (lenient).

For health, we define two indicators as opportunities. For one-year-old children, we use full immunization and for children under three years, we use an indicator for whether the child is stunted (low height-for-age). The first is an indicator of the opportunities for prevention against deadly but easily protectable diseases. The second indicator, which is the opportunity to be adequately nourished, is a key measure of health status in childhood, with implications for human potential and lifelong earnings. As opposed to the other opportunities considered here, which are in most cases inputs that can be directly influenced by sectoral policies and programs, not being stunted is a function of the availability of a complex bundle of inputs, which includes access to safe water and adequate sanitation, breastfeeding, and food intake with adequate calories and micronutrients, mapping to different sectors like infrastructure and health. Moreover, unlike the other opportunities that are about access to services, not being stunted (a proxy for "being nourished") involves a "functioning"—namely, a previous process through which nourishment is achieved.

Finally, in one part of the analysis in subsequent chapters, we use a particular definition of opportunities, which yields a "composite HOI" that reflects access to multiple goods and services for the same child. For this part of the analysis, "opportunity" refers to a child being covered by *all* the goods and services that are relevant for a child of that age, and this definition is then used to compute the HOI exactly the same way as before. For each country, children are classified into two age groups—1-year-olds and 6- to 11-year-olds—and the goods and services relevant for each age group are considered. This exercise yields two "composite" HOIs, one for each age group in each country for a given year. The composite HOI has an intuitive interpretation: it reflects the extent to which children of a particular age group are covered by *all* the basic opportunities relevant for their age and how unequal is the coverage between different groups of children. It is derived from the idea that none of the basic opportunities listed earlier are substitutes for one another, and the absence of any one of them constitutes an inadequacy in human opportunities that society must care about.

Defining a Set of Circumstances for SSA Countries

Circumstances are exogenous characteristics of the child which, in order to satisfy the principle of equality of opportunities in a society, should not be correlated with having access to a basic good or service. In reality, however, a number of such characteristics could matter for access and the analysis in this report will attempt to identify how much they actually matter. The exact criteria for determining which characteristics should be considered "circumstances" are complex. Ideally, each society should choose its own set of circumstances that it believes should not interfere with access to basic goods and services. At the same time, for results of a multicountry analysis to be comparable across countries, the circumstances chosen should be identical for all countries. For the purposes of our analysis, a set of circumstances common across all countries is selected, taking into account the characteristics that most societies would accept as *should not* be mattering for a child's access to basic goods and services, but *may in fact* matter. The list of circumstances is also informed by the choices made for previous work on the HOI in the LAC region by Barros et al. (2009, 2012), albeit with some changes reflecting differences in the regional context of Africa and Latin America and the nature of the data available for each region.

The circumstances we select can be categorized into five main groups: characteristics of the child, household composition, location, characteristics of the household head (or mother), and socioeconomic status of the household. Table 2.2 shows the complete list of circumstances within each category considered for every type of opportunity. While the categories are the same for all types of opportunities, three of the individual circumstances—gender of the child, presence of an elderly person (65 years and older) in the household, and location (urban or rural) of the household—are identical across all opportunities. For the rest, *there are some differences in the definition of the circumstances used for education and infrastructure opportunities versus those used for health opportunities* (see table 2.2). These differences occur due to a combination of two factors: data availability and the relevance of a particular circumstance for an opportunity.[18]

As mentioned earlier, the list of circumstances selected for constructing the HOI for an opportunity matters a great deal for the measure. Given this, all results that follow in subsequent chapters are subject to the caveat that the HOI is estimated for a specified list of circumstances and therefore subject to change if this list were to change. This is quite different, for instance, from a standard inequality measure (like Gini coefficient of income), which has a unique value for a given distribution of income. But another property of the HOI, mentioned in the second section mitigates this concern. While the HOI for an opportunity is not unique and depends on the number of circumstances considered, it can not be higher if more circumstances are added to the existing list.

Table 2.2 List of Circumstances

Dimension	Education opportunities	Infrastructure opportunities	Health opportunities
Child characteristics	Child's gender	Child's gender	Child's gender
			Birth order
Household composition	Children (0–15 years) in the household	Children (0–15 years) in the household	Siblings living in the household
	Presence of elderly (65+ years)	Presence of elderly (65+ years)	Presence of elderly (65+ years)
	Presence of both parents in the household	Presence of both parents in the household	Mother living with a husband or not
	Both parents alive	Both parents alive	
Location	Location (urban/rural)	Location (urban/rural)	Location (urban/rural)
Household head/mother characteristics	Education of household head	Education of household head	Education of mother
	Age of household head	Age of household head	Age of mother
	Gender of household head	Gender of household head	
Socioeconomic status	Wealth quintiles	Wealth quintiles	Wealth quintiles

Note: The set of circumstances for Senegal in period 1 does not include education of the household head, Nigeria in period 1 does not include wealth quintiles, and Kenya in period 2 does not include orphan status and presence of parents. The reason for the omission in all these cases is that the information is not available.

Do African Children Have an Equal Chance? · http://dx.doi.org/10.1596/978-1-4648-0332-1

In other words, if a society wants to measure equality of opportunity with reference to a *larger* number of groups than we have considered, the measure of the HOI we provide will serve as an *upper bound* to the "true" HOI that would consider all circumstance groups.

Having a common set of circumstances for a given opportunity across all countries also implies that certain circumstances important for inequality in a particular country are absent from the list. This could lead to the HOI (D-Index) estimated for that country to be over-(under) estimated and not reflect the "true" inequality of opportunity in the country. Ethnicity is a notable example of such an omitted circumstance (see the detailed discussion below). Given this potential issue, the results throughout this report should be interpreted as the upper (lower) bounds of the HOI and D-Index for an opportunity in a particular country, computed for a set of circumstances common to all countries. In other words, country-specificity is sacrificed for comparability across countries, a trade-off that seems appropriate for a multicountry study.

Finally, it is important to take into account the effect of excluding any interaction between circumstances from the logit estimation model to compute predicted probability of access (see box 2.4). As explained there, the simplified specification is essential for the analysis to be tractable, and implies that the HOI (D-Index) should be interpreted as the upper (lower) bound of what the estimates would be if interactions were included. The omission of interactions also means that the additional effect of "double disadvantages" on access to a service cannot be taken into account. This could occur, for example, when the cumulative disadvantage of being a girl child in a rural area is different from what is suggested by the marginal effects of gender and location on school attendance. Such disadvantages have been analyzed in the literature in various contexts— Lewis and Lockheed (2006), for example, show that girls in rural areas are doubly disadvantaged in access to education in a number of countries.[19] While the inability to account explicitly for a double disadvantage in our analysis is no doubt a limitation, its effect on HOI and D-Index measures is likely to be small in most cases. The caveat would, however, apply more strongly to the analysis of how each individual circumstance contributes to inequality, the subject of chapter 4 of this volume.

Ethnicity as a "Missing" Circumstance

In the case of SSA countries, the absence of any circumstance related to differences in ethnicity (or race or tribal affiliation) in this study is a notable omission. Anecdotal as well as empirical evidence suggests that these differences, which have arisen or accumulated due to a combination of historical factors, can be important in explaining inequality of opportunities in some of the SSA countries (see box 2.7).

At the same time, the fact that these differences are always country-specific is an argument against including them as circumstances in a multicountry study like this one, where the need for a cross-country comparison requires that the same set (and definition) of circumstances be used across all countries.[20]

Box 2.7 Ethnic Inequalities in Sub-Saharan Africa and the Example of Kenya

According to the 2004 UN Human Development Report, "more than 150 countries have significant minority ethnic or religious groups, and only 30 countries do not have a religious or ethnic minority that constitutes at least 10% of the population" (p. 29). The divisions between ethnic groups can be deeper in the case of colonial states, especially African ones, where colonial powers could utilize ethnic segmentations to their advantage, and post-independence boundaries did not always overlap with the geographic separation of ethnic minorities. Not all ethnic groups are necessarily subject to discrimination or suffer from socioeconomic disadvantages, but conflict and socioeconomic needs often combine to aggravate initial differences in opportunity outcomes between groups.

Consider the case of inequality in education and health in Kenya. Kenya's data (Alwy and Schech 2004) suggest that geographical location and proximity to the ruling elite led to an uneven distribution of educational resources and an accumulation of advantages of certain ethnic affiliations over the rest of the national population. Large differences persist in both access to and quality of primary education, as measured by the Gross Enrollment Rates and the examination results in the different provinces. Differences are seen in the low performance of North Eastern regions and the Coast Province, where the Somali and the Swahili reside, juxtaposed against the high school enrollment rates in Nairobi, the Central Province, and the Rift Valley Province. Inequality can be traced back in time, to the 1960s and 1970s, when regions where the ethnic group of the President (the Kikuyu) predominated may have received preferential treatment. Inequalities were also not limited to education only, nor did the same ethnic group always receive preferential treatment. During the period of President Moi in the 1980s and 1990s, advantages accrued to his ethnic group (the Kalenjin). Brockerhoff and Hewett (1998) found that children of this ethnic group were 50 percent less likely than others to die before age five years. More broadly, groups with high levels of government representation display better childhood immunization outcomes given that their political influence placed them closer to the infrastructure of health clinics and well-paved roads.

Sources: "Ethnicity and Child Mortality in Sub-Saharan Africa" (Brockerhoff and Hewett), Population Council (1998). "Ethnic Inequalities in Education in Kenya" (Alwy and Schech), *International Education Journal* 5(2), (2004). *Human Development Report: Cultural Liberty in Today's Diverse World* (UNDP 2004).

One practical solution could have been to use geographic location as an (imperfect) proxy for ethnic differences—given that ethnic groups are concentrated by location in most countries. But this also proves to be unworkable in a multi-country setting because we cannot define "regions" using available data in a way that applies to all countries, which also simultaneously serves as a proxy for ethnic differences in each country.[21] Moreover, even if one were to ignore or circumvent the need for an identical definition of a circumstance across countries, the lack of available data on ethnicity (or its proxies like language or even location) for many countries in the DHS data would still make it very difficult to include these as circumstances. Therefore, the list of circumstances lacks any indicator or proxy for ethnicity or tribal affiliation. The only circumstance that even remotely approaches capturing these differences is urban/rural location of the child, and only if a certain ethnic group(s) in a country is more concentrated in urban (or rural) parts of a country than others.

What does the exclusion of ethnicity (or its proxies) from the list circumstances imply for our analysis of inequality of opportunities in the chapters that follow? There are two main points to consider. *First*, as is the case with the omission of any potential circumstances of importance, the HOI (D-Index) can be lower (higher) only if ethnicity were to be included as a circumstance. Thus, our estimated HOI (D-Index) for any opportunity would continue to be an upper (lower) bound of what we would have estimated had ethnicity been included as a circumstance. *Second*, to the extent that ethnicity may be correlated with one or more of the socioeconomic circumstances we do include (e.g., household wealth, parental education), our measure of inequality of opportunities and the HOI would reflect differences between ethnic groups as well. What it would *not* reflect are the differences between ethnic groups *net of the effects* of other circumstances—an important point to consider for the discussion on how different circumstances contribute to inequality (chapter 5).

We conclude by noting that the discussion in this chapter sets the stage for what is to follow in chapters 3 to 6 of this study, which will focus on the main results with an HOI analysis for 20 countries, for the opportunities described above. The HOI for an opportunity in each country will measure the inequality adjusted coverage rate for the opportunity, where the adjustment is the penalty assigned for inequality in coverage between different groups. The groups will be defined by the circumstances listed in table 2.2, reflecting the consensus in society about exogenous factors that should not influence a child's access to basic goods and services.

Annex 2A

A Graphical Interpretation of an HOI

Figure 2A.1 shows a simple graphical interpretation of an HOI. It graphs the probability of a child of a particular circumstance (e.g., percentile of per capita income or wealth) completing sixth grade on time, with circumstance (on the horizontal axis) improving from left to right. The horizontal line is the average coverage rate for the entire population of children. The curved line shows access rates for different levels of circumstance. There is *inequality* of opportunity in this case, since probability of access to the opportunity is positively correlated with circumstance, which is shown by the fact that the curved line does not coincide with the horizontal line. Opportunities allocated in the red area above the horizontal line violate the equality of opportunity principle: they show dependence of the access to education on income or wealth. There is an intuitive interpretation of the red area: it is the share of the total number of opportunities that are "misallocated" in favor of children with better circumstances so that they have higher than average access to the opportunity.[22]

Figure 2A.1 A Simple Graphical Interpretation of an HOI

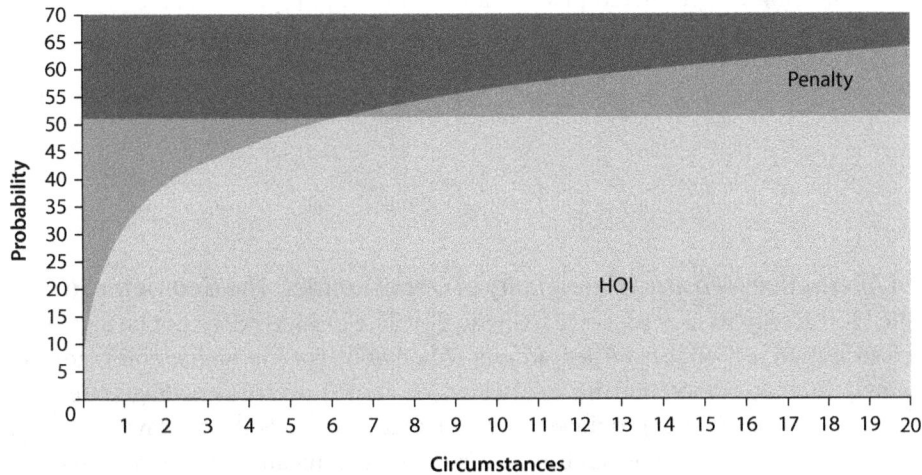

Source: Adapted from Barros, Molinas Vega, and Saavedra 2010.
Note: HOI = Human Opportunity Index.

Computing the Human Opportunity Index from Household Survey Data

In order to construct the HOI, we need to obtain the conditional probabilities of access to opportunities for each child based on his or her circumstances. In order to do so, one can estimate a logistic model, linear in the parameters β, where the event I corresponds to accessing the opportunity (e.g., access to clean water), and x the set of circumstances (e.g., gender of the child, education, and gender of the head of the household, etc.). We fit the logistic regression using survey data:

$$Ln\left(\frac{P\left[I=1\middle|X=(x_1,...,x_m)\right]}{1-P\left[I=1\middle|X=(x_1,...,x_m)\right]}\right) = \sum_{k=1}^{m} x_k\beta_k. \tag{9}$$

where x_k denotes the row vector of variables representing the k-dimension of circumstances, hence, $x=(x_1,...,x_m)$ and $\beta'=(\beta_1,...,\beta_m)$ a corresponding column vector of parameters. From the estimation of this logistic regression, one obtains estimates of the parameters $\{\beta_k\}$ to be denoted by $\{\hat{\beta}_{k,n}\}$, where n denotes the sample size.

Given the estimated coefficients, one can obtain for each individual in the sample his or her predicted probability of access to the opportunity in consideration:

$$\hat{p}_{i,n} = \frac{Exp\left(x_i\hat{\beta}_n\right)}{1+Exp\left(x_i\hat{\beta}_n\right)}. \tag{10}$$

Finally, compute the overall coverage rate, C, the D-Index, the penalty, P, and the HOI using the predicted probability $\hat{p}$ and sampling weights, w:

$$C = \sum_{i=1}^{n} w_i \hat{p}_{i,n} \quad D = \frac{1}{2C} \sum_{i=1}^{n} w_i \left| \hat{p}_{i,n} - C \right| \tag{11}$$

$$P = C * D; \text{ and } HOI = C - P.$$

An Alternative Measure of Inequality of Opportunities: The Geometric HOI

The HOI is only weakly sensitive to inequality. The D-Index does not change with redistribution of opportunities among vulnerable (or nonvulnerable) groups, namely, among groups that have a below (or above) average coverage rate. The geometric HOI (GHOI), defined as the average of a strictly concave function, avoids this limitation. The GHOI is the geometric mean of the circumstance-specific coverage rates and happens to be subgroup consistent. For instance, the GHOI for a country is equivalent to the geometric mean of the GHOI of all regions in the country, that is, $GHOI = \prod_r \left(GHOI_r \right)^{\infty_r}$, where $GHOI_r$ is the population weighted geometric mean of the circumstance group specific coverage rates

Table 2A.1 List of Countries with DHS Surveys, by Year

Country	Period 1 (circa 1998)	Period 2 (circa 2008)	Origin	Region
Cameroon	1998	2004	Francophone	Central
Congo, Dem. Rep.[a]		2007	Francophone	Central
Ethiopia	2000	2011		Eastern
Ghana	1998	2008	Anglophone	Western
Kenya	1998	2008–09	Anglophone	Eastern
Liberia[a]		2007	Anglophone	Western
Madagascar	1997	2008–09	Francophone	Eastern
Malawi	2000	2010	Anglophone	Eastern
Mali	1995–96	2006	Francophone	Western
Mozambique	1997	2003		Eastern
Namibia	2000	2006–07	Anglophone	Southern
Niger	1998	2006	Francophone	Western
Nigeria	1999	2008	Anglophone	Western
Rwanda	2000	2010	Francophone	Eastern
Senegal	1997	2010–11	Francophone	Western
Sierra Leone[a]		2008	Anglophone	Western
Tanzania	1996	2010	Anglophone	Eastern
Uganda	1995	2006	Anglophone	Eastern
Zambia	1996	2007	Anglophone	Eastern
Zimbabwe	1994	2010–11	Anglophone	Eastern

Source: Demographic and Health Surveys, various years (as of August 2012).
Note: DHS = Demographic and Health Surveys.
a. Countries for which a DHS of only one year is available.

in region r and α_r is the fraction of the population in region r. As a consequence, the country index would always increase when all regional indexes increase.

Combining the use of an HOI and a GHOI allows us to benefit from the relative strengths of these two indexes that share the basic idea (of measuring an inequality-sensitive coverage rate) and many of their properties. The HOI is accessible to a broad audience and includes an intuitive interpretation of the D-Index. The advantages of the GHOI over the HOI are its sensitivity to any change in the distribution of circumstance-specific coverage rates and its sub-group consistency, which can be important for analyzing changes in the HOI at subpopulation (or group) levels. But the GHOI is less intuitive than the HOI and does not have an easy graphical interpretation; and if the coverage of an opportunity for any circumstance group is very low, so is the GHOI. This is not very intuitive, especially when the number of circumstances is relatively large: a measure that approaches zero when an opportunity is rare among a relatively small segment of the population has limited use to policy makers in the real world. For these reasons, the GHOI will be used only for a few specific parts of the analysis in this volume, namely when subgroup consistency is a requirement.

Notes

1. This section draws in part from Barros et al. (2009, 2012); Barros, Malinas Vega, and Saavedra (2010); and Abras et al. (2013).

2. The process involves a transformation function, which depends on individual, social, and contextual (institutional) aspects. A larger set of options ("life plans" or combinations of functionings) in the capability set implies more "effective freedom" (see Basu and Lopez-Calva 2011 and Sen 2001).

3. There may be some ambiguity about when effort actually becomes relevant for a child, which is likely to depend on the social, cultural, and ethical norms that vary across societies. A more pragmatic approach is to consider effort as being irrelevant for children below age 16, which would dilute the concern about possible correlations between effort and circumstances.

4. Estimating health effects on income is difficult due to problems in measuring health and the potential endogeneity of health (see Deaton, 2006). Studies like Bloom, Canning, and Sevilla (2004), Weil (2007), Lorentzen, McMillan, and Wacziarg (2008), Bloom, Canning, and Fink (2009), and Cervelatti and Sunde (2009), using different methods, have shown health effects on income or growth to be important and probably exceeding the reverse effect, namely that of income on health. The debate is, however, not fully settled yet, due to the difficulties previously mentioned.

5. This section is a much shorter version of the detailed conceptual discussion in Barros et al. (2009, 2012). For a complete description of the measure, its rationale, properties, and limitations, see Barros, Malinas Vega, and Saavedra (2010).

6. The penalty depending on circumstances implies that the penalty will change if we change the set of circumstances, and will be zero if no circumstances are considered.

7. A "circumstance group" is a group of children that share the same circumstances. For example, a circumstance group can be all children who share the traits of living in a rural area with parental income in the lowest quintile and parental education of

primary level. The number of circumstance groups will depend on the number of circumstances being considered and the number of categories within each circumstance.

8. More formally, $D = D(x)$, where x is the vector of circumstances. It can be shown that $D(x) \leq D(x, z)$ for any set of circumstances z (see Barros, Malinas Vega, and Saavedra 2010 for a formal proof). Note, however, that this property may not hold for a change in the *definition* of a circumstance, as opposed to an increase in the number of circumstances. In other words, if the same circumstance were to be defined in a different way, for example, by changing the categories within a circumstance, there is no guarantee that the HOI will always move in the same direction.

9. To illustrate what this means, consider a country where the average school enrollment rate for 12- to 15-year-olds is 50 percent and enrollment rates for circumstance groups H and L are 40 percent and 30 percent, respectively. A shift of enrollment in favor of the more vulnerable group (group L) that results in an enrollment rate of 35 percent for both groups will leave the D-Index and HOI unchanged.

10. Combining the use of the HOI and Geometric HOI (GHOI) can allow us to benefit from the relative strengths of these two indexes that share the basic idea and many of their properties. The advantages of the GHOI are its sensitivity to any change in the distribution of circumstance-specific coverage rates and its subgroup consistency. But the GHOI is less intuitive than the HOI and does not have an easy graphical interpretation. For these reasons, the GHOI is typically used in HOI analysis only when subgroup consistency is a requirement, which is not the case in this study since subregional- or subgroup-level analysis is not attempted for any country.

11. It is easy to see that the number of circumstance groups multiplies rapidly as the number of circumstances (and the number of categories within each circumstance) increases. When the number of circumstance groups becomes large, the non-parametric method of computing the index, which will require computing D as given by equation (3), becomes unwieldy and runs into problems due to extremely small sample sizes for some of the groups.

12. For more details, see Barros, Malinas Vega, and Saavedra (2010).

13. This refers to availability of surveys as of August 2012, when the analysis for this study was completed.

14. This estimation is based on the most recent estimates of the World Development Indicators.

15. For 1 of the 17 countries (Senegal), information on education and health opportunities is not available for the earlier year (circa 1998).

16. Francophone countries in the sample of 20 countries are Cameroon, the Democratic Republic of Congo, Madagascar, Mali, Niger, Rwanda, and Senegal. Anglophone countries are Ghana, Kenya, Liberia, Malawi, Namibia, Nigeria, Sierra Leone, Tanzania, Uganda, Zambia, and Zimbabwe. Ethiopia and Mozambique are classified as "other."

17. The SACMEQ project has collected test scores for sixth graders in 15 countries in southern and eastern Africa, with the latest data being available for 2007. The PASEC project has tested second and fifth graders in 22 Francophone countries. However, even if the two sets of data are combined, test scores are not available for five countries included in our study—Ethiopia, Ghana, Liberia, Nigeria, and Sierra Leone. Moreover, data from the two sources are not designed to be comparable, due to differences in the content and methodology of the tests.

18. Health opportunities are available from a module of the DHS survey that is quite separate from the modules that yield information on education and infrastructure. This essentially means that certain types of circumstances, which can be used for constructing an HOI of health opportunities, either were not available for other opportunities or had to be replaced with circumstances that served as proxies (e.g., education of household head substituting for education of mother). In some cases, circumstances used for a particular opportunity are not relevant for another type of opportunity—for example, birth order is relevant for health opportunities but not for infrastructure, access to which is at the household rather than child level.

19. Also see Lockheed (2008) and Lewis and Lockheed (2008). Also see Filmer (2008), who analyzes education inequality in a large number of countries along a dimension such as income quintiles, gender, and orphanhood, and documents some of the effects of double disadvantages. For example, when being female is associated with lower educational attainment, the shortfall is largest among the poor.

20. One way around the problem of the lack of common ethnic groups across countries is to classify children according to the minority (or majority) status of their ethnic group in a country. But even this proves to be very difficult without using some highly arbitrary means of classification, given that many of the SSA countries are composed of multiple ethnic groups, none of which have a "majority" status in terms of their share of the population. Using language (instead of ethnic) groups leads to the same problem.

21. In some countries, the number of regions is also too large to be incorporated in our analysis as a circumstance—a large number of regional "dummies" as independent variables in the logistic regression, given the sample sizes we have, leads to insurmountable problems in the estimation process.

22. This also implies that the red area is the share of total opportunities that would have to be reallocated to children with lower than average opportunities, in order to achieve equality of opportunities, for a given level of coverage.

References

Abras, A., A. Hoyos, A. Narayan, and S. Tiwari. 2013. "Inequality of Opportunities in the Labor Market: Evidence from Life in Transition Surveys in Europe and Central Asia." *IZA Journal of Labor & Development* 2: 7. http://www.izajold.com/content/2/1/7.

Alderman, H., J. Hoddinott, and B. Kinsey. 2006. "Long-Term Consequences of Early Childhood Malnutrition." *Oxford Economic Papers* 58 (3): 450–74.

Alwy, A., and S. Schech. 2004. "Ethnic Inequalities in Education in Kenya." *International Education Journal* 5 (2): 266–74.

Arneson, R. 1989. "Equality and Equality of Opportunity for Welfare." *Philosophical Studies* 56: 77–96.

———. 1990. "Liberalism, Distributive Subjectivism, and Equal Opportunity for Welfare." *Philosophy and Public Affairs* 19 (2): 158–94.

Barro, R. 2001. "Human Capital and Growth." *American Economic Review* 91 (2): 12–17.

Barros, R., F. Ferreira, J. Molinas Vega, and J. Saavedra. 2009. *Measuring Inequality of Opportunities in Latin America and the Caribbean*. Washington, DC: World Bank.

Barros, R., J. Molinas Vega, and J. Saavedra. 2010. "Measuring Progress Toward Basic Opportunities for All." *Brazilian Review of Econometrics* 30 (2): 335–67.

Barros, R., J. Molinas Vega, J. Saavedra, and M. Giugale. 2012. *Do Our Children Have a Chance? A Human Opportunity Report for Latin America and the Caribbean.* Washington, DC: World Bank.

Basu, K., and L. Lopez-Calva. 2011. "Functionings and Capabilities." In *Handbook of Social Choice and Welfare*, vol. 2, edited by K. Arrow, A. Sen, and K. Suzumura, 153–87. Amsterdam: North Holland.

Betts, J., and J. Roemer. 2007. "Equalizing Opportunity for Racial and Socioeconomic Groups in the United States through Educational Finance Reform." In *Schools and the Equal Opportunity Problem*, edited by L. Woessman and P. Peterson. Cambridge, MA: MIT Press.

Bloom, D., D. Canning, and G. Fink. 2009. "Disease and Development Revisited." NBER Working Paper 15137, National Bureau of Economic Research, Cambridge, MA.

Bloom, D., D. Canning, and J. Sevilla. 2004. "The Effect of Health on Economic Growth: A Production Function Approach." *World Development* 32: 1–13.

Bourguignon, F., F. Ferreira, and M. Menendez. 2007. "Inequality of Opportunity in Brazil." *Review of Income and Wealth* 53 (4): 585–619.

Brockerhoff, M., and P. Hewett. 1998. "Ethnicity and Child Mortality in Sub-Saharan Africa." Policy Research Division Working Papers No. 107, Population Council, New York.

Case, A., and C. Paxson. 2006. "Stature and Status: Height, Ability, and Labor Market Outcomes." NBER Working Paper 12466, National Bureau of Economic Research, Cambridge, MA.

Cervellati, M., and U. Sunde. 2009. "Life Expectancy and Economic Growth: The Role of the Demographic Transition." IZA Discussion Paper 4160, Institute for the Study of Labor, Bonn.

Checchi, D., and V. Peragine. 2010. "Inequality of Opportunity in Italy." *Journal of Economic Inequality* 8: 429–50.

Chetty, R., J. Friedman, N. Hilger, E. Saez, D. Schanzenbach, and D. Yagan. 2010. "How Does Your Kindergarten Classroom Affect Your Earnings? Evidence from Project STAR." NBER Working Paper 16381, National Bureau of Economic Research, Cambridge, MA.

Cogneau, D., and S. Mesplé-Somps. 2008. "Inequality of Opportunity for Income in Five Countries of Africa." *Research on Economic Inequality* 16: 99–128.

Cohen, G. 1989. "On the Currency of Egalitarian Justice." *Ethics* 99: 906–44.

Currie, J., and D. Thomas. 1999. "Does Head Start Help Hispanic Children?" *Journal of Public Economics* 74 (2): 235–62.

Deaton, A. 2006. "Global Patterns of Income and Health: Facts, Interpretations, and Policies." NBER Working Paper 12735, National Bureau of Economic Research, Cambridge, MA.

Demographic and Health Surveys. Various years. USAID. http://www.dhsprogram.com.

Dworkin, R. 1981a. "What Is Equality? Part 1: Equality of Welfare." *Philosophy and Public Affairs* 10: 185–246.

———. 1981b. "What Is Equality? Part 2: Equality of Resources." *Philosophy and Public Affairs* 10: 283–345.

Ferreira, F., and J. Gignoux. 2011. "The Measurement of Inequality of Opportunity: Theory and an Application to Latin America." *Review of Income and Wealth* 57 (4): 622–57.

Ferreira, F., J. Gignoux, and M. Aran. 2011. "Measuring Inequality of Opportunity with Imperfect Data: The Case of Turkey." *Journal of Economic Inequality* 9 (4): 651–80.

Filmer, D. 2007. "If You Build It, Will They Come? School Availability and School Enrollment in 21 Poor Countries." *Journal of Development Studies* 43 (5): 901–28.

Filmer, D. 2008. "Inequalities in Education: Effects of Gender, Poverty, Orphanhood, and Disability." In *Girls' Education in the 21st Century: Gender Equality, Empowerment and Economic Growth*, edited by M. Tembon and L. Fort. Washington, DC: World Bank.

Filmer, D., and L. Pritchett. 2001. "Estimating Wealth Effects without Expenditure Data—or Tears: An Application to Educational Enrollments in States of India." *Demography* 38 (1): 115–32.

Grimm, M. 2011. "Does Inequality in Health Impede Economic Growth?" *Oxford Economic Papers* 63: 448–74.

Hild, M., and A. Voorhoeve. 2004. "Equality of Opportunity and Opportunity Dominance." *Economics and Philosophy* 20: 117–45.

Hoddinott, J., J. Maluccio, J. Behrman, R. Flores, and R. Martorell. 2008. "The Impact of Nutrition during Early Childhood on Income, Hours Worked, and Wages of Guatemalan Adults." *The Lancet* 371 (February): 411–16.

Lefranc, A., N. Pistolesi, and A. Trannoy. 2008. "Inequality of Opportunities vs. Inequality of Outcomes: Are Western Societies Alike?" *Review of Income and Wealth* 54 (4): 513–46.

———. 2009. "Equality of Opportunity and Luck: Definitions and Testable Conditions, with an Application to Income in France." *Journal of Public Economics* 93 (11–12): 1189–207.

Lewis, M., and M. Lockheed. 2006. "Inexcusable Absence: Why 60 Million Girls Still Aren't in School and What to Do about It." Center for Global Development, Washington, DC.

———. 2008. "Social Exclusion and the Gender Gap in Education." Policy Research Working Paper 4562, World Bank, Washington, DC.

Lockheed, M. 2008. "The Double Disadvantage of Gender and Social Exclusion in Education." In *Girls' Education in the 21st Century: Gender Equality, Empowerment, and Economic Growth*, edited by M. Tambon and L. Fort, 115–26. Washington, DC: World Bank.

Lorentzen, P., J. McMillan, and R. Wacziarg. 2008. "Death and Development." *Journal of Economic Growth* 13: 81–124.

Marrero, G., and J. Rodríguez. 2013. "Inequality of Opportunity and Growth." *Journal of Development Economics* 104(C): 107–22.

Molina, E., A. Narayan, and J. Saavedra. 2013. "Outcomes, Opportunity and Development: Why Unequal Opportunities and Not Outcomes Hinder Economic Development." Policy Research Working Paper 6735, World Bank, Washington, DC.

Nozick, R. 1974. *Anarchy, State, and Utopia*. New York: Basic Books.

Ooghe, E., E. Schokkaert, and D. Van de Gaer. 2007. "Equality of Opportunity versus Equality of Opportunity Sets." *Social Choice and Welfare* 28: 383–90.

Rawls, J. 1971. *A Theory of Justice*. Cambridge, MA: The Belknap Press of Harvard University Press.

Roemer, J. 1993. "A Pragmatic Theory of Responsibility for the Egalitarian Planner." *Philosophy & Public Affairs* 22 (2): 146–66.

———. 1998. *Equality of Opportunity*. Cambridge, MA: Harvard University Press.

Roemer, J., R. Aaberge, U. Colombino, J. Fritzell, S. Jenkins, A. Lefranc, I. Marx, M. Page, E. Pommer, J. Ruiz-Castillo, M. Segundo, T. Tranaes, A. Trannoy, G. Wagner, and I. Zubiri. 2003. "To What Extent Do Fiscal Regimes Equalize Opportunities for Income Acquisition among Citizens?" *Journal of Public Economics* 87 (3–4): 539–65.

Rutstein, S., and K. Johnson. 2004. *The DHS Wealth Index*. DHS Comparative Reports No. 6, Calverton, MD.

Sen, A. 1979. "Utilitarianism and Welfarism." *The Journal of Philosophy* 76: 463–89.

———. 1985. "Well-Being, Agency, and Freedom: The Dewey Lectures 1984." *Journal of Philosophy* 82: 169–221.

———. 2001. *Development as Freedom*. Oxford, U.K.: Oxford University Press.

UNDP (United Nations Development Programme). 2004. *Human Development Report: Cultural Liberty in Today's Diverse World*. New York: Oxford University Press.

UNICEF. 2007. "Children and the Millennium Development Goals: Progress towards a World Fit for Children." Secretary General of the United Nations, New York.

Van der Gaer, D. 1993. "Equality of Opportunity and Investment in Human Capital." PhD Dissertation, Catholic University of Leuven, Leuven, Belgium.

Van der Gaer, D., E. Schokkaert, and M. Martinez. 2001. "Three Meanings of Intergenerational Mobility." *Economica* 68: 519–38.

Weil, D. 2007. "Accounting for the Effects of Health on Economic Growth." *Quarterly Journal of Economics* 122: 1265–306.

CHAPTER 3

Opportunities for Children in Africa: Recent Evidence

Economic growth has been robust in many of the sub-Saharan African (SSA) countries over the past two decades, due to better global macroeconomic conditions, an enhanced environment for trade, higher commodity prices, and more foreign aid and debt relief.[1] As a result, the overall poverty rate for the continent has fallen from 58 percent in 1990 to 48 percent in 2008. Largely, this growth has led to improvements in human opportunities, an example of which is the rise in net primary enrollment rate from 56 percent in 1999 to 73 percent in 2007. That said, as discussed in chapter 1, large differences remain in access to opportunities for children across countries and among different groups within countries. Whether these gaps have narrowed over time, despite the progress seen in many countries, remains an open question.

This chapter will present the analysis of human opportunities for children in 20 SSA countries, using DHS data from the late-2000s. The analysis will rely on the Human Opportunity Index (HOI) described in chapters 1 and 2, a metric that is best understood as the inequality-adjusted coverage rate of a particular good or service, where "inequality" refers to the variation in coverage rate between children of different circumstances. The first section will focus on education opportunities. The second section will examine access to safe water, sanitation, and electricity, the most basic opportunities in infrastructure. The third section will present the findings for access to health opportunities, where the analysis is limited to just two indicators, full immunization and nutrition (not being stunted).

The fourth section of this chapter examines the question: what is the status of opportunities among children in a country, when "human opportunities" is defined to include *all basic goods and services relevant* for a child of a certain age? To address this question, we consider two age groups—1 year and 6–11 years—and define a child's "access" as coverage by *all* the basic services relevant for the age group he or she belongs to. The HOI computed with these definitions, referred to as the "composite HOI" for each age group, reflects the inequality-adjusted coverage rate of all basic goods and services for children in each age group in a country.

Human Opportunities in Education

The four main education opportunities selected for African countries, as discussed in chapter 2, are school attendance for children of age 6–11 years and 12–15 years, starting primary school on time (for children of age 6–7 years), and finishing primary school (for children of age 12–15 years).[2] The HOI for each of these varies greatly across countries. Some countries, namely Zimbabwe, Kenya, Namibia, Malawi, Ghana, and Uganda, have an HOI of over 80 for school attendance among 6- to 11-year-olds; whereas others, such as Mali, Liberia, and Niger, have an HOI of around 30 or less. For an opportunity such as finishing primary school, the variation is even more marked, with the HOI ranging from 78 (Zimbabwe) to 6 (Mozambique).

Figure 3.1 shows the HOI ranking for each of the four education opportunities examined in this study. The bars represent the HOI and the dots represent the overall coverage rate, with the gap between the two reflecting the penalty due to inequality of opportunity among children of different circumstances. Note that the ranking of countries by an HOI does not necessarily mimic the ranking by coverage rates. This would occur between two countries when a larger share of children in one country has access to the education opportunity, but access is more equally distributed in the other country. Examples of this are Sierra Leone and Nigeria for school attendance (6–11 years), the Democratic Republic of Congo and Tanzania for school attendance (12–15 years), Madagascar and Zimbabwe for starting primary school on time, and Senegal and Malawi for finishing primary school among 12- to 15-year-olds.

The HOI varies significantly between two *types* of education opportunity—those related to access to school (attendance) and those related to, however imperfectly, the quality of education (starting school on time and finishing primary school). *First*, children in SSA do much better overall in school attendance than in starting school on time or finishing primary school among 12- to 15-year-olds. The average HOIs across 20 countries for school attendance are 63 (ages 6–11) and 72 (ages 12–15), compared to 27 for starting primary school on time and for completion of primary school among 12- to 15-year-olds. *Second*, how countries are ranked relative to each other by the HOI can change significantly from one type of opportunity to another. For example, Kenya and Namibia are very high on the HOI ranking scale for primary school attendance but much lower for starting primary school on time. These are thus examples of countries where the primary education system has expanded rapidly, while indicators of "quality" have not quite kept pace with the expansion. Conversely, Nigeria ranks much better in starting primary school on time and finishing primary school than in attendance for the two age groups considered.

Figure 3.1 shows that attendance improves with age of children for most countries in the sample (compare panels a and b), which is consistent with a low HOI for starting primary school on time. Liberia and Zambia, the countries with the highest increase in school attendance with age, also have low metrics for children starting primary school on time, suggesting that late start in schooling contributes

Figure 3.1 HOI for Access to Education in Sub-Saharan Africa (circa 2008)

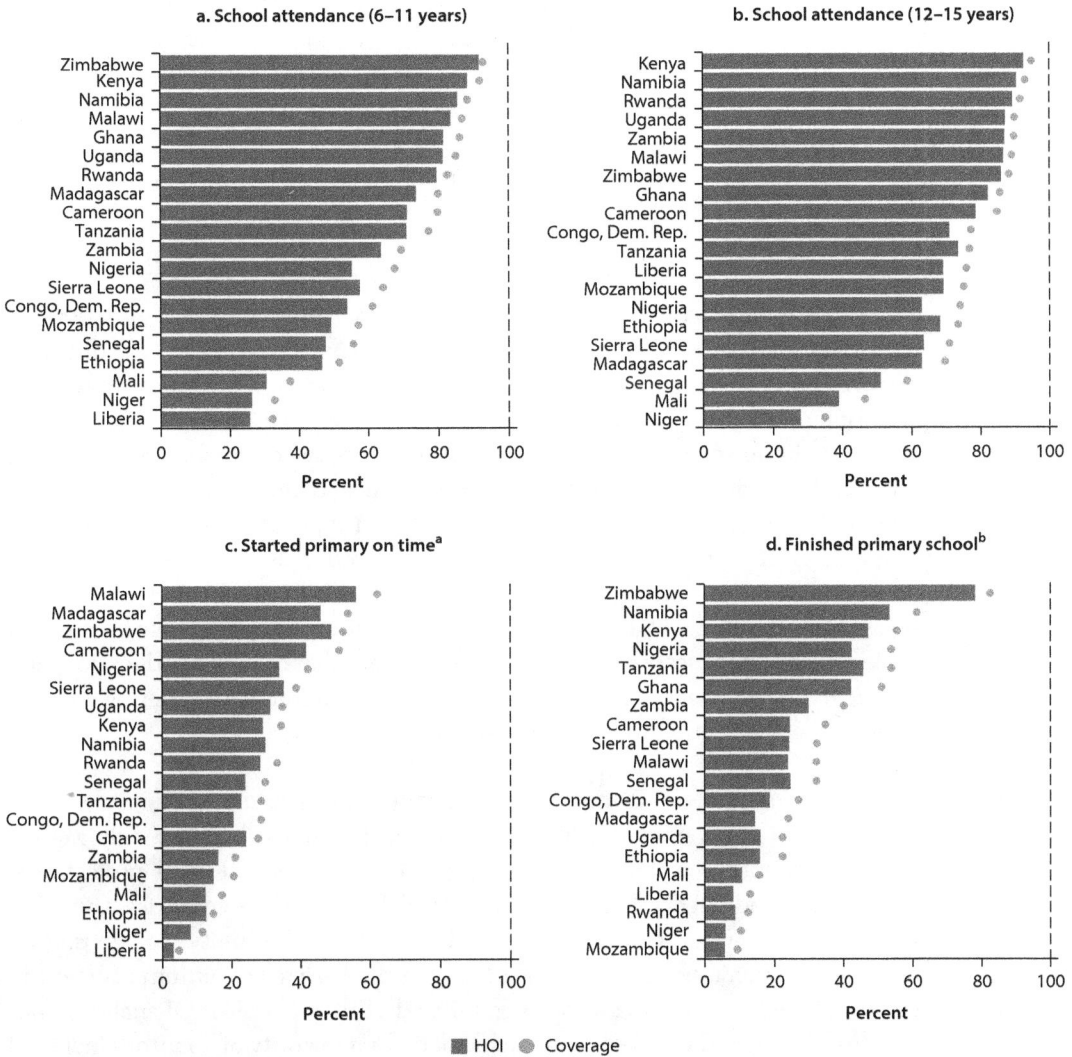

a. School attendance (6–11 years)

b. School attendance (12–15 years)

c. Started primary on time[a]

d. Finished primary school[b]

■ HOI ● Coverage

Source: Authors' calculations using Demographic and Health Surveys data, various years.
Note: HOI = Human Opportunity Index.
a. Started primary school on time (by age 6 years), measured among a cohort of 6- to 7-year-olds.
b. Finished primary school, measured among a cohort of 12- to 15-year-olds.

to the rise in school attendance with age. Also, the gap between the HOI and coverage seems to reduce with age, which suggests that circumstances matter more for attendance of younger children in school than for that of older children.

The cross-country correlations between the HOIs for the four education opportunities (table 3.1) indicate that countries that do well in one dimension tend to do relatively well in others as well. The highest correlations are seen between the two HOIs for attendance, and between attendance for 6- to 11-year-olds and starting primary school on time—which appear to be intuitive.

Table 3.1 Cross-Country Correlations between HOIs in Education Opportunities

	Attendance (6–11)	Attendance (12–15)	Started primary on time	Finished primary school
Attendance (6–11)	1	0.82	0.75	0.63
Attendance (12–15)	0.82	1	0.44	0.47
Started primary on time	0.75	0.44	1	0.46
Finished primary school	0.63	0.47	0.46	1

Source: Authors' calculations using Demographic and Health Surveys data, various years.
Note: HOI = Human Opportunity Index.

To conclude the discussion on education opportunities in the late-2000s in SSA, two main insights are worth highlighting. *First*, coverage of all education opportunities is far below universal in most countries; and opportunities are distributed in most cases with a high degree of inequality between children of different circumstances. *Second*, a vast gulf exists between opportunities related to attendance and those related to completion and on time start of primary school. A low HOI and coverage for the second type of opportunities suggest that quality of schooling, which these indicators reflect to a limited extent, is an important area of concern with regard to education opportunities of children across SSA countries. The following subsection shows some evidence on student achievement (from secondary sources) to illustrate that quality of education, and inequality in the quality of education received by children with differing circumstances, merit attention in a number of countries.

Quality of Education—Evidence from Secondary Literature

Test scores of children comparable across countries are available for only a small subset of countries included in this study from the SACMEQ-III project (see chapter 2). Had such information been available for more countries, the HOI analysis would have been conducted defining the "opportunity" (of getting an education of minimum standard) as achieving the basic or minimum standard in literacy reading and numeracy for a certain grade. But while the HOI analysis is not worthwhile, given the lack of comparable data for a majority of countries included in our study, it is instructive to examine some *simple indicators from available publications* for eight of our countries that are a part of the SACMEQ project.

The SACMEQ-III scores for tests administered to sixth-grade children in 2007, available for eight countries in our sample, show wide variation in the percentage of children in a country with basic skills in reading or numeracy (figure 3.2). The percentage of sixth graders with basic skill in reading ranges from 56 in Zambia to 97 in Tanzania, while that in numeracy ranges from 33 in Zambia to 89 in Kenya. Most countries do better on reading than numeracy, but countries doing well in one are likely to do relatively well in the other as well, suggesting that similar underlying factors are driving achievements on both fronts.

Breaking down the numbers by *location* and *socioeconomic status* of children, one finds significant gaps between urban and rural children, and between children with high and low socioeconomic status. Urban-rural gaps in both

Figure 3.2 Basic Proficiency in Reading and Numeracy in Select SSA Countries, 2007

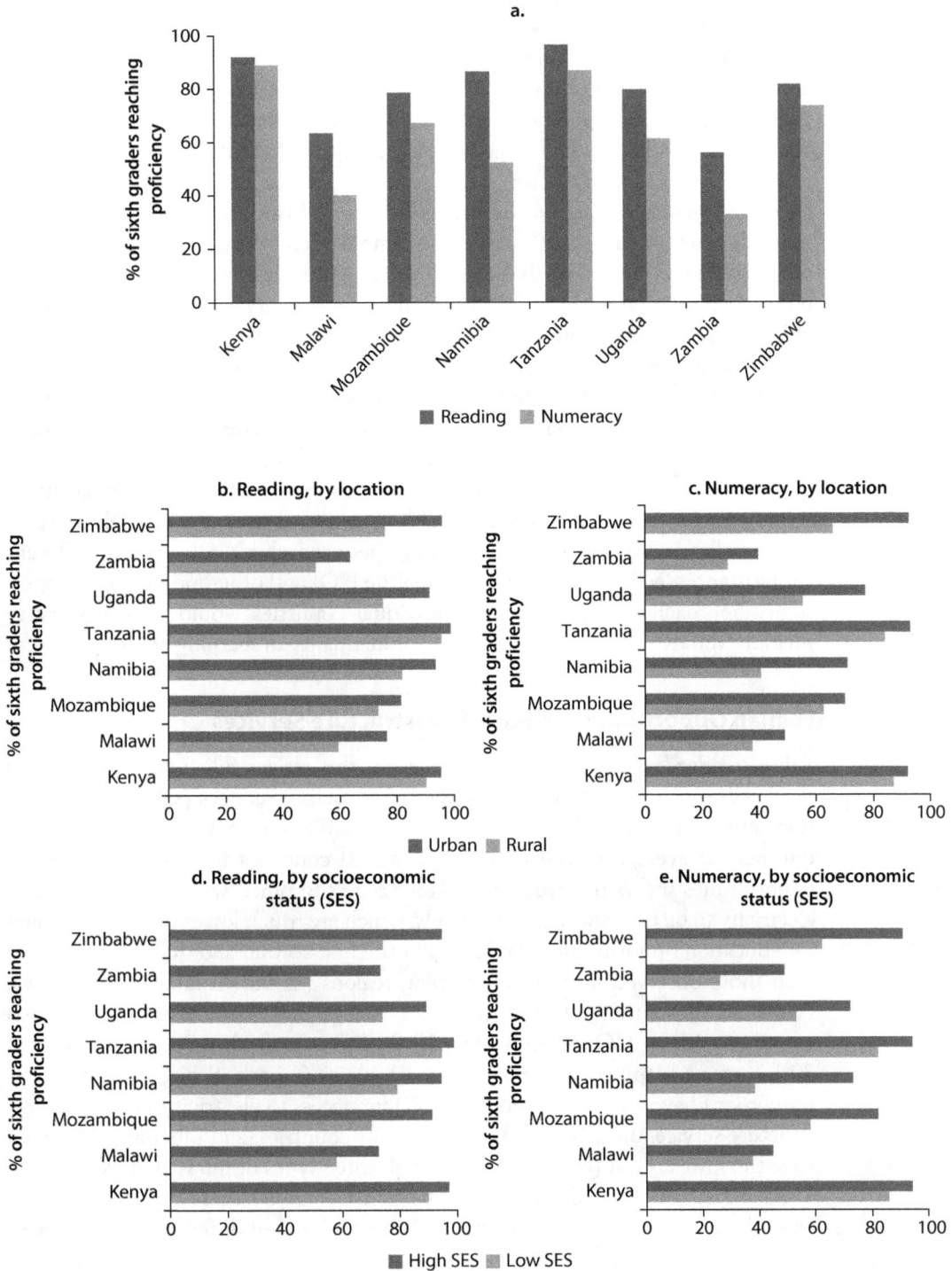

a.

Reading   Numeracy

b. Reading, by location

c. Numeracy, by location

Urban   Rural

d. Reading, by socioeconomic status (SES)

e. Numeracy, by socioeconomic status (SES)

High SES   Low SES

Source: SACMEQ III 2010; Hungi et al. 2010.
Note: SES = socioeconomic status; SSA = Sub-Saharan Africa.

Do African Children Have an Equal Chance? • http://dx.doi.org/10.1596/978-1-4648-0332-1

reading and numeracy are large in Malawi, Uganda, and Zimbabwe; and gaps between children with high and low socioeconomic status in reading and numeracy are the largest in Mozambique, Namibia, Zambia, and Zimbabwe. On the other hand, Kenya and Tanzania show consistently smaller gaps between urban and rural children, and between children of different socioeconomic status. The gaps indicate that inequality of opportunity in education, as measured by student achievement, is likely to be large in many countries in SSA.

How well do the indicators of education opportunities used in our analysis (figure 3.1) correlate, across countries, with the indicators of education opportunities shown in figure 3.2? Based on the sample of eight countries, the percentage of sixth graders who have basic proficiency in reading or numeracy has some positive correlation with the HOIs for finishing primary school (12- to 15-year-olds) and school attendance of 6- to 11-year-olds.[3] While correlations from such a small sample are not very meaningful, they are at least consistent with intuition and the argument made earlier that primary school attendance and completion of primary school by a certain age provide useful information about education opportunities of children, including the quality of learning.

Quality of education is thus an important source of concern in a majority of SSA countries for which data are available, not just in terms of low levels of learning overall but also inequality in learning between children born into different circumstances. More in-depth work using the HOI and other inequality of opportunity approaches at the level of individual countries would be necessary to measure the extent, trends, and drivers of inequality of learning achievements.

Human Opportunities in Basic Infrastructure Services

When standards of services similar to those in other regions (like Latin America and the Caribbean) are used, access to basic infrastructure services (safe water, sanitation, and electricity) is found to be extremely limited in SSA countries. A simple unweighted average of the HOI across all 20 countries for each of the three opportunities shows the average HOIs for access to piped water, flush toilet, and electricity to be 6, 3, and 10, respectively, which are much lower than the averages for education opportunities considered in the first section and dramatically lower than those observed in other developing regions (as shown later in chapter 6). Figure 3.2 shows that out of 20 countries, Senegal and Namibia are the only two countries with an HOI of more than 10 for access to flush toilet and more than 20 for access to piped water; and four countries (Ghana, Senegal, Nigeria, and Cameroon) have an HOI of more than 20 for access to electricity. For each infrastructure service, there is large variation across countries; and Liberia and Uganda have the lowest HOI (of 1 or below) for all three types of infrastructure.

For most countries, the problem of low coverage by these facilities is vastly exacerbated by inequality in coverage among children of different circumstances (figure 3.3). In fact, for almost all cases where overall coverage of a service is nontrivial (more than 5 percent of all children covered by the service), the HOI is significantly different from coverage. Countries that are in the top five for

Figure 3.3 HOI for Access to Basic Infrastructure in Sub-Saharan Africa (circa 2008)

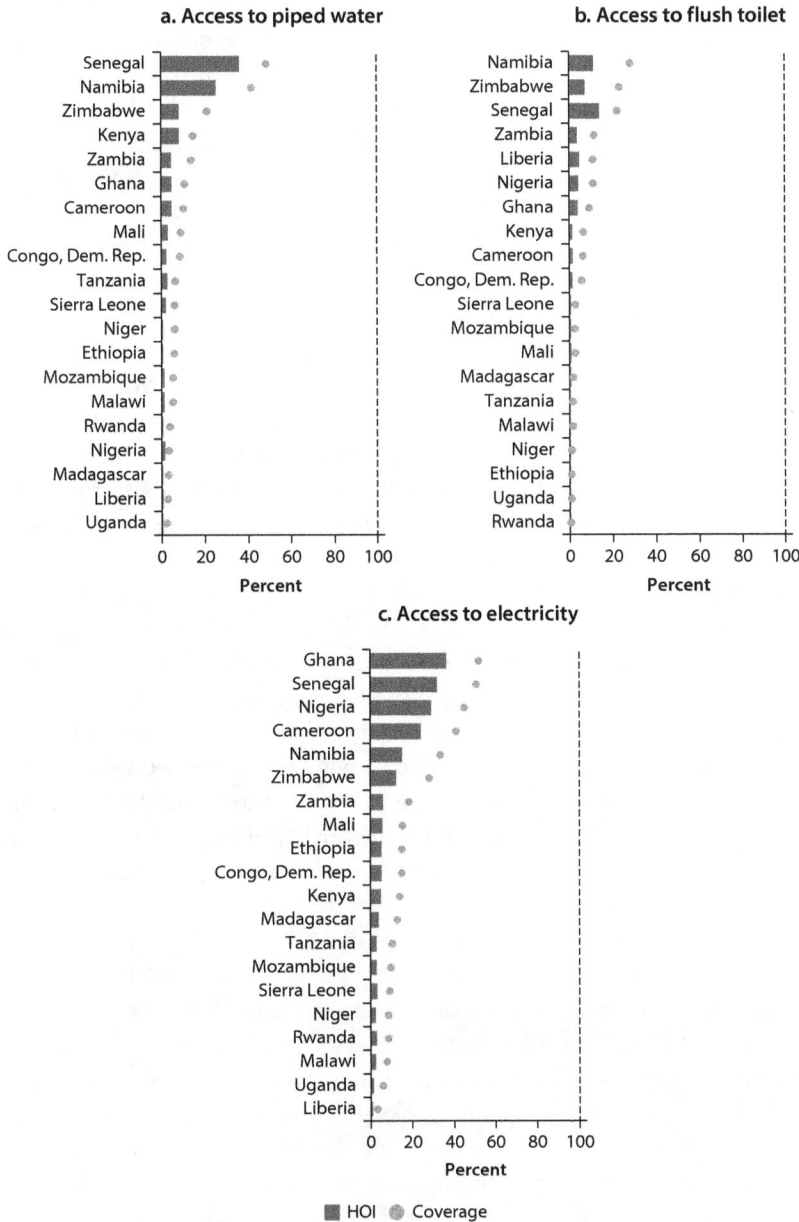

a. Access to piped water

b. Access to flush toilet

c. Access to electricity

■ HOI ● Coverage

Source: Authors' calculations using Demographic and Health Surveys data, various years.
Note: HOI = Human Opportunity Index.

coverage of piped water and electricity all have HOIs that are significantly lower than the coverage rate for these services.

Access to electricity is defined by the commonly used standard of availability of electricity in the household, which is also comparable with the standard used for other regions like LAC. Even using this minimalistic definition, which does not take into account the quality (e.g., how many hours during a day) of electricity that is available, access to electricity is extremely limited and unequally distributed among children of different circumstances in SSA countries. The highest ranked country (Ghana) registers an HOI of only 37; and in seven countries, coverage of electricity among all children is less than 10 percent, with the HOI being much lower due to inequality in access. In the countries with the highest coverage (Ghana, Senegal, Nigeria, and Cameroon), 30–40 percent of electricity access that is provided is skewed toward groups with more favorable circumstances.

More Liberal Standards for Safe Water and Adequate Sanitation

As is evident from figure 3.3, access rates are so low for piped water and flush toilets that it is difficult to differentiate between countries. In order to conduct a more nuanced analysis of the differences in equality of opportunity between countries, we expand our definitions of these opportunities. We operationalize this by defining "safe water" as access to piped-, well-, or rainwater instead of just piped water, and by defining "adequate sanitation" as the presence of a flush or pit toilet in the household instead of just a flush toilet. As expected, we see a marked increase in coverage and HOI scores because of using more liberal standards for these opportunities (figure 3.4).

Although safe water is still more widely available (the average HOI is 68) than adequate sanitation (the average HOI is 62), the gap between the two opportunities shrinks when the more liberal standards are applied. The average distance between the HOI and the coverage rate (which is the average penalty for inequality of opportunity) is 4.8 for access to water and 7.4 for access to a toilet or pit latrine. Thus, access to adequate sanitation is more closely related to circumstances than access to safe water, which appears to be more equitably distributed. Interestingly, for both water and sanitation, inequality of opportunity (gap between the HOI and coverage) is lower when the less demanding standards are used. In other words, as an opportunity is defined by a higher standard, the association between circumstances and the opportunity increases, which is quite intuitive.

Using the two different definitions for safe water and adequate sanitation yields entirely different rankings of the countries by an HOI. For example, Niger has the highest HOI (98) for access to safe water using the more liberal standard, but has among the lowest HOIs (equal to one) when using the more restrictive standard. Kenya, on the other hand, ranks 4th when using the more restrictive standard for safe water but 16th when using the more liberal standard. This suggests that the types of infrastructure considered in the two standards for the same opportunity are quite different, and that each country has a different capacity to provide access to each type of infrastructure, even for the same opportunity. In fact, very few countries rank relatively well in providing safe water according to *both* standards—Senegal and Namibia stand out as exceptions, with HOIs of over 25 in access to piped water and over 85 using the more liberal standard. Similar conclusions apply to access to sanitation as well, comparing figures 3.3 and 3.4.

Given the large differences in the HOI under the two sets of standards for safe water and adequate sanitation, it is important to select the set of standards that is more appropriate for the purposes of analyzing human opportunity in Africa.

Figure 3.4 HOI for Access to Basic Infrastructure: Reasonable Standards (circa 2008)

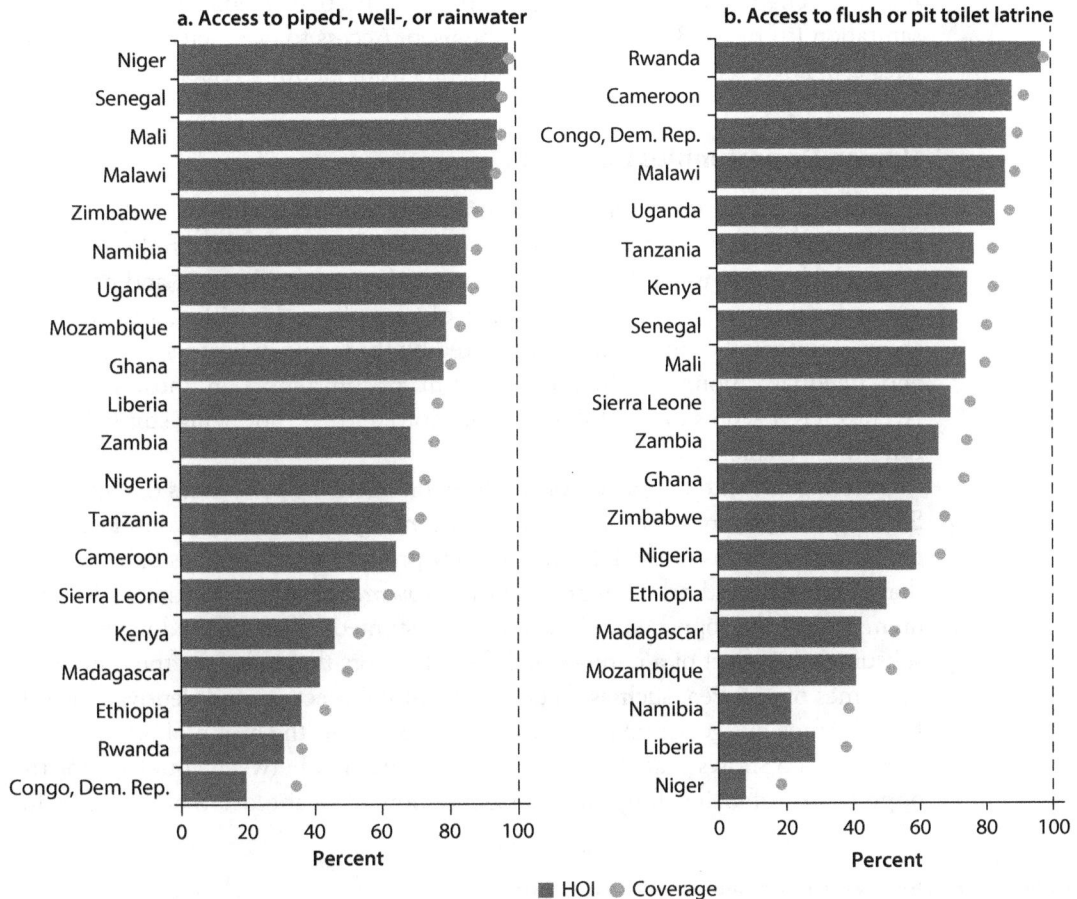

a. Access to piped-, well-, or rainwater

Niger	
Senegal	
Mali	
Malawi	
Zimbabwe	
Namibia	
Uganda	
Mozambique	
Ghana	
Liberia	
Zambia	
Nigeria	
Tanzania	
Cameroon	
Sierra Leone	
Kenya	
Madagascar	
Ethiopia	
Rwanda	
Congo, Dem. Rep.	

b. Access to flush or pit toilet latrine

Rwanda	
Cameroon	
Congo, Dem. Rep.	
Malawi	
Uganda	
Tanzania	
Kenya	
Senegal	
Mali	
Sierra Leone	
Zambia	
Ghana	
Zimbabwe	
Nigeria	
Ethiopia	
Madagascar	
Mozambique	
Namibia	
Liberia	
Niger	

Percent

■ HOI ● Coverage

Source: Authors' calculations using Demographic and Health Surveys data, various years.
Note: HOI = Human Opportunity Index.

The more liberal standards (those in figure 3.4) appear to be more relevant and will be the focus of analysis in the rest of the study. Using a standard that yields extremely low coverage rates for most countries is not particularly useful, since HOI in these cases would add little to the analysis—inequality of opportunity is irrelevant when almost no one has coverage. Using the more liberal standards yields higher coverage and HOI and meaningful differences across countries. It also helps countries identify more reasonable targets to strive toward. Consequently in subsequent chapters, the more liberal standards of figure 3.4 will be the ones used for further analysis.

Our preference for the more liberal standards for safe water and sanitation, however, is not intended to impose a value judgment on which standards are the most appropriate benchmark for an individual country to use. The choice of standard for a country should ultimately depend on the norms of the country and society in determining what is acceptable as a basic right for children. Notably, the use of the more liberal standards has important implications for comparability of results for Africa with those from other regions. For comparisons with the LAC region in chapter 6, for example, the more restrictive standards for water and sanitation (in figure 3.3) will have to be used. Access to electricity in SSA countries can, however, be compared with results from all other regions.

Human Opportunities for Health

In order to determine human opportunities related to health, we focus on two key indicators that are available for all countries from DHS data: full immunization, which serves as a proxy for basic protection against diseases, and not being stunted, which represents the absence of chronic malnutrition. Our analysis shows opportunities in health, as measured by these two indicators, to be limited and unequal among children of different circumstances in most countries. Average HOI scores of 53 (full immunization) and 59 (not being stunted) illustrate these challenges.

Before going into the details of the story on health opportunities of children in SSA, two caveats are important to mention. *First*, the opportunities considered here are limited in terms of the information they provide, which implies that the story that emerges would not be representative of *overall* health opportunities for children. *Second*, the "opportunity" of "not being stunted," as mentioned in chapter 2, subsumes the effect of a number of different factors that influence the nutritional outcomes of children, such as dietary and cultural practices and deprivations suffered by previous generations (that affect, for example, the health of mothers).

Figure 3.5 shows that there is a lot more variation between countries for the opportunity of being fully immunized (among 1-year-olds) than there is for

Figure 3.5 HOI for Health in Sub-Saharan Africa (circa 2008)

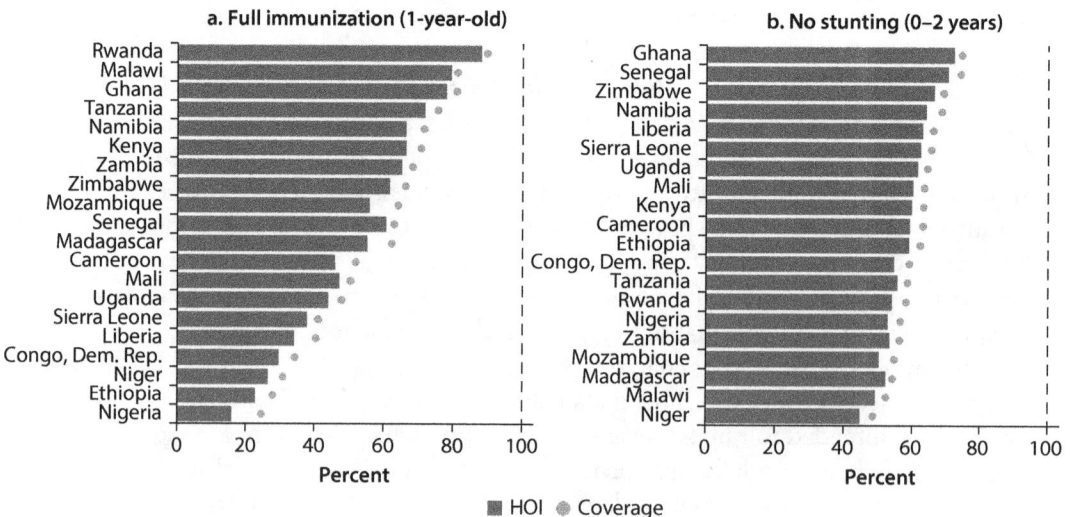

Source: Authors' calculations using Demographic and Health Surveys data, various years.
Note: HOI = Human Opportunity Index.

nutrition ("not being stunted" among 0- to 2-year-olds). HOI scores for full immunization range from a low of 16 in Nigeria to a high of 88 in Rwanda with a standard deviation (not weighted by country population) of around 20. In contrast, the HOI for nutrition ranges between 46 (Niger) and 73 (Ghana), with a standard deviation of around seven.[4] Unlike what was seen for education opportunities, cross-country correlation between HOIs for immunization and nutrition is low (around 0.18). Among numerous examples, two countries particularly stand out: Liberia and Sierra Leone rank in the top six on the HOI scale on nutrition but among the bottom six on full immunization.

The lack of cross-country correlation between the two sets of HOIs and the fact that cross-country variation in the HOI for immunization is much higher than that for nutrition merit a discussion. A plausible hypothesis, which remains to be explored in future work, would be that access to immunization is more directly related to a government's capacity to provide a particular service than nutrition, and variation in the quality of government services across countries is likely to be higher than (and uncorrelated with) factors such as dietary and cultural practices. And the same hypothesis could also explain why inequality across children of different circumstances is higher for full immunization than for stunting in most countries.

Access to a Bundle of Basic Goods and Services: The "Composite" HOI

Previous sections of this chapter have focused on the coverage and inequality in opportunities, taken individually or one at a time, among children. Now we turn to an important and related question: what can we say about children's opportunities in a country when "opportunities" are defined as the relevant *set* or basket of basic goods and services that should be available to a child of a particular age? Implicit behind this question is the idea that basic opportunities like school attendance (for a child of school age), water, and sanitation are not substitutes for one another, but rather constitute a minimal bundle of opportunities that a child must have in order to have a fair chance of fulfilling his/her potential in life.

As mentioned in chapter 2, we can also define opportunity as access to a *combination* of goods and services relevant for a certain age group. For children of *1 year of age*, this consists of *access to safe water, adequate sanitation, full immunization, and not being stunted*. For children of *age 6–11 years*, it is a combination of *water, sanitation, and school attendance*. Consequently, two HOI numbers are generated, one for each age group, in every country. These indicate how countries compare with each other in terms of access to the relevant bundle of opportunities for that age group; and how for the same country, access to basic goods and services for the older cohort of children compares with that for the younger cohort.

This method of computing a composite HOI, which can be loosely described as "aggregating" across different opportunities, has some attractive features.[5] *First*, it yields a single country-level scalar that is a composite measure of "human opportunity," defined as a child's access to a bundle of critical goods and services. Thus, the scalar has an intuitive interpretation linked to how "opportunity" is defined for every individual child. *Second*, the method can differentiate between the opportunities relevant for children of different age groups. Immunization status, for example, is not even known for children of age 6–11 years from the surveys we use, whereas school attendance is not relevant for children of 1 year of age.

Before discussing the results, it is important to mention a few caveats. The *first* caveat relates to the subjective *choice* of goods and services that goes into the definition of a composite HOI. The choices we have made are not intended in any way to suggest that *other* goods and services do not matter or matter less for a child. Rather, our choice of goods and services for either age group is motivated by common sense and expediency. More precisely, the motivation has been to define a set of goods and services that most societies would agree is essential for a child and, equally important, for which data are available from the DHS. Safe water and adequate sanitation satisfy these criteria for all age groups of children, as do nutrition and immunization for the younger children and school attendance for the older cohort. Clearly, more comprehensive surveys, if they were to become available, would allow us to construct more complete composite indexes for all age groups of children; and more frequent surveys would ensure that these measures can even be tracked over time for a cohort of children.[6] The choice of indicators is also guided by the fact that these should be as "different" from each other as possible, to ensure that the composite HOI reflects access to a true *combination* of basic goods and services, as opposed to access to multiple similar or interrelated services.

The *second* caveat relates to the "weighting" of different opportunities that is implicit in how we define our composite HOI. By construction, the absence of *any* one of the opportunities in a composite HOI for a child (e.g., water, sanitation, or school attendance for someone of age 6–11 years) counts as a "zero" in terms of her access to the "bundle of opportunities." The main criticisms of this assumption are that it is somewhat arbitrary *and* does not allow for any country-level variation in how the components of the bundle are weighted in the bundle. While these are valid criticisms, our simple assumption has two advantages: it allows for cross-country comparison by a composite HOI *and* does not suggest any hierarchy of importance or any degree of substitution among opportunities included in a bundle. This seems to be the most intuitive approach, given that each composite HOI refers to a minimalistic list of basic goods and services that, most countries agree, should be universally available to children (and the lack of any one cannot be compensated by any of the others).

The *third* caveat relates to the age groups we considered for computing the composite HOI. Our choice of age groups (1 year and 6–11 years) is not intended to suggest that other age groups are less "important" in some way. Rather, the choice of age groups reflects what we consider to be sensible: age groups that are nonoverlapping, one of which reflects the opportunity set available to a child very early in life, and another that shows opportunities available to children during their early school years. With these constraints, the precise choice of age groups was driven by the nature of the indicators and the age of the children for whom these were available.

Figure 3.6 shows the composite HOI corresponding to the two age groups—1 year and 6–11 years—in the latest year for which DHS data are available, all of which are from the late-2000s (circa 2008). Looking across countries, a few broad facts and patterns are apparent. *First*, there is very large variation across countries for both the HOI, which is expected given the large variation in the HOI for some of the individual indicators. The HOI for 1 year ranges from around 2 in Niger to nearly 28 in Senegal, and that for 6–11 years goes from 3 in Niger to 69 in Malawi.

Second, the HOI for 1 year is lower than that for older children for all countries. Consistent with these numbers, the HOI for children of 1 year of age has an unweighted average of 13 across countries, compared to the corresponding figure of 29 for children of 6–11 years. The difference between the two HOIs for each country is driven mainly by the differences between access to school attendance on the one hand and nutrition and immunization on the other.

Third, the two composite HOIs are correlated to a high degree across countries, with a correlation coefficient of 0.78. But even though the country rankings by the two composite HOIs are highly correlated,[7] there are notable exceptions where the rank of a country by one HOI is significantly different from its rank by the other (figure 3.7). Nigeria ranks much better in the HOI for older children

Figure 3.6 Composite HOI for Access to Bundle of Opportunities (circa 2008)

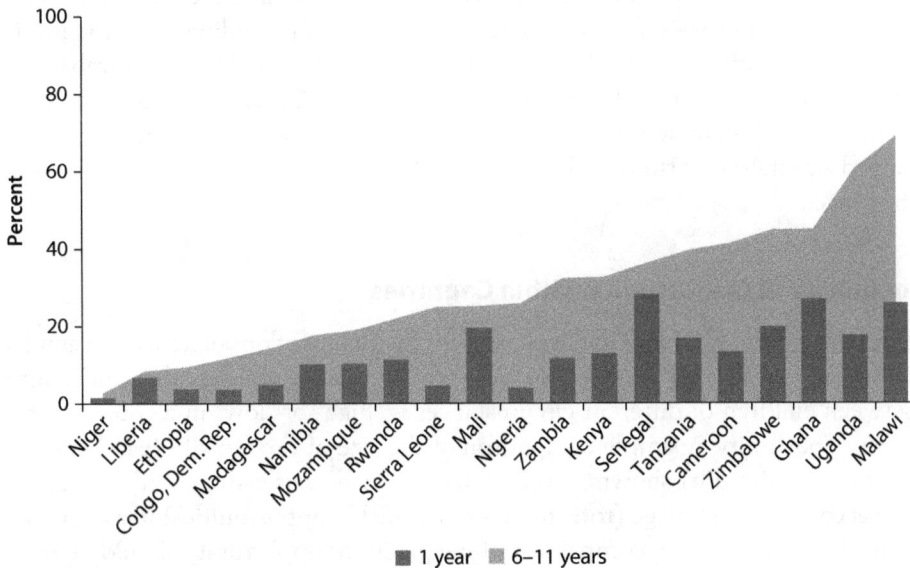

■ 1 year   ▨ 6–11 years

Source: Authors' calculations using Demographic and Health Surveys data, various years.
Note: (1) Children 1 year: opportunities included are access to water (piped-, well-, or rainwater), access to sanitation (pit or flush toilet), full immunization, and no stunting. (2) Children 6–11 years: opportunities included are school attendance, access to water (same as above), and access to sanitation (same as above). (3) A child has access to bundle of opportunities if meeting the standard (of coverage) for all the opportunities defined above, corresponding to his or her age group. (4) Countries are sorted in increasing order by the HOI for 6–11 years. HOI = Human Opportunity Index.

Figure 3.7 Ranking of Countries, by Composite HOIs (circa 2008)

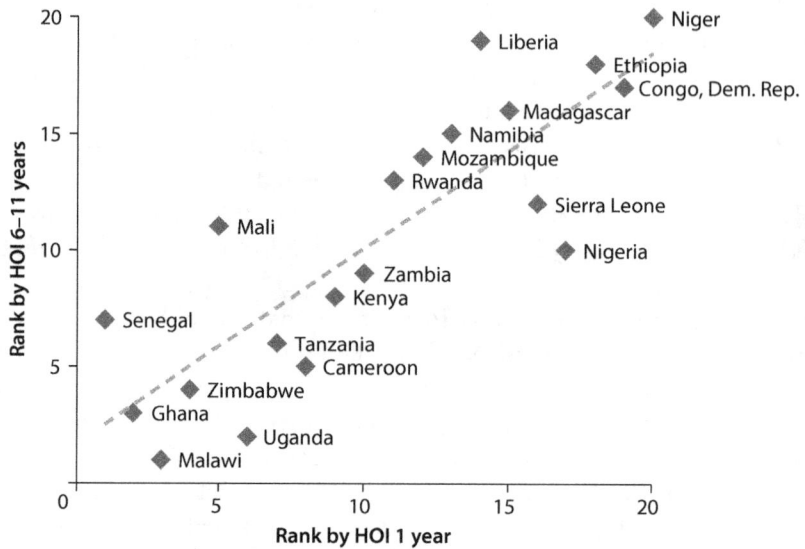

Source: Authors' calculations using Demographic and Health Surveys data, various years.
Note: Lower number indicates higher rank. HOI = Human Opportunity Index.

than for younger children. Mali and Senegal rank much better by HOI for younger, as opposed to older, children.

Some countries rank high in both types of HOIs, which indicates that relative to other countries, they are doing a better job of providing the basic minimum opportunities to children regardless of age. Ghana, Malawi, Zimbabwe, and Uganda are all ranked in the top six by either HOI measure. On the other hand, Niger, the Democratic Republic of Congo, Ethiopia, and Madagascar are ranked among the bottom six by either HOI, indicating the daunting challenges they face.

Inequality of Opportunity within Countries

Even though the HOI includes a penalty for inequality of opportunity, the graphs shown so far in this chapter do not provide clarity on whether inequality between children of different circumstances is "high" or "low" in a country for a given opportunity. A simple comparison of the size of the penalty (gap between the bar and the dot) shown in these graphs can be misleading, without taking into account the coverage (total number of available opportunities) in a country.[8] Instead, a cross-country comparison of inequality of opportunity should be conducted by the *ratio of the penalty to the coverage rate* for a given opportunity, which is the *dissimilarity* or *inequality of opportunity* index (D-Index for short). Intuitively, as stated in chapter 2, the D-Index is the share of available opportunities that are distributed inequitably among circumstance groups, that is, in violation of the principle of equality of opportunity.

Even a direct comparison of D-Indexes across countries can be misleading if coverage is not taken into account, since the D-Index is negatively correlated with coverage. Therefore, the relevant question to consider is whether a country has a higher (or lower) D-Index, in comparison to what would be expected *given* the coverage of the opportunity in that country. To show this, a linear regression line is fitted through scatter plots of D-Index and coverage rates of composite bundles for 1-year-olds and 6- to 11-year-olds in figure 3.8. The distance of each point from the fitted line in each graph indicates how inequality of opportunity in a country, given the coverage of the opportunity in the country, compares with the expected D-Index based on the sample of countries included in the study.

In terms of the opportunity of having the composite bundles for 1-year-olds (figure 3.8a) and 6- to 11-year-olds (figure 3.8b), Niger, the Democratic Republic of Congo, and Namibia are the clear outliers—with inequality of opportunity being much *higher than what would be expected*, given the coverage rate of the opportunity. On the flip side, Uganda and Mali are the most significant outliers—countries with *lower than expected* inequality of opportunity for their coverage rates—for 1-year-olds and 6- to 11-year-olds, respectively. Finally, the fitted line is steeper in figure 3.8a than in figure 3.8b, implying that inequality of opportunity is higher, on average, for the composite bundle of younger children than that of the older children.

Similar analysis for other opportunities (see annex 3A, figures 3A.1 and 3A.2) shows the following countries are the most significant outliers in terms of higher than expected inequality of opportunity: Nigeria for school attendance among 6- to 11-year-olds and 12- to 15-year-olds and full immunization; the Democratic Republic of Congo for starting primary on time and access to safe water; Madagascar for finishing primary school; and Niger and Namibia for access to adequate sanitation. Inequality of opportunity is the highest (given coverage rates) for access to electricity and sanitation, and finishing primary school on time; and lowest for not being stunted, immunization, and school attendance. Access to electricity and nutrition, which have the highest and lowest inequality of opportunity, on average, respectively, have a key feature in common: no country qualifies as an outlier with higher (or lower) than expected inequality of opportunity. For electricity, the average inequality of opportunity is high for *all* countries, even after taking the low coverage into account. Conversely, for nutrition, inequality of opportunity is low for *all* countries.

Conclusion

It is useful to recap some of the key findings of this chapter, all of which are from the late-2000s (circa 2008), the latest period for which DHS data are available.

- *The extent of cross-country variation in the HOI differs significantly across opportunities.* To show this, figure 3.9 graphs the coefficient of variation for each HOI (the ratio of standard deviation to the average). Cross-country differences are much larger in the case of access to electricity and finishing primary school

Figure 3.8 D-Index and Coverage across Countries in Access to Composite Bundles

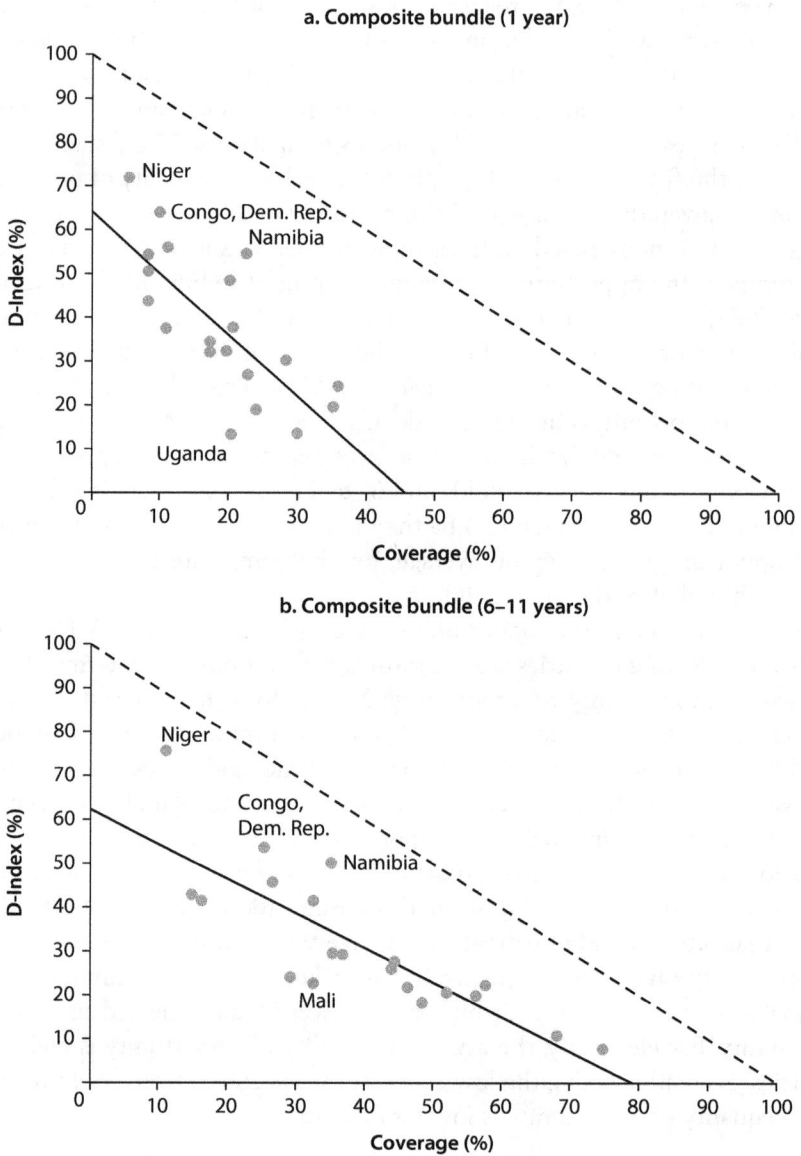

a. Composite bundle (1 year)

b. Composite bundle (6–11 years)

Source: Authors' calculations using Demographic and Health Surveys data, various years.
Note: D-Index = dissimilarity index.

than for the other opportunities. The extent of cross-country variation in the two composite HOIs is quite high and similar for the two measures.

- *In most countries, school attendance is higher and more equitably distributed than completion and on-time start of primary school.* Thus, even as some countries have a long way to go in school enrollment (e.g., Mali and Niger),

Figure 3.9 Cross-Country Variation for Each Type of HOI (circa 2008)

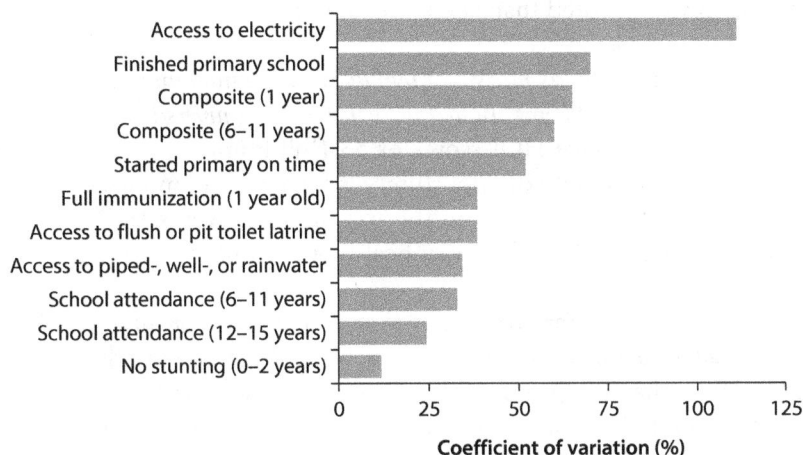

Source: Authors' calculations using Demographic and Health Surveys data, various years.
Note: CV is the ratio of standard deviation to the average of the HOI across all countries. Higher CV indicates higher cross-country variation. HOI = Human Opportunity Index.

late entry into and noncompletion of primary school are important challenges across *all* SSA countries. Even in Malawi, the country with the *highest* HOI for timely start to primary school, 62 percent of 6- to 7-year-old children have started school on time and the "penalty" due to inequality results in an HOI of only 56. And with an HOI of just 78, Zimbabwe ranks the highest in the HOI for completion of primary school among 12- to 15-year-olds.

• *The low and variable HOIs in starting primary on time and finishing primary school suggest important challenges in the quality of education in most SSA countries.* Student achievement test scores (from SACMEQ-III) in eight of the countries suggest wide cross-country variation across countries in the percentage of sixth graders who have basic skills in reading and mathematics, as well as large gaps in achievement between children of different circumstances (location and socioeconomic status) in most countries.

• *Depending on the standard used to define "adequacy," access to safe water, sanitation, and electricity in SSA countries ranges from uneven to poor.* Access to electricity is extremely low across the board and inequality is high—the HOI is below 10 for 14 out of 20 countries. The HOIs for water and sanitation are very low as well, when the more demanding standards for adequacy are used. On average, countries fare somewhat better on access to electricity and worse on access to a flush toilet, compared to access to piped water.

• *Using more liberal standards for water and sanitation—more appropriate for the level of income of SSA countries—the picture gets significantly better but remains highly uneven across countries.* Safe water continues to be more widely available and equitably distributed than adequate sanitation.

- *Opportunities in health, as measured by full immunization and not being chronically malnourished (not being stunted), are well below universal in most countries,* as illustrated by average HOI scores of 53 (full immunization) and 59 (not being stunted). Inequality of opportunity is higher for immunization than for nutrition in most countries. To put this in context, however, these two indicators provide a highly limited view of health opportunities among children.

- *The HOI for immunization varies more than that for nutrition, and there is almost no correlation between the two opportunities.* Niger, Nigeria, and Ethiopia have an HOI of lower than 27 for immunization, in contrast to an HOI of more than 75 for the top three (Ghana, Malawi, and Rwanda). Low correlation between the two HOIs suggests that the factors influencing a country's performance in immunization are quite different from those influencing nutrition. The former is more closely related to the quality of child health services provided by the government, whereas the latter is a result of myriad and complex factors such as dietary practices.

- *For a few countries, an HOI in one or more of the health opportunities is so low as to merit special attention.* Nigeria, Ethiopia, Niger, and the Democratic Republic of Congo have an HOI below 30 for full immunization; and Niger is also the only country with an HOI below 50 for not being stunted. In immunization, Nigeria, Liberia, Madagascar, and Mozambique have particularly high penalties for inequality of opportunity. While inequality of opportunity tends to be low for nutrition, Tanzania, Uganda, and the Democratic Republic of Congo have higher penalties compared to other countries.

- *The composite HOI, measured separately for 1-year-olds and 6- to 11-year-olds, shows that all countries do better in an HOI for the older children than that for younger children.* High correlation between the two measures indicates that countries that do relatively well in terms of access to opportunities for young children tend to do so for older children as well, albeit with some exceptions. Ghana, Malawi, Zimbabwe, and Uganda, all of which are ranked in the top six by either HOI measure, are the relative success stories. Niger, the Democratic Republic of Congo, Ethiopia, and Madagascar are ranked among the bottom six by either HOI. Mali and Senegal rank much better by an HOI for younger children than that for older children, and the converse is true for Nigeria.

- *Inequality of opportunity within countries is higher, on average, for the composite bundle of younger children than that of the older children.* Niger, the Democratic Republic of Congo, and Namibia have the highest inequality of opportunity for the composite bundles relative to what would be expected given their coverage rates. Conversely, Uganda and Mali have the *lowest* inequality of opportunity given their coverage rates, for the younger and older children, respectively. Among single opportunities, inequality of opportunity is high for access to electricity and sanitation, and finishing primary school; and low for not being stunted, immunization, and school attendance. The countries with significantly higher than expected inequality of opportunity include Nigeria for school attendance and full immunization, and the Democratic Republic of Congo for starting primary on time and access to safe water.

In concluding this chapter, it is important to highlight three implications of the findings. *First*, if the concerns embedded in an HOI are consistent with the implicit social welfare function of policy makers in SSA (see the discussion in chapter 2), improving welfare would require a combination of expanding coverage and enhancing equity in coverage in varying degrees. The optimum weights on the two objectives would depend on the individual opportunity and country. Generally speaking, a focus on equity, along with expansion of coverage, is likely to yield the best results for opportunities with relatively high inequality in most countries—access to electricity and sanitation, and finishing primary school. Where inequality of opportunity is relatively low in most countries—namely for nutrition, immunization, and school attendance—an HOI increase would primarily come from expanding coverage.

Second, lack of access to basic opportunities in infrastructure and health is a source of serious concern in most SSA countries. Safe water, adequate sanitation, and vaccination are perhaps the most important predictors of a child's health status and even school attendance and performance.[9] If access to these services—particularly among children of disadvantaged circumstances—does not improve rapidly, children in many countries will remain significantly at risk, even as opportunities such as school attendance show progress. Different sets of standards for safe water and adequate sanitation yield very different rankings of countries by an HOI, suggesting that the capacity of each country to provide different types of facilities varies widely, even within the same class of facilities.

Third, as education opportunities among children in SSA countries improve, the attention of policy makers is likely to focus more and more on the quality of learning imparted in schools. The variation in SACMEQ-III test scores of sixth graders across eight countries, and among children with different circumstances *within* countries, hints at significant inequality of opportunity in learning. The indicators used in the HOI analysis here reflect only a small part of the story, even as there is some correlation (based on a small cross-country sample) between countries with a higher HOI in primary school completion and student performance in reading and numeracy. In-depth analysis using students' test scores, as and when they become available for most countries in SSA, would help to complete the picture on how the opportunity of receiving quality education is influenced by the circumstances a child is born into and what that suggests for policy.

Annex 3A

Figure 3A.1 D-Index and Coverage across Countries in Education Opportunities

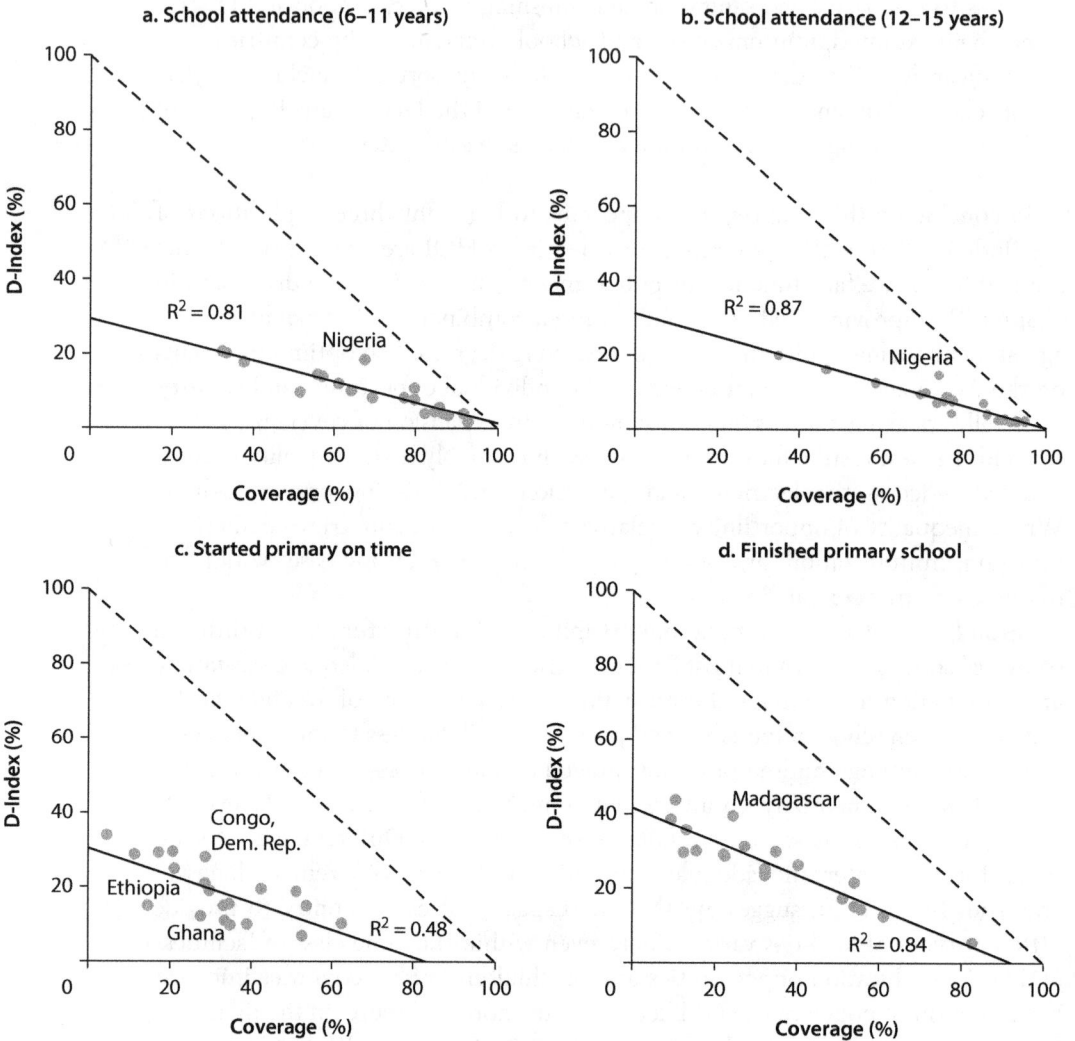

a. School attendance (6–11 years)

$R^2 = 0.81$

Nigeria

D-Index (%)

Coverage (%)

b. School attendance (12–15 years)

$R^2 = 0.87$

Nigeria

D-Index (%)

Coverage (%)

c. Started primary on time

Congo,
Dem. Rep.

Ethiopia

Ghana

$R^2 = 0.48$

D-Index (%)

Coverage (%)

d. Finished primary school

Madagascar

$R^2 = 0.84$

D-Index (%)

Coverage (%)

Source: Authors' calculations using Demographic and Health Surveys data, various years.
Note: D-Index = dissimilarity index.

Figure 3A.2 D-Index and Coverage across Countries in Infrastructure and Health Opportunities

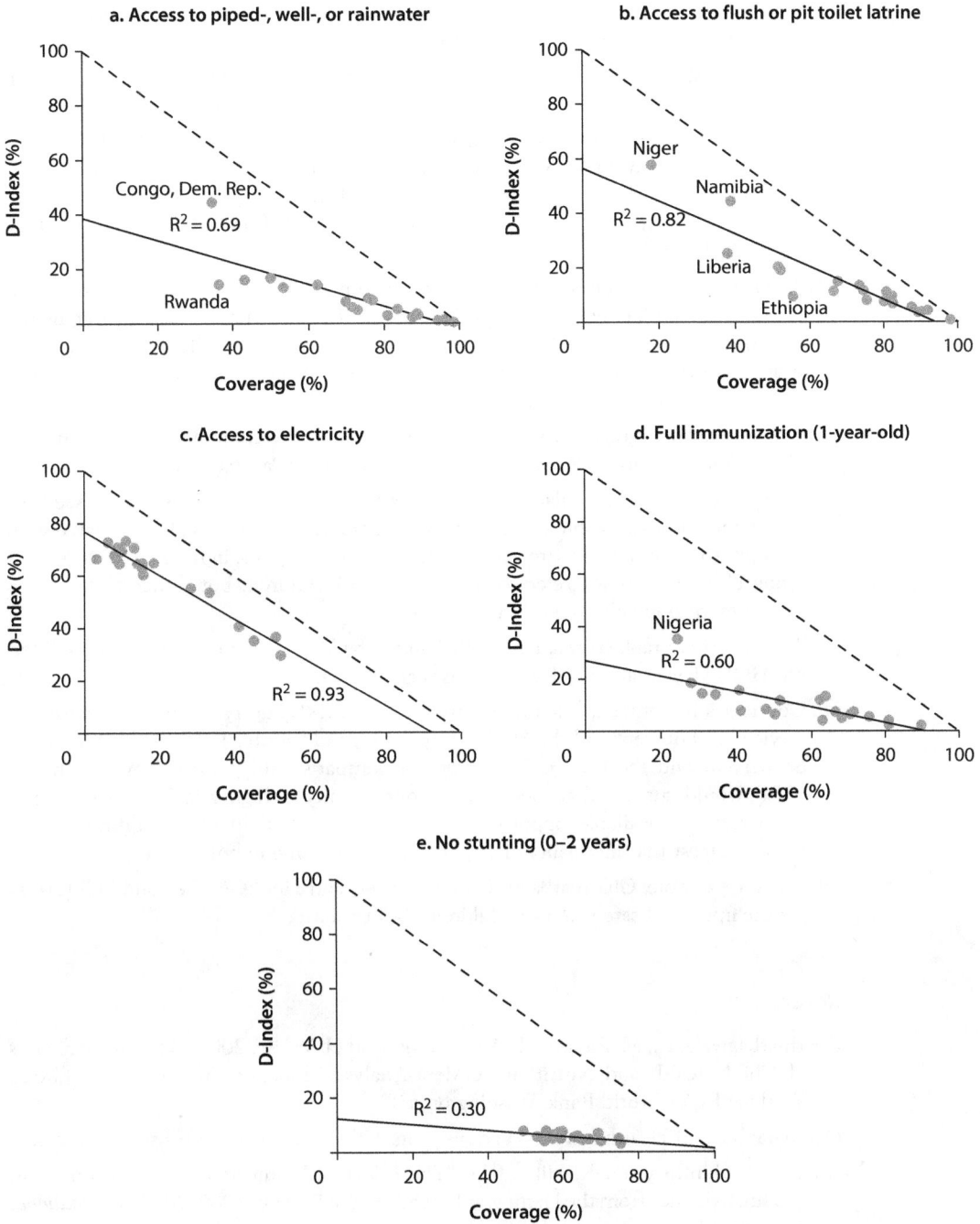

a. Access to piped-, well-, or rainwater

b. Access to flush or pit toilet latrine

c. Access to electricity

d. Full immunization (1-year-old)

e. No stunting (0–2 years)

Source: Authors' calculations using Demographic and Health Surveys data, various years.
Note: D-Index = dissimilarity index.

Notes

1. United Nations Economic Commission for Africa (2010); McKinsey Global Institute (June 2010); World Bank's *Africa's Pulse* (September 2011, Volume 4).

2. Attending sixth grade for 12-year-olds and completing six or more years of education for those of age 13–15 years.

3. The cross-country correlations (based on eight countries) between the HOI for finishing primary school (12- to 15-year-olds) and the percentage of children with basic skills in reading or mathematics are around 0.4 and 0.35, respectively. The corresponding correlations with school attendance (6- to 11-year-olds) are 0.26 and 0.16, respectively.

4. The extent of variation is similar if, instead of stunting, the indicator for nutrition used is "not being underweight" for 0- to 2-year-olds. The HOI levels are, however, higher for not being underweight, compared to not being stunted, reflecting the fact that most countries do much better on weight-for-age of children (acute malnutrition) than for height-for-age (chronic malnutrition).

5. One method of aggregation, seen in some publications, is to compute a weighted average of HOI measures for different opportunities to create an "average" HOI for a country.

6. If DHS surveys were available six years apart for each country, it is easy to see how the opportunities available to a cohort of 1 year of age in time t can be compared with the opportunities for the same cohort, now of age 6–8 years, in time $(t+1)$. Note that "cohort" here does not refer to the *same* set of children, but rather to the same *circumstance group* observed six years apart.

7. The Spearman rank correlation coefficient for ranking of countries by the two different HOIs (1 year and 6–11 years) is as high as 0.84.

8. Consider a hypothetical example with two countries: country A where coverage of a service is 50 percent and the HOI is 45 percent, and country B where the coverage is 80 percent and the HOI is 72 percent. A comparison of penalty (coverage minus HOI) would suggest that inequality of opportunity is higher in B than in A. But 10 percent of available opportunities are "misallocated" in both countries, which would suggest that inequality of opportunity is the same in both.

9. See, for example, Charmarbagwala et al. (2004) and Fink, Günther, and Hill (2011) for the impact of safe water on children's health status.

References

Charmarbagwala, R., M. Ranger, H. Waddington, and H. White. 2004. "The Determinants of Child Health and Nutrition: A Meta-Analysis." Independent Evaluation Group Working Paper, World Bank, Washington, DC.

Demographic and Health Surveys. Various years. USAID. http://www.dhsprogram.com.

Fink, G., I. Günther, and K. Hill. 2011. "The Effect of Water and Sanitation on Child Health: Evidence from the Demographic and Health Surveys 1986–2007." *International Journal of Epidemiology* 40: 1196–204.

Hungi, N., D. Makuwa, K. Ross, M. Saito, S. Dolata, F. van Cappelle, L. Paviot, and J. Vellien. 2010. "SACMEQ III Project Results: Pupil Achievement Levels in Reading and Mathematics, Working Document No. 1." Southern and Eastern Africa Consortium for Monitoring Educational Quality, Paris.

McKinsey Global Institute. 2010. *Lions on the Move: The Progress and Potential of African Economies*. McKinsey & Company.

SACMEQ (The Southern and Eastern African Consortium for Monitored Educational Quality) III. 2010. "Project Results: Pupil Achievement Levels in Reading and Mathematics." Working Document 1. http: www.sacmeq.org.

United Nations Economic Commission for Africa. 2010. *Promoting High-Level Sustainable Growth to Reduce Unemployment in Africa*. Economic Report on Africa. UNECA, Addis Ababa, Ethiopia.

World Bank. 2011. *Africa's Pulse*, Vol. 4, September, Washington, DC.

CHAPTER 4

Progress toward Opportunities for All

In chapter 3, we took stock of where sub-Saharan African (SSA) countries are in terms of equitable access to opportunities for children in the late-2000s. The analysis has served two major purposes. *First*, it has helped in identifying how countries fare—in comparison to each other and across different types of indicators for the same countries—in terms of access to opportunities and where the challenges lie. *Second*, with the reasonable idea that some basic goods and services are equally important for a child at a particular stage of life, the composite Human Opportunity Index (HOI) computed for two different age groups for each country illustrates the distance that most countries have to travel to achieve universal access to even the most basic set of opportunities for children.

As important as taking stock of where countries are, is to trace the paths that have led countries to where they are. Accordingly, this chapter will focus on the trends in the HOI for all the opportunities considered so far. It will address two key questions. *First:* how has the HOI evolved for each country and every opportunity considered so far, over the roughly 10-year period between the late-1990s and late-2000s? *Second:* what does the change in the HOI for an opportunity in a country tell us about the underlying changes in coverage, inequality, and child characteristics? To shed light on this issue, we decompose the changes in the HOI into the effects of scale (distribution-neutral change in coverage), redistribution (change in inequality of coverage), and composition (changes in circumstances of the children). This exercise shows the dynamics of access to services in each country and the promises and challenges they suggest for policy makers looking ahead to the future.

Uneven Progress: The Decade of the 2000s

In looking at how the HOI has evolved for countries between the late-1990s and late-2000s, we have to take into consideration the fact that the survey years used for the analysis and the length of time between the two surveys are not the same for all countries.[1] To enable a meaningful comparison across countries, the results are presented in terms of annualized (average annual) change in the HOI for each opportunity between the two survey years for a particular country. Considering all 17 countries for which some data for both years are available, the average length of time between the two survey years is 10.3 years, with the average concealing some variation in the length of time across countries.[2]

Education Opportunities

Figure 4.1 shows the *average annual change* in the HOI between the late-1990s and late-2000s for each of the education opportunities discussed in the second section, in 16 countries for which data are available for both periods.[3] The opportunities are school attendance (6–11 years), school attendance (12–15 years), started primary on time (ages 6–7), and finished primary school (12- to 15-year-olds). The *dots* in each figure represent the point estimates for the average annual change in the HOI for a particular opportunity in a country, while the bars represent the 95 percent confidence interval around each estimate. An average annual change can be accepted as statistically significant when the bar does not overlap with zero (marked on the horizontal axis). The point estimate depicted by the dot for Cameroon in figure 4.1c, for example, shows a positive change. But the bar shows that the change in Cameroon is not significantly different from zero, at 95 percent level of confidence.

Encouragingly, all 16 countries have made statistically significant improvements in the HOI for school attendance of children aged 6–11 years. For school attendance among the older age group (12–15 years), the HOI has improved significantly in all but three countries. Looking across countries, Nigeria, Kenya, and Zimbabwe rank the lowest in terms of change in the HOI for attendance for young children (figure 4.1a), while Nigeria, Zimbabwe, and Tanzania rank the lowest in change in the HOI for attendance of older children (figure 4.1b). Nigeria is the only country with a statistically significant reduction in the HOI for attendance of 12- to 15-year-olds. Between the two countries that rank near the bottom in terms of improvements for *both* age groups, Nigeria and Zimbabwe, the former has more reason to be concerned since Zimbabwe had a much higher level of the HOI to start with in the late-1990s than Nigeria.[4] On the other hand, Ethiopia and Rwanda fare particularly well, with an HOI advancement of over two percentage points annually. Tanzania is an interesting case, with a very high increase in the HOI for attendance of younger children, but hardly any improvement in that of older children. This might be explained by an already high rate of attendance among older children in the 1990s due to late enrollment in school.

Progress is more uneven in the opportunity of starting primary school on time, with 5 out of 16 countries showing no statistically significant improvement, including 3 that show a significant decline (figure 4.1c). Improvements in the HOI for completion of primary school among 12- to 15-year-olds are on par with that in school attendance in the same age group—13 out of 16 countries show a statistically significant average annual gain in the HOI (figure 4.1d). Namibia shows the largest improvements on both starting on time and completion of

Figure 4.1 Progress in Education Opportunities between circa 1998 and circa 2008

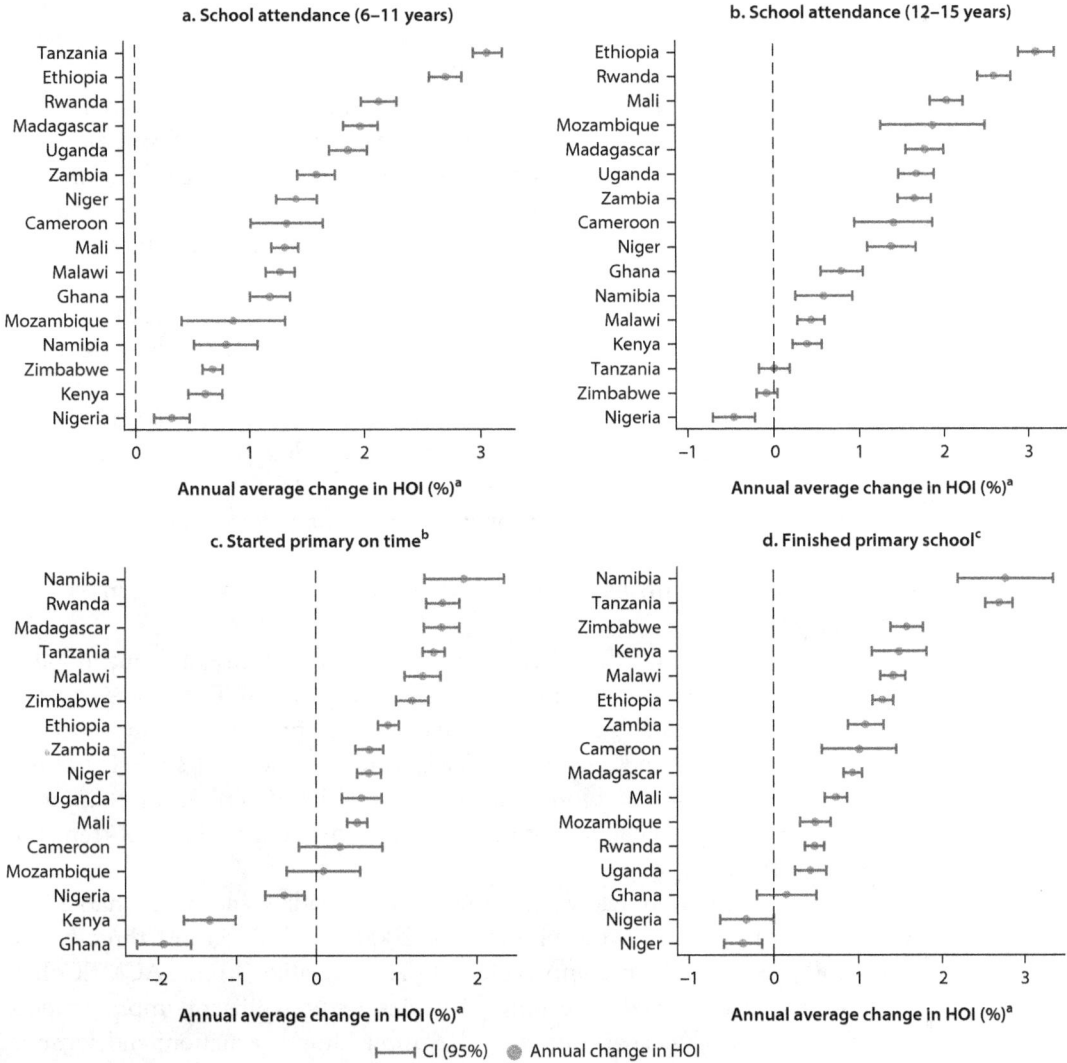

a. School attendance (6–11 years)

b. School attendance (12–15 years)

c. Started primary on time[b]

d. Finished primary school[c]

$\vdash\!\!-\!\!-\!\!\dashv$ CI (95%) ● Annual change in HOI

Source: Authors' calculations using Demographic and Health Surveys data, various years.
Note: CI (95%) refers to 95% confidence intervals of the point estimate of the annual percentage point change. HOI = Human Opportunity Index.
a. Annual change in the HOI is the average annual percentage point change between two survey years (circa 1998 and circa 2008).
b. Started primary school by age 6 years, measured among a cohort of 6- to 7-year-olds.
c. Finished primary school, measured among a cohort of 12- to 15-year-olds.

primary school, whereas Nigeria shows significant declines for both indicators. In addition to Namibia, Tanzania and Malawi are among the top five improvers for both opportunities. And in addition to Nigeria, Ghana is ranked among the bottom three in improvement for both opportunities. Kenya, interestingly, shows a statistically significant reduction in the HOI for starting primary in time, while being ranked among the top five improvers in the HOI for completion of primary school among 12- to 15-year-olds.

Statistically significant improvement for all four education opportunities in a country would indicate unequivocal progress—gains in enrollment on the one hand, and timely entry into school and retention through primary school years on the other. Such progress is shown by eight countries: Ethiopia, Madagascar, Malawi, Mali, Namibia, Rwanda, Uganda, and Zambia. Among the other countries, some interesting facts are worth mentioning. Kenya, Ghana, Cameroon, and Mozambique have made some gains in HOIs for school attendance but not for starting primary school on time and/or completion of primary. Nigeria seems to have slipped backwards in all but one education opportunity, and its slow progress in school attendance among 6- to 11-year-olds lags behind that of every other country. Finally, the story of Rwanda is worth highlighting: the country is ranked among the top three in improvements in attendance (both age groups) and starting primary in time, but in the bottom five for improvement in the HOI for primary school completion. This seems to tell the story of a postconflict country that has been highly successful in getting children into school, including a generation of children whose schooling has been delayed or interrupted by conflict, which has slowed the improvement in primary completion.

Trends for Select Countries in Learning Achievement—Evidence from Secondary Source

Has the improvement in education opportunities in a majority of countries been accompanied by improvement in the quality of education? Test scores of sixth graders from the SACMEQ-III project (see chapter 2) provide some evidence for seven of the countries included in our analysis. While the HOI analysis has not been conducted with test scores due to the reasons described in chapter 2, average scores for the small subset of countries provide some hints of trends in student achievement.

Figures 4.2a and 4.2b below show that average reading and mathematics test scores for sixth graders have risen between 2000 and 2007 in just three of the seven countries for which comparable data are available (from SACMEQ-III). Tanzania and Namibia are the only countries with significant improvements in both test scores; Malawi, Kenya, and Zambia show stagnation; and Uganda and Mozambique show a significant decline in at least one average test score. Therefore, this subsample of countries shows mixed progress in average learning achievement—a sound indicator for the opportunity of access to quality education—with a majority of countries showing stagnation or worse.

For these seven countries, progress in average test scores clearly lags behind progress in the education opportunities analyzed using the HOI. But is there a *correlation* between progress in these education opportunities and learning achievements, as measured by test scores? While the small sample of countries precludes any robust conclusion about correlations, figures 4.2c and 4.2d show that countries with the largest improvements in average test scores (Namibia, Tanzania, and Malawi, in that order) are also those with the largest increase in the HOI for finishing primary school and starting primary school on time. At the other end of the spectrum are Mozambique, Uganda, and Zambia, with stagnating

Figure 4.2 Change in Student (Sixth Grade) Test Scores in Select SSA Countries

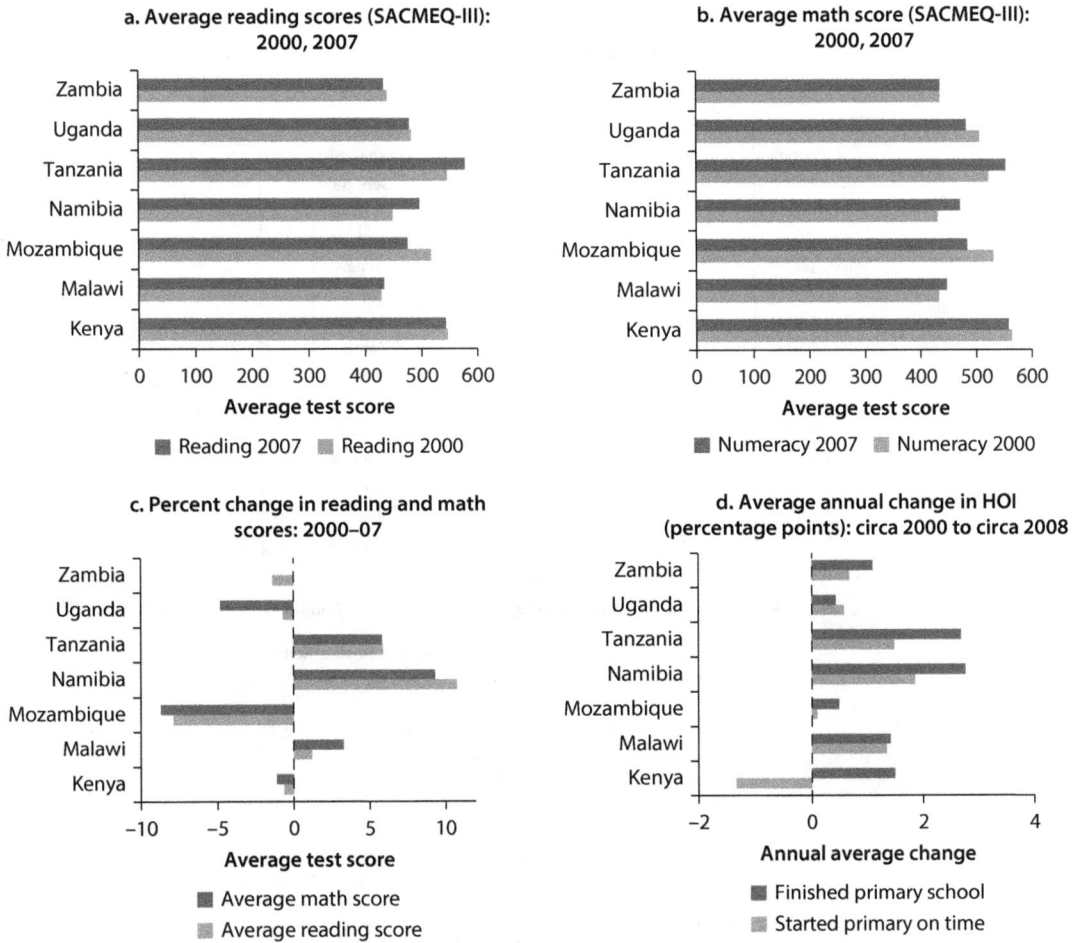

a. Average reading scores (SACMEQ-III): 2000, 2007

Zambia
Uganda
Tanzania
Namibia
Mozambique
Malawi
Kenya

0   100   200   300   400   500   600
Average test score

■ Reading 2007   ■ Reading 2000

b. Average math score (SACMEQ-III): 2000, 2007

Zambia
Uganda
Tanzania
Namibia
Mozambique
Malawi
Kenya

0   100   200   300   400   500   600
Average test score

■ Numeracy 2007   ■ Numeracy 2000

c. Percent change in reading and math scores: 2000–07

Zambia
Uganda
Tanzania
Namibia
Mozambique
Malawi
Kenya

−10   −5   0   5   10
Average test score

■ Average math score
■ Average reading score

d. Average annual change in HOI (percentage points): circa 2000 to circa 2008

Zambia
Uganda
Tanzania
Namibia
Mozambique
Malawi
Kenya

−2   0   2   4
Annual average change

■ Finished primary school
■ Started primary on time

Source: Makuwa 2010.
Note: HOI = Human Opportunity Index; SACMEQ = Southern and Eastern Africa Consortium for Monitoring Educational Quality; SSA = Sub-Saharan Africa.

or declining test scores along with small increases in the HOI. Thus, at least for this small group of countries, a rising HOI for the opportunities that were selected as indirect proxies for quality of education (finishing primary school and on time start of primary school) appears to be associated with a rise in average learning achievement among sixth grade students.

Opportunity of Access to Basic Infrastructure

Improvement in access to basic infrastructure, namely water, sanitation, and electricity, has been mixed (figure 4.3). Using the more liberal definitions for access to safe water and adequate sanitation (as in figure 3.4 in chapter 3), 11 out of the 17 countries experienced a statistically significant average annual increase in the HOI for safe water and 12 out of 17 had the same for sanitation.

Figure 4.3 Progress in Infrastructure Opportunities between circa 1998 and circa 2008

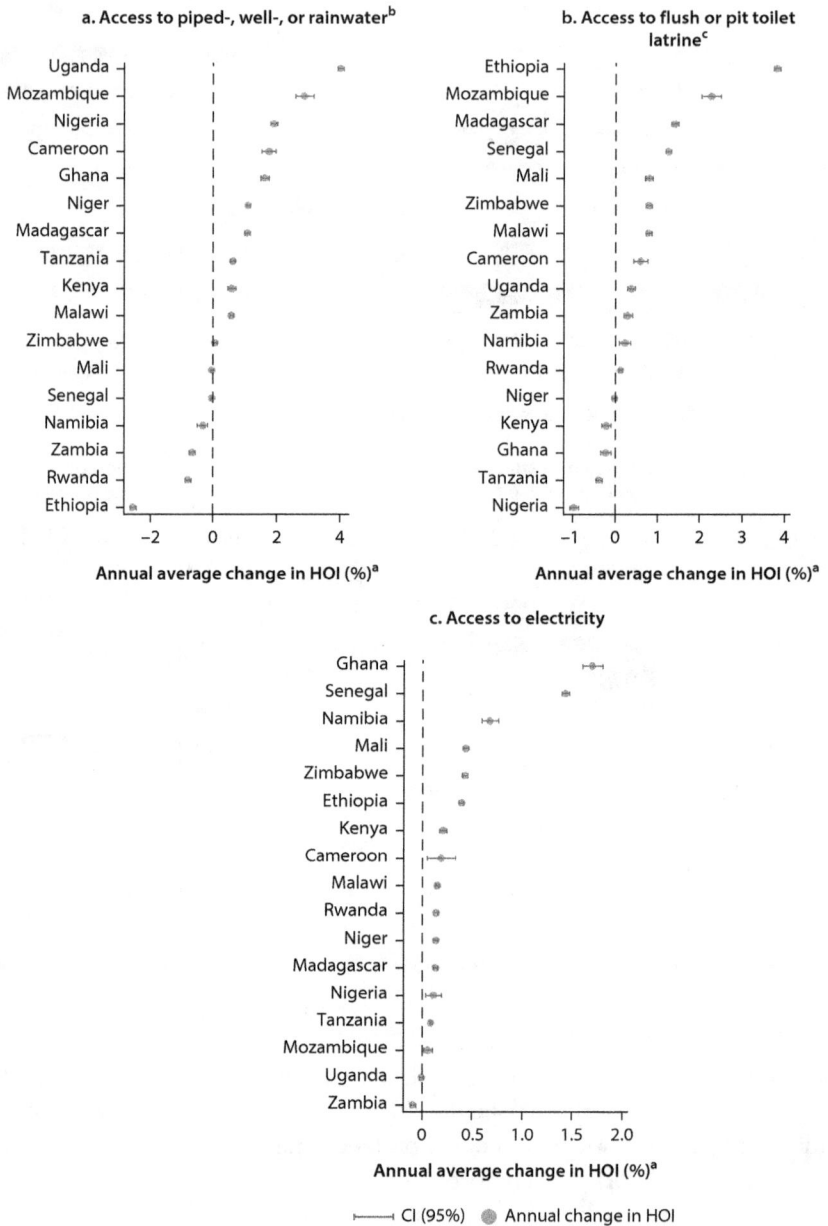

a. Access to piped-, well-, or rainwater[b]

Uganda
Mozambique
Nigeria
Cameroon
Ghana
Niger
Madagascar
Tanzania
Kenya
Malawi
Zimbabwe
Mali
Senegal
Namibia
Zambia
Rwanda
Ethiopia

−2   0   2   4

Annual average change in HOI (%)[a]

b. Access to flush or pit toilet latrine[c]

Ethiopia
Mozambique
Madagascar
Senegal
Mali
Zimbabwe
Malawi
Cameroon
Uganda
Zambia
Namibia
Rwanda
Niger
Kenya
Ghana
Tanzania
Nigeria

−1   0   1   2   3   4

Annual average change in HOI (%)[a]

c. Access to electricity

Ghana
Senegal
Namibia
Mali
Zimbabwe
Ethiopia
Kenya
Cameroon
Malawi
Rwanda
Niger
Madagascar
Nigeria
Tanzania
Mozambique
Uganda
Zambia

0   0.5   1.0   1.5   2.0

Annual average change in HOI (%)[a]

├───┤ CI (95%)   ● Annual change in HOI

Source: Authors' calculations using Demographic and Health Surveys data, various years.
Note: CI (95%) refers to 95% confidence intervals of the point estimate of the annual percentage point change.
HOI = Human Opportunity Index.
a. Annual change in the HOI is the average annual percentage point change between two survey years (circa 1998 and circa 2008).
b. Piped-, well-, or rainwater is the main source of drinking water for the household.
c. Presence of flush toilet or pit toilet latrine in the household.

Notably, the ranking of countries by improvement in the HOI is markedly different between the two indicators. For example, Ethiopia, Mali, Namibia, Rwanda, Senegal, and Zambia experienced some average annual increase in the HOI for access to sanitation, but a stagnant or falling HOI for access to safe water. Conversely, Ghana, Kenya, Niger, Nigeria, and Tanzania showed an increase in the HOI for access to safe water but stagnation or decline in the HOI for sanitation. While no country experienced a decrease in both HOIs, only six countries (Cameroon, Madagascar, Malawi, Mozambique, Uganda, and Zimbabwe) showed at least some improvement in the HOI for *both* water and sanitation. Uganda and Mozambique had an average annual improvement of three percentage points or more in the HOI for access to safe water; Ethiopia had the same for access to sanitation, along with a reduction of more than two percentage points for access to safe water.

The HOI in access to electricity shows little improvement—a sobering fact given the low access to electricity in most countries at the beginning of the period. Fifteen out of 17 countries show some increase in the HOI, but for 12 of these countries the average annual increase in the HOI is less than 0.5 percentage point. Only two countries—Ghana and Senegal—have an increase of one percentage point or more in the HOI annually. Ghana is the only country where an increase in the HOI averaged nearly two percentage points annually, which occurred even as Ghana had the third highest the HOI in electricity (around 20) to start with in the late-1990s. On the flip side, the HOI for electricity showed a slight annual decline for Zambia, which also had a very low HOI (less than 10) to start with. The overall story on access to electricity is thus one of stagnation and lack of convergence among countries, with countries with low and unequal access in the late-1990s being unable to expand access in subsequent years.

Access to Health Opportunities

Figure 4.4 shows the change in the HOI related to health opportunities—full immunization and not being stunted. The confidence intervals for changes in the HOI for health opportunities are larger than those for education or infrastructure, implying that, for some countries, the direction of change in the HOI for health opportunities is statistically ambiguous. Just 12 (out of 16) and 7 (out of 16) countries show a statistically significant increase in the HOI for immunization and not being stunting, respectively; and statistically significant declines are seen for Zambia and Zimbabwe in immunization and for Niger and Namibia in nutrition.

Uganda and Zambia show HOI improvements for nutrition but not immunization. Ethiopia, Madagascar, Malawi, Nigeria, and Tanzania show significant increases in the HOI for both opportunities. Cameroon, Ghana, Kenya, Mali, Mozambique, Niger, and Rwanda show significant improvements for immunization but not for nutrition; Namibia and Zimbabwe show no improvement in the HOI for either indicator. Mozambique and Nigeria show the highest rate of improvement in the HOI for immunization and nutrition, respectively, far outpacing the progress achieved by any other country.

Figure 4.4 Progress in Health Opportunities between circa 1998 and circa 2008

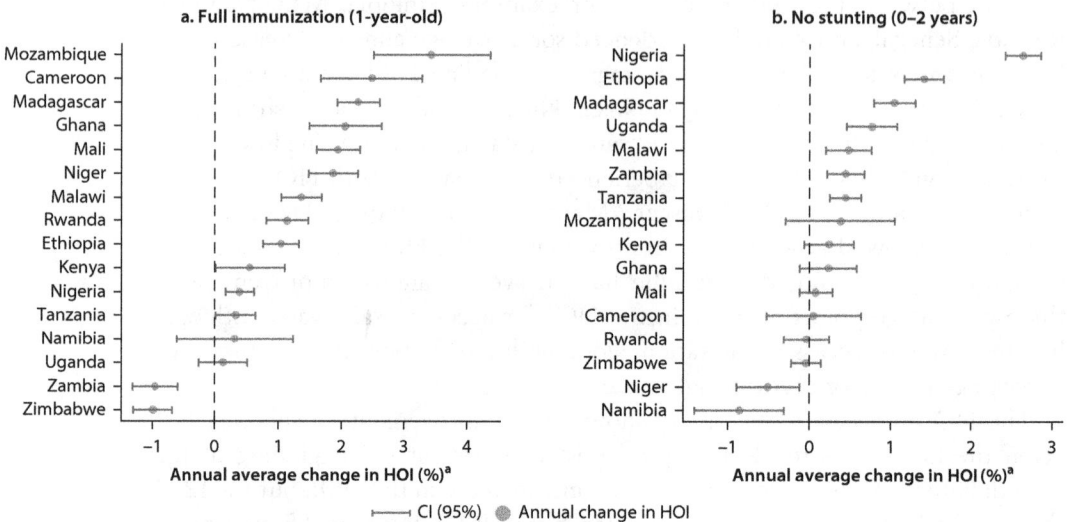

a. Full immunization (1-year-old)

b. No stunting (0–2 years)

Annual average change in HOI (%)ᵃ

Annual average change in HOI (%)ᵃ

├──┤ CI (95%)   ● Annual change in HOI

Source: Authors' calculations using Demographic and Health Surveys data, various years.
Note: CI (95%) refers to 95% confidence intervals of the percentage point estimate of the annual change. HOI = Human Opportunity Index.
a. Annual change in the HOI is the average annual percentage point change between two survey years (circa 1998 and circa 2008).

Access to All Opportunities Relevant for an Age Group—The Composite HOI

Having looked at the trends in the HOI for each individual opportunity between the late-1990s and late-2000s, we now look at how access to a minimum bundle of goods and services relevant for a certain age group has evolved across countries during this period. To see this, we bring back the composite HOI defined in chapter 3, which is anchored in the idea that basic services are not substitutes for one another, but constitute a minimal set of opportunities that a child must have in order to have a fair chance of fulfilling his/her potential in life. As in chapter 3, for children of 1 year of age, the basic set of opportunities consists of access to safe water, adequate sanitation, full immunization, and not being stunted. For children of age 6–11 years, the bundle is a combination of safe water, adequate sanitation, and school attendance. Figure 4.5 below shows the average annual change in each of the two composite HOIs for each country, along with the statistical significance of these changes.

Two points are worth highlighting. *First*, the improvement tends to be larger and more consistent across countries for the composite HOI for older children compared to that for the younger children. This is partly attributable to what was seen earlier, that improvements in school attendance (relevant for 6- to 11-year-olds) are more common than those in immunization (1 year of age). In case of the younger children, the composite HOI increases for only 10 out of 16 countries, remains unchanged for 4 (Kenya, Namibia, Rwanda, and Zimbabwe), and declines for Zambia, when the statistical significance of the changes is taken into account. In contrast, all countries with the exception of Namibia show

Figure 4.5 Progress in Access to Bundle of Opportunities between circa 1998 and circa 2008

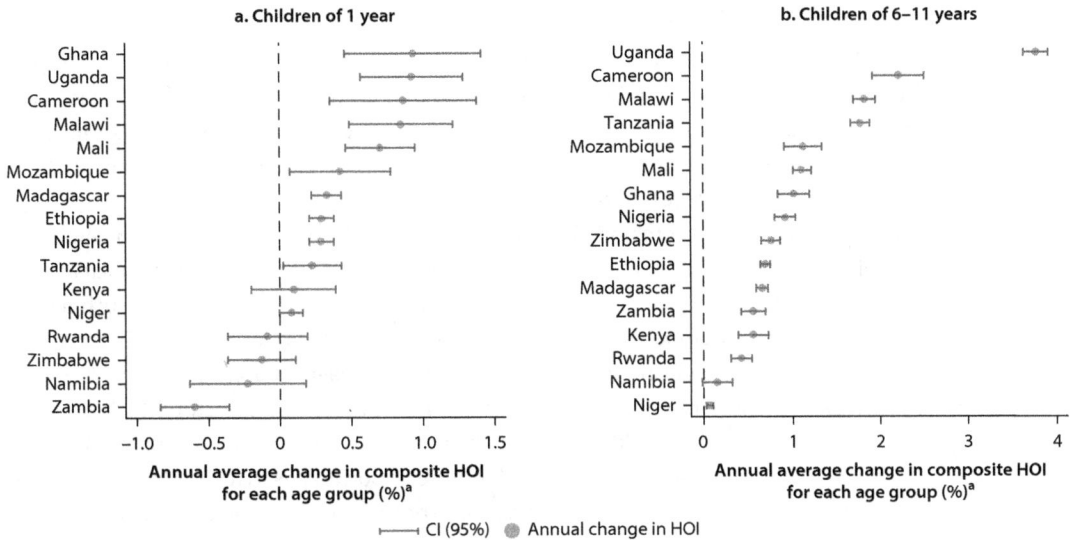

a. Children of 1 year

b. Children of 6–11 years

Annual average change in composite HOI
for each age group (%)[a]

├───┤ CI (95%)   ● Annual change in HOI

Source: Authors' calculations using Demographic and Health Surveys data, various years.
Note: (1) CI (95%) refers to 95% confidence intervals of the point estimate of the annual change; HOI = Human Opportunity Index. (2) Children 1 year: opportunities included are access to water (piped-, well-, or rainwater), access to sanitation (pit or flush toilet), full immunization, and no stunting. (3) Children 6–11 years: opportunities included are school attendance, access to water (same as above) and access to sanitation (same as above). (4) A child has access to a bundle of opportunities if meeting the standard (of coverage) for all the opportunities. (5) The sample includes only 16 countries for which information on all the opportunities used here is available.
a. Annual change in the HOI is computed as the average annual change in the period between two survey years.

statistically significant improvement in the composite HOI for children of age 6–11 years.

Second, a small group of countries stands out as being highly successful—relative to other countries—in improving access to a set of opportunities for children in both age groups. Uganda, Cameroon, and Malawi are among the top three countries in improvements for both age groups, with an average annual increase in the composite HOI of nearly one percentage point for 1-year-olds and two or more percentage points for 6- to 11–year-olds. For the younger age group, Ghana and Mali represent the other relative success stories; and the same is true for Tanzania for the older age group. Uganda is also worth a special mention for achieving an average annual increase of nearly four percentage points in the composite HOI for 6- to 11-year-olds—an impressive rate of improvement that far outpaces any other country for this age group. In Uganda, the main contributor to this improvement has been a rapid increase in access to safe water, along with that in school attendance (see box 4.1).

A Comparison of How Many Opportunities a Country Has Improved in

While the trends in the composite HOI reflect the progress in providing access to an age-specific *set* of relevant opportunities, a *simple count of the number of opportunities* for which the HOI has improved shows how broad the improvements have been in each country. Figure 4.6 shows the number of opportunities,

Box 4.1 Improving Opportunities for 6- to 11-Year-Olds: The Story of Uganda

Uganda achieved an average annual increase of nearly four percentage points in the composite Human Opportunity Index (HOI) for 6- to 11-year-olds between 1995 and 2006, higher than any other Sub-Saharan Africa country in this study by quite a margin (see figure 4.4). In terms of the components of the composite opportunity, Uganda led all countries (out of 16) in increase in the HOI for access to safe water, with an average annual increase of four percentage points; and placed just ninth and fifth in improvement in the HOI for access to sanitation and school attendance for 6- to 11-year-olds, respectively, with average annual HOI increases of 1.9 and 0.4 percentage points, respectively. How did these changes add up to such a high improvement in the composite opportunity (access to all three opportunities)?

The graph below, showing the coverage (but not inequality of opportunity) of all combinations of the three opportunities in both years, tells part of the story. In 1995, only 26 percent of 6- to 11-year-olds in Uganda had access to all three opportunities. Between 1995 and 2006, coverage expanded more for those opportunities that were lagging in 1995: coverage of safe water increased from 45 percent to 88 percent, and school attendance increased from 67 percent to 85 percent, while that of sanitation increased from 84 percent to 87 percent. This resulted in the share of 6- to 11-year-old children with all three opportunities rising from 26 percent to 68 percent. Increase in coverage of safe water made the biggest difference: 32 percent of children of 6–11 years had sanitation and school attendance in 1995 but no access to safe water; this share shrunk to 8 percent in 2006. While this breakdown ignores the underlying changes in inequality that also contributed to the change in composite HOI, it helps illustrate a point: the more a country improves in the opportunity it lags the most, the higher its improvement in composite HOI is likely to be.

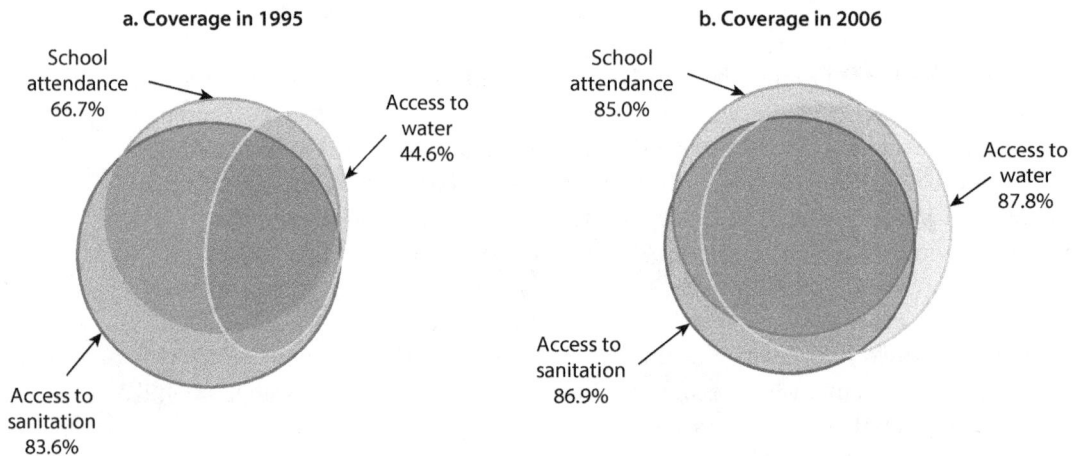

a. Coverage in 1995

School attendance 66.7%

Access to water 44.6%

Access to sanitation 83.6%

b. Coverage in 2006

School attendance 85.0%

Access to water 87.8%

Access to sanitation 86.9%

Figure 4.6 Number of Opportunities with Statistically Significant Increases in HOI

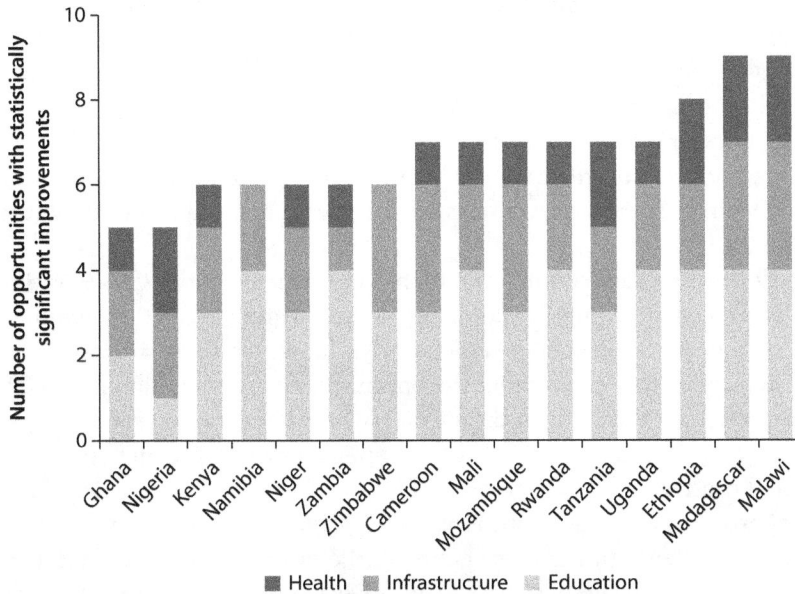

Source: Authors' calculations using Demographic and Health Surveys data, various years.
Note: (1) Total no. of opportunities: four in education, three in infrastructure, and two in health. (2) Does not take into account the *size* of improvement. HOI = Human Opportunity Index.

disaggregated by type, for which each country has made statistically significant average annual improvements between the late-1990s and late-2000s.

Improvements are more common in education than in health and basic infrastructure. Ethiopia, Madagascar, and Malawi are the relatively better performers by this count, showing a statistically significant increase in the HOI for at least eight of the nine opportunities included in the analysis. Ghana and Nigeria are the lowest performers by this count, with improvements in only five opportunities. The "average" country in our full sample of 16 SSA countries shows a statistically significant HOI improvement in 6.8 opportunities.[5]

How a country ranks in terms of the number of improving opportunities can be quite different from how it fares in terms of improvements in the composite HOI. For example, while Ghana ranks at the bottom by the first measure, it is one of the most rapid improvers in the composite HOI for younger children. But there is an unambiguous success story. For Malawi, rapid improvements in the composite HOI for both age groups are consistent with being the country with the highest number of opportunities that have improved.

Cross-Country Variation in the HOI over Time

How has cross-country variation in access to opportunities for children evolved between the late-1990s and late-2000s? As mentioned in chapter 3, the coefficient of variation (CV)—the ratio between the standard deviation and the mean—is a widely used summary measure of variation. Figure 4.7 compares the CV for each type of HOI in the two periods. Two facts stand out.

First, the CV has declined over time for all the HOIs, including those for individual and composite opportunities, with the extent of decline being quite similar (as a proportion of the initial CV) across all opportunities. *Second*, there are significant differences in the extent of cross-country variation across opportunities in both periods. Access to electricity, finishing primary school, and starting primary school on time have the highest cross-country variation (as measured by the CV) in both periods, whereas school attendance and health opportunities have the lowest.

The decline in cross-country variation, as measured by the CV, over time for all HOIs is an encouraging development, as it indicates a reduction in differences in access to opportunities between countries. However, there are two factors to take into account that can temper the optimism. *First*, a reduction in the CV can be in part due to an increase in the average, which has occurred for all opportunities in varying degrees, since for all the opportunities, improving countries outnumber those that have deteriorated. It turns out, however, that for six out of nine opportunities (finishing primary school, access to piped-, well-, or rainwater, and electricity being the only exceptions), the cross-country *standard deviation* actually fell between the two periods. In other words, in a vast majority of cases, the dispersion of the HOI across countries has declined, indicating that differences between countries have indeed narrowed.

Second, the decline in cross-country variation shown in figure 4.7 applies to the group of 16 or 17 countries where DHS data are available for both years to allow

Figure 4.7 Cross-Country Variation of HOIs in Each Period

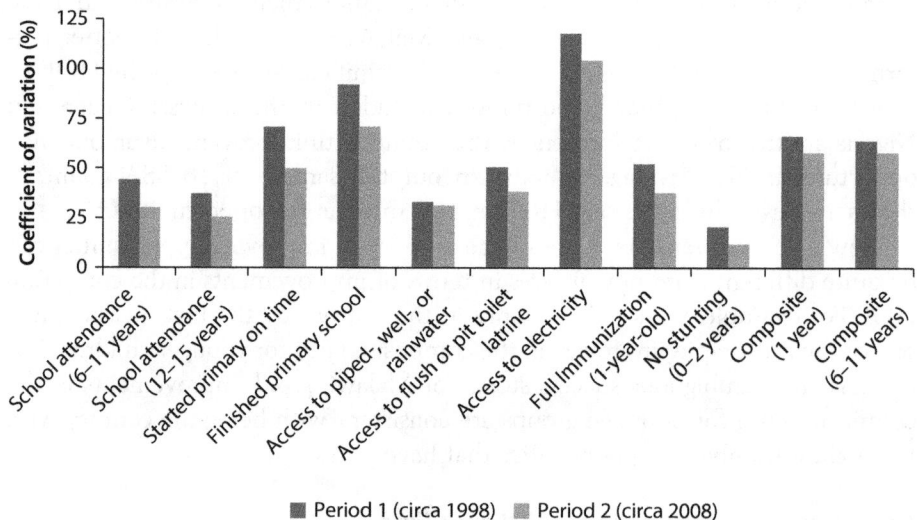

■ Period 1 (circa 1998)   ■ Period 2 (circa 2008)

Source: Authors' calculations using Demographic and Health Surveys data, various years.
Note: CVs are calculated using the sample of countries for which the HOI is available for *both* years (17 for water, sanitation, and electricity, 16 for others), to ensure comparability across years. CVs for period 2 may be different from those shown in figure 3.9, which were for all 20 countries. HOI = Human Opportunity Index.

for computation of the HOI. Given that three of the missing countries, the Democratic Republic of Congo, Liberia, and Sierra Leone, are fragile states with low HOIs, it is possible that their inclusion would have led to different results. This is, however, unlikely, since the decline in the CV from the late-1990s to the late-2000s—albeit smaller in size than what is seen in figure 4.7—occurs even after including these countries in the computation of the CV for the later period.[6]

Therefore, notwithstanding the two caveats above, for the countries in our sample, the reduction in cross-country variation in opportunities among children appears to be real, and possibly indicates some degree of convergence over time among countries in providing access to basic opportunities.

Assessing Progress: Decomposing Changes in the HOI

Now that we have seen how the HOI has changed for opportunities in every country, it is important to focus on the dynamics underlying these changes. Recalling the discussion in chapter 2, change in an HOI can be decomposed into three components: (a) the *scale* effect, which reflects a change in the coverage rate proportionately for all circumstance groups; (b) the *equalization* effect, which reflects a pro-vulnerable transfer of opportunities across circumstance groups; and (c) the *composition* effect, which reflects changes in population shares among circumstance groups. These effects reflect the extent to which the measured change in the HOI is attributable to change in access to the opportunity among all groups (scale), redistribution of opportunities among groups, or change in the circumstances of the population itself.

Decomposing Changes in the HOI for Education

Most of the changes in the HOI for education opportunities can be explained by the scale and equalization effects (figure 4.8). In regions with relatively greater upward mobility such as Latin America, the shift in circumstance groups will naturally create a composition effect (e.g., as more people get richer and *therefore* get access to better health care). In SSA there is relatively little evidence of a composition effect driving improvements in the HOI. In fact, in several countries, there are small negative composition effects; in such cases groups with circumstances that put them at a relative disadvantage compared to the rest of the population (say, children whose parents are less educated) are growing more rapidly than others.

The predominance of scale effect over equalization effect (figure 4.8) suggests that there have been improvements in access to education across all circumstance groups, as opposed to "reallocation" of access in favor of particular groups. That said, the equalization effect is important for countries like Ethiopia, Madagascar, and Mali across all education opportunities. This seems to suggest that public policies in these countries are helping to close the gap between traditionally underserved children and others, not just in terms of attending school but also timely entry into school and completion of primary school.

It is perhaps no coincidence that Ethiopia, Madagascar, and Mali also show (along with five other countries) a statistically significant improvement in

Figure 4.8 Changes in HOIs for Education Opportunities: Contribution of Each Factor

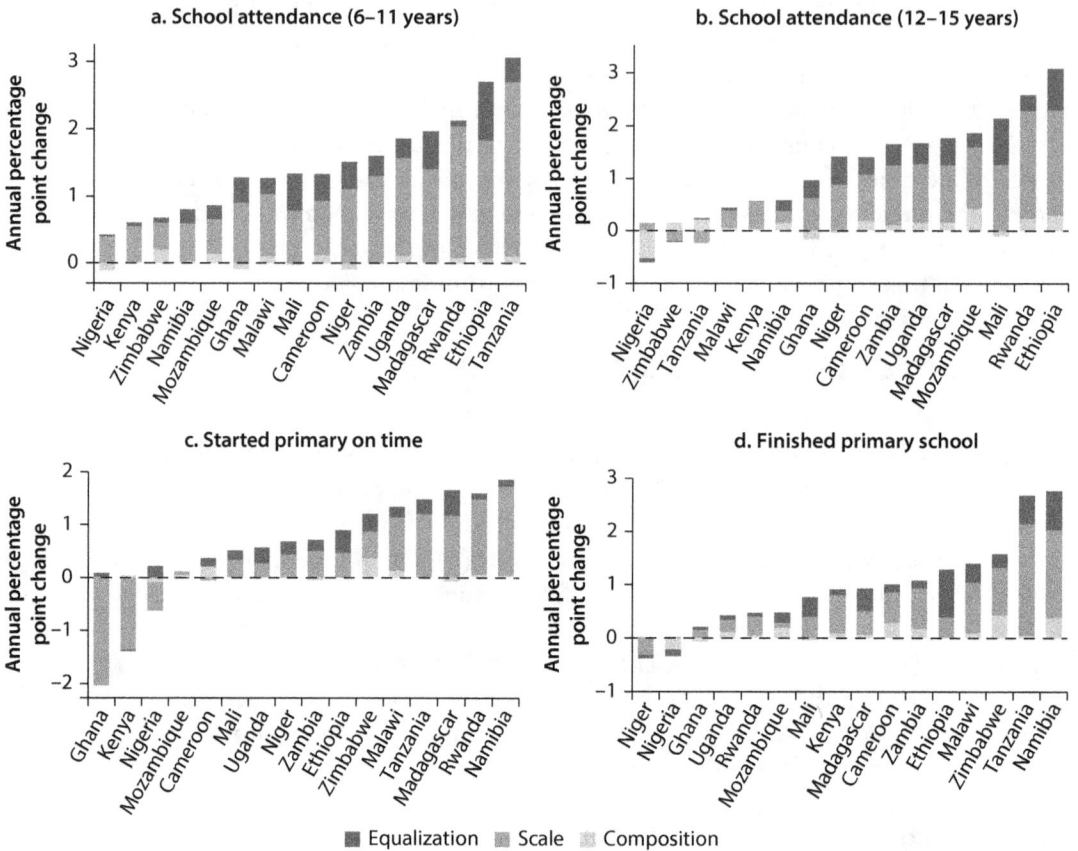

a. School attendance (6–11 years)

b. School attendance (12–15 years)

c. Started primary on time

d. Finished primary school

■ Equalization ■ Scale ■ Composition

Source: Authors' calculations using Demographic and Health Surveys data, various years.
Note: HOI = Human Opportunity Index.

the HOI, measured in terms of annual average, for *all four* education opportunities during this period (see figure 4.6). While the scale factor still dominates in terms of contribution to improvement in the HOI for all three countries, it is fair to say that greater "equalization" of opportunities among groups has played an important role in their success. A positive and significant contribution of the equalization effect also implies that the HOI for these countries has improved more than the average coverage rate of each opportunity.

Decomposing Changes in the HOI for Basic Infrastructure

Figure 4.9 shows the decomposition of the HOI for access to basic infrastructure, using the expanded definitions for safe water and adequate sanitation (as in figures 3.4 and 4.3). The patterns for water and sanitation are broadly similar to those seen for education. The scale effect dominates for almost all countries, the equalization effect is important in some countries but not in others, and the composition effect is negligible with a few exceptions. Interestingly, the equalization effect is significant for all the countries that show relatively large

Figure 4.9 Changes in HOIs for Infrastructure Opportunities: Contribution of Each Factor

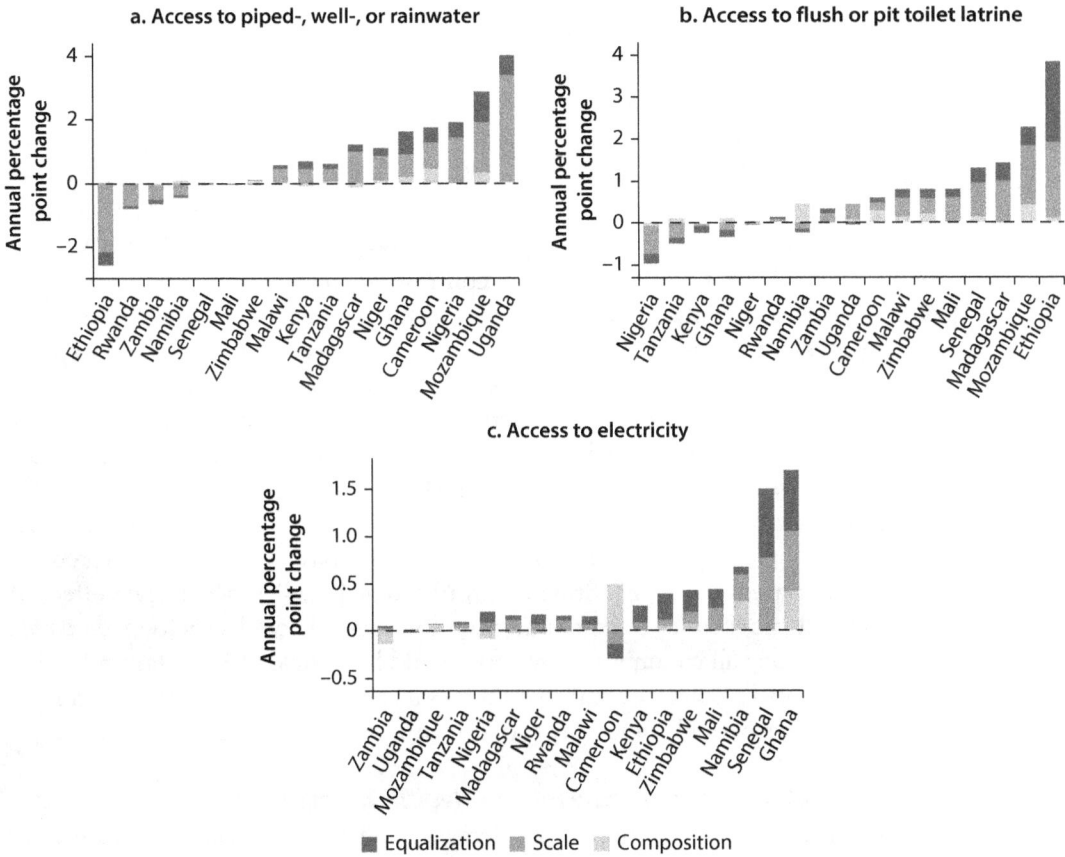

a. Access to piped-, well-, or rainwater

b. Access to flush or pit toilet latrine

c. Access to electricity

■ Equalization ▨ Scale ▧ Composition

Source: Authors' calculations using Demographic and Health Surveys data, various years.
Note: HOI = Human Opportunity Index.

improvements in the HOI, for example, when the top five "improvers" in water and sanitation are considered. The equalization effect is particularly important, almost as much as the scale effect, for improving the HOI in Ghana (for safe water) and Ethiopia (for sanitation). Some of the small declines in the HOI (for water in Ethiopia and sanitation in Nigeria) are partly attributable to a negative equalization effect as well, indicating some redistribution away from the underserved groups.

Compared to all the opportunities we have seen so far, the decompositions for access to electricity turn out to be quite different. *First*, cross-country variation in the decomposition results for change in the HOI in electricity is very high. This may be in part because there is marked variance in the extent of change in the HOI for electricity, with many more countries showing little or no change compared to what is seen for other opportunities. *Second*, equalization and composition effects play a much larger role for access to electricity than they do for water, sanitation, and other opportunities. Among the top 10 improvers in the HOI for access to the electricity, the equalization effect is the dominant driver of change in five countries (Ghana, Zimbabwe, Kenya, Malawi, and Ethiopia), while the composition effect dominates for two others (Namibia and Cameroon).

The importance of equalization in improving access to electricity is an encouraging trend: access to electricity is less unequal than it used to be roughly a decade ago. However, the optimism must be tempered by concern about how *small* the improvements in electricity access have been. As mentioned earlier, just 3 out of 17 countries show an improvement in the HOI that averaged more than 0.5 point per year and no country tops two percentage points per year (see figure 4.3).

The small size of the scale effect, contributing an improvement of less than 0.5 percentage point annually for all except the top two improvers, points to the main problem: access to electricity is extremely low across the board with little improvement over time. Starting from a very low base in the late-1990s—the highest HOI and coverage rate were just 28 and 44, respectively (both for Nigeria)—improving opportunities would have required a broad-based expansion in access, beyond what is seen for any of the countries. Since the HOI takes into account the distance between actual and universal coverage *and* inequality among groups, improving the HOI from a low base will necessarily require expansion in coverage benefiting all groups, that is, a significant scale effect. A simple statistic illustrates the point: given the coverage of electricity, even *perfect* equality among all circumstance groups would have yielded a maximum HOI of 52 among all 17 countries (this would be Ghana) in the late-2000s, and further improvements would come only if coverage were to improve among all groups.

Decomposing Changes in the HOI for Health Opportunities

The results of decomposition of the changes in health opportunities (figure 4.10) are qualitatively similar to those for education opportunities. The equalization

Figure 4.10 Changes in HOIs for Health Opportunities: Contribution of Each Factor

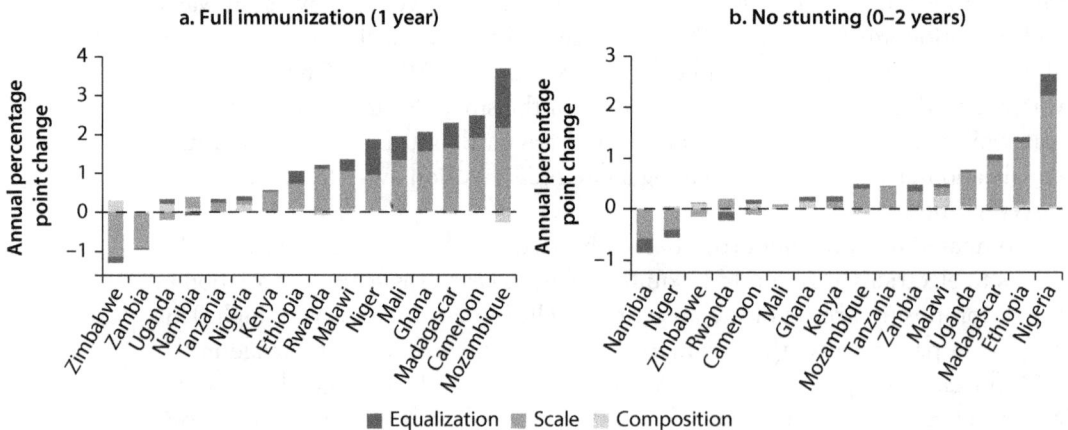

Source: Authors' calculations using Demographic and Health Surveys data, various years.
Note: HOI = Human Opportunity Index.

effect tends to be weaker for nutrition than immunization. Most of the improvement in the HOI for not being stunted among children of 0–2 years of age is explained by the scale effect, suggesting that these improvements have occurred among the general population in a fairly uniform manner. The composition effect plays little or no role in most countries.

The scale effect is dominant in all cases, regardless of the direction of change. The equalization effect also plays an important role for the six countries with the highest improvement in the HOI in full immunization, and for the country with the highest improvement in nutrition (Nigeria). The scale effect was the main driver of change in countries where the HOI in immunization fell (Zimbabwe and Zambia), which indicates a broad-based fall in immunization in these countries that affected all circumstance groups.

Conclusion

In concluding this chapter, it is useful to revisit some of the main findings about the progress achieved by SSA countries in providing opportunities to children between the late-1990s (circa 1998) and late-2000s (circa 2008).

- *HOIs for school attendance have shown the most consistent progress among the opportunities considered here*. Thirteen countries show a statistically significant annual average increase in HOIs for school attendance among children of ages 12–15, and all 16 countries show a statistically significant annual average increase in HOIs for school attendance among children of age 6–11 years. Progress is more uneven across countries in primary school completion among 12- to 15-year-olds and timely entry into school. Eight countries show statistically significant improvements in the HOI for *all four* education opportunities: Ethiopia, Madagascar, Malawi, Mali, Namibia, Rwanda, Uganda, and Zambia.

- According to student achievement data (from SACMEQ-III) for seven countries over a comparable period, *progress in average reading and mathematics test scores of sixth graders has been patchy and lagged behind other education opportunities*. Countries with significant progress in average test scores (Tanzania and Namibia) also had the largest improvement in HOIs for completion of and timely start to primary school. While correlations from such a small sample can be misleading, at least in this group of seven countries, rising opportunities in completing and timely start to primary school seem to be associated with improved learning among students.

- *The scale effect (increase in access proportionally for all circumstance groups) contributes the most toward the improvements in HOIs for education*. The equalization effect (reallocation of opportunities among groups, holding the overall coverage constant) is less important but significant in many cases, and particularly so in three of the countries (Ethiopia, Mali, and Madagascar) that have shown improvements in all education opportunities.

- *Trends in access to safe water, adequate sanitation, and electricity are more mixed than those for education.* Using the more liberal standards, 11 out of 17 countries and 12 out of 17 countries experienced a statistically significant increase in the HOI for water and sanitation, respectively. Even though no country experienced a fall in the HOI for *both* water and sanitation, only six (Cameroon, Madagascar, Malawi, Mozambique, Uganda, and Zimbabwe) showed improvements in both, illustrating the low correlation between improvements in water and sanitation. In access to electricity, the story is that of stagnation: out of 15 countries that show statistically significant increases in the HOI, 12 show an average annual increase of less than 0.5 percentage point and none exceeds an annual increase of two percentage points.

- *For water and sanitation, the scale effect dominates and the composition effect is negligible in most cases.* The equalization effect is more likely to be important when the improvements in the HOI are relatively large, for example, among the top five improving countries in water or sanitation. *Equalization and composition effects are much more important for explaining changes in access to electricity.* Among the top 10 improvers in the HOI for access to electricity, equalization is the dominant force in five countries.

- *Twelve and 7 (out of 16) countries show a statistically significant increase in the HOI for immunization and not being stunted,* respectively; while Zambia and Zimbabwe experienced significant decreases in the HOI for immunization and Niger and Namibia in the HOI for nutrition. Mozambique and Nigeria show the highest rate of improvement in the HOI for immunization and nutrition, respectively, by a large margin relative to other countries.

- *For health opportunities, the scale effect again dominates in all cases and the equalization effect is weaker for nutrition than immunization.* Even as the scale effect predominates, it is important to note that in countries with the highest rate of improvement in the HOI—Mozambique for immunization and Nigeria for nutrition—equalization has also contributed substantially. Improvements in the HOI for nutrition in most other countries seem to have occurred for all circumstance groups. But a rise in the HOI for immunization has occurred with some degree of equalization across groups, particularly in cases where the improvements have been large.

- *Trends in the composite HOI indicate how much progress countries have made in providing an age-relevant bundle of opportunities to children of certain age groups.* The progress tends to be larger and more consistent across countries for the older children compared to the younger children. All countries other than Namibia show a statistically significant improvement in the composite HOI for children of age 6–11 years. In the case of children of age one, the composite HOI increases for only 10 out of 16 countries and actually declines for 1 country (Zambia).

- *Uganda, Cameroon, and Malawi make up the top three countries in improvements in the composite HOI for both age groups,* with an annual average increase of nearly one percentage point for 1-year-olds and two or more percentage points for 6- to 11–year-olds. Uganda stands out for achieving rapid progress in the composite HOI for 6- to 11-year-olds in particular, far outpacing any other country in this age group.

- *A simple count of the number of opportunities for which a country has experienced a statistically significant increase in the HOI shows three countries—Ethiopia, Madagascar, and Malawi—with improvements in at least eight out of the total of nine opportunities.* At the other end of the spectrum are Nigeria and Ghana with improvements in only five opportunities.

Notably, almost all improvements in access to opportunities in education, health, water, and sanitation are due to effects that are likely to reflect, at least to a large degree, the result of *policy* initiatives in service delivery. The dominance of the scale effect—seen in almost every instance where there is a substantial improvement in the HOI—suggests that progress almost always comes with expansion of services to all groups in the population. In some cases, such as Mali (for education), Ethiopia (education and sanitation), Mozambique (water and immunization), Nigeria (nutrition), and Senegal (electricity), the expansion has favored underserved groups to some extent. The trend toward higher equity, wherever it has occurred, probably reflects policy successes and/or changes in behaviors and attitudes in society.

If scale effects indicate the likely effects of broad-based policy initiatives to expand access, the lack of scale effects for access to electricity in most countries points to a serious problem. Given the extremely low HOI of electricity in the late-1990s, tangible gains would have required improving coverage across all groups, which clearly did not occur in the period up to the late-2000s. Consequently during this period, the HOI for electricity improved to some extent in only two countries (Ghana and Senegal) due to a combination of scale and equalization effects.

The negligible composition effects seen in most cases indicate that changes in children's circumstances over time, in terms of the distribution of demographic, socioeconomic, or parental attributes among children, are *not* important drivers of change in access to basic services. While such structural changes in a society are bound to have impacts on access to basic services for children over time, the period under consideration is probably too short for such effects to occur. Instead, the evidence is strong that SSA countries that have made rapid progress toward universalization of basic opportunities for children have achieved so through expansion of services to all groups and, to a lesser extent, by improving equity in access to services among groups.

Notes

1. See annex (table 2A.1), for the list of countries and DHS survey years for each country.

2. With regard to the first period, the survey years range from 1994 (Zimbabwe) to 2000 (Ethiopia, Malawi, Namibia, and Rwanda). For the second period, the survey years range from 2003 (Mozambique) to 2011 (Ethiopia). The length of time that has elapsed between the two survey years ranges between 6 years (Mozambique) and 16.5 years (Zimbabwe) and average length of time between the two survey years is 10.3 years.

3. Average annual change in an HOI for a particular opportunity is calculated as the difference in the HOI between period two and period one, divided by the difference in years between the two periods. Since an HOI is in percentage terms, the average annual change is in percentage point terms.

4. Nigeria had HOIs of 52 and 67 for school attendance among 6- to 11-year-olds and 12- to 15-year-olds, respectively, in the late-1990s, which changed to 55 and 63, respectively, in the late-2000s. Zimbabwe had HOIs of 80 and 87 for school attendance among 6- to 11-year-olds and 12- to 15-year-olds in the late-1990s, which changed to 92 and 86, respectively, in the late-2000s.

5. The number 6.8 represents a simple, unweighted average of the number of opportunities in which each country shows a statistically significant HOI improvement.

6. Note that in this case, the comparison is between the variation across 16 (or 17 in the case of infrastructure) countries in the 1990s and 20 in the 2000s, which is not a like-for-like comparison.

Reference

Makuwa, D. 2010. "What Are the Levels and Trends in Reading and Mathematics Achievement?" SACMEQ Policy Issues Series, No. 2, September. http://www.sacmeq .org/sites/default/files/sacmeq/reports/sacmeq-iii/policy-issue-series/002-sacmeqpoli cyissuesseries-pupilachievement.pdf.

CHAPTER 5

Unpacking Inequality: How Do Circumstances Matter for Opportunities?

Earlier chapters of this study have provided a view of how sub-Saharan African (SSA) countries are placed in terms of providing opportunities for basic services in education, health, and infrastructure to their children and how much progress they have made in these dimensions. But there is a critical question left unanswered: what are the circumstances of children that contribute the most to the inequality of opportunity that is observed? This chapter will address this gap by analyzing the relative importance of different circumstances in explaining inequality of opportunity.

The evidence so far shows that most SSA countries, despite some improvements that vary across countries, are characterized by significant distance from universal provision of basic services among children and persistent inequality in how available opportunities are distributed. Given this, it is all the more important to better understand the socioeconomic characteristics that influence a child's likelihood of belonging to a group that is vulnerable (or underserved) in terms of access to opportunities. While a cross-country study like this one is more about diagnostics than policies, a better understanding of the drivers of inequality can be a useful starting point for future analysis of policy options focusing on individual countries and opportunities.

The question of interest is framed as follows: what is the "contribution" of a specific circumstance (or a group of related circumstances) to inequality of opportunities, among the key set of circumstances included in the analysis? The measure of inequality used is the dissimilarity or D-Index, which can be interpreted as a component of the Human Opportunity Index (HOI; see chapter 2), and the period we focus on is the *most recent* one for which Demographic and Health Survey (DHS) data are available for each country (late-2000s, circa 2008). The methodology we use is to decompose the D-Index according to the Shapley value concept, by which the contribution of each circumstance to the index of inequality can be estimated such that the contributions add up to the value of the D-Index computed with all the circumstances, so that the relative contribution of each circumstance can be assessed. The first section discusses the concepts and methodology used for the analysis; the second section presents the main decomposition results; the third section illustrates how opportunities vary by circumstance profiles, using a select few examples; and the fourth section concludes the chapter with a brief discussion of the results and their broader implications.

Methodology for Decomposing Inequality of Opportunities

We begin by briefly recalling some of the discussion in chapter 2 of this study. The D-Index, also known as the "inequality of opportunity index" for a good or service, has the intuitive interpretation of being equivalent to the proportion of available opportunities that needs to be reallocated among circumstance groups in order for equality of opportunity to prevail. A high D-Index implies that the coverage rate of that good or service varies sharply across circumstances groups, which implies that a larger share of the total number of opportunities has to be reallocated. One implication of the way it is defined, that is, measuring the inequality *between* circumstance groups, is that the D-Index can change according to the set of circumstances used to define groups.

An important property of the D-Index is that the measure of inequality can only increase or stay constant when more circumstances are added to the existing set of circumstances. As explained in chapter 2, this property implies that the measured D-Index is always a lower bound of the actual inequality that would be estimated if one were to use the set of *all* relevant circumstance variables. The property also allows defining the contribution of each circumstance to inequality as the *marginal value added by a "new" circumstance* to the D-Index. Circumstances that add more to the D-Index are interpreted as "contributing" a larger share of the inequality between groups. This is the basic intuition behind the decomposition we use, based on the Shapley value solution concept in cooperative game theory that estimates the contribution of each circumstance to inequality, such that the contributions add up to full value of the D-Index estimated with all circumstances (see box 5.1 for a more detailed discussion).[1]

Among a number of caveats to the analysis,[2] two are especially important. *First*, this approach provides a statistical decomposition of the index and the results do not indicate causality or channels through which unequal access to opportunities is manifested. *Second*, the estimated contributions of circumstances depend on the choice and definition of opportunities and circumstances, which are identical all through the study. Any change to these definitions will yield a change in all results, including the measure of inequality of opportunities (D-Index) and the contribution of each circumstance to inequality.

The circumstances are grouped into six dimensions, as discussed in chapter 2 (see table 2.2): (a) *child characteristics* (e.g., gender of the child); (b) *household composition* (e.g., orphanhood, presence of children and elderly in the household); (c) *location of the child* (urban or rural); (d) *education of the household head*

Box 5.1 Decomposition Based on the Shapley Value Concept

The D-Index or inequality of opportunity index measures the inequality between circumstance groups. For a given set of circumstances, the "contribution" of an additional circumstance to the index can be interpreted as the *marginal change in the value of the D-Index* after adding the "new" circumstance. Circumstances that add more to the D-Index are then considered as contributing to (or explaining) a larger share of the inequality between groups. However, estimating the marginal contribution of each circumstance is complicated. This is because the change in the value of the D-Index as a "new" circumstance is added depends on the *existing* set of circumstances to which the circumstance is added, which in turn implies that the contributions of circumstances would change depending on the sequence in which different circumstances are added. Simply put, the contribution of each circumstance is not unique. Moreover, the contributions of all circumstances estimated this way may not add up to the full D-Index (based on all circumstances), which is not appealing.

The decomposition based on the Shapley value, which is a solution concept in cooperative game theory, is a method that offers a unique, intuitive solution to the above problem The approach is based on the decomposition method proposed by Shorrocks (2012). The Shapley value (Shapley 1953) assigns a unique distribution among the players of a total surplus generated by the coalition of all players using the following rule. In the coalition each player is assigned their marginal contribution to the surplus as a fair compensation, where the player's contribution is calculated as the *average addition to the surplus over all possible different permutations* in which the coalition can be formed. We apply the same concept to the decomposition of the D-Index, with the circumstances being analogous to the players, the total D-Index is analogous to the surplus, and the different combinations of circumstances are equivalent to the coalitions in a cooperative game. In other words, the contribution of a circumstance to the D-Index is the average addition to the value of the D-Index over all possible different permutations in which circumstances can be combined. See the annex for a detailed example that illustrates the method.

Source: Hoyos and Narayan (2011).

(or mother); (e) *other characteristics* (like age) *of the household head* (or mother); and (f) *the socioeconomic status of the child*, measured by the wealth quintile the household belongs to. The inequality contributed by some of the circumstances, for example, wealth and household head's education, may suggest lack of economic and social mobility, while that due to gender of the child or the household head may indicate the influence of social factors on a child's access to opportunities.

Contributions of Circumstances to Inequality: Results from Decompositions

In presenting the results from Shapley decompositions graphically, we focus primarily on the *average* contribution of each circumstance in the D-Index for a particular opportunity, where the average is computed over all or a subset of countries in the sample. Focusing on the averages makes it possible for us to present and identify the broad patterns in how circumstances matter for inequality of different opportunities. This would be difficult if we were to use more disaggregated graphs, given the large number of decompositions (involving 20 countries, nine opportunities, and multiple circumstances) that have to be taken into account.

Three points are important to note before we present the results. *First*, all averages presented here are simple averages (across countries) computed from the decompositions conducted for each country and each opportunity separately, and provides a broad picture for this large sample of SSA countries. The results from decompositions for every country and opportunity are presented in the annex (see figure 5A.1). *Second*, a key limitation of averages is the inability to identify country-specific variations from the average or the "norm." While this is unavoidable in a study covering multiple countries and sectors, we pay some attention to country-specific variations (referring to figure 5A.1 in the annex), particularly when they are significant departures from the average in terms of how circumstances matter for inequality of a certain opportunity.

The *third* point of note is our additional focus on averages for countries that are in the top 50 percent in terms of the D-Index for a particular opportunity, since the question of how much a certain circumstance contributes to inequality is especially relevant when inequality is relatively high. The group of 10 "high-inequality" countries for every opportunity is also the group for which inequality is more likely to be a cause for concern. The list of the 10 most unequal countries does *not* remain the same from one opportunity to another. Also, as we know already, the D-Index varies significantly across opportunities, as it depends on the coverage and distribution of an opportunity. This implies that the *level* of inequality among the 10 most unequal countries in one opportunity can be quite different from that for the 10 most unequal countries in another opportunity.

Therefore, differences in the *level* of inequality across both countries and opportunities need to be taken into account when interpreting the results of our decomposition. Figure 5.1 demonstrates the point about differences across opportunities with a simple graph, which shows for each opportunity the average D-Index and coverage rates for all countries and the average D-Index of the 10 most unequal countries (sorted by the D-Index for each opportunity).

The averages in figure 5.1 tell an interesting story. *First*, there are large differences in the D-Index across opportunities, which are important to keep in mind when interpreting the contributions of specific circumstances to inequality.[3] The level of inequality is particularly low for the opportunity of not being stunted and higher but still low for immunization, school attendance for 12- to 15-year-olds, finishing primary school, and access to safe water. The highest levels of inequality are seen for access to electricity and starting primary school on time. The graph also shows that the difference in average D-Index between the 10 most unequal countries and the full sample of countries is significant in

Figure 5.1 Inequality and Coverage by Opportunity

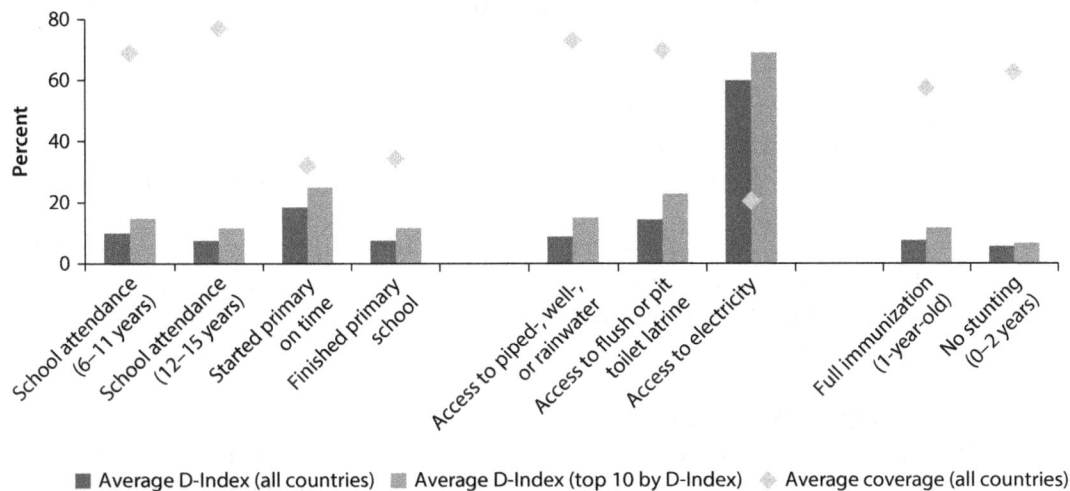

■ Average D-Index (all countries)　■ Average D-Index (top 10 by D-Index)　◆ Average coverage (all countries)

Source: Authors' calculations using Demographic and Health Surveys data, various years.
Note: Average D-Index and coverage for each opportunity is calculated as the simple unweighted average of D-Index and coverage across all countries. Top-10 countries by D-Index for each opportunity are the same group of countries considered as "high-inequality" countries in figure 5.2b. D-Index = dissimilarity index.

most cases, suggesting that it is useful to include both groups of countries in discussing the relative importance of circumstances in explaining the inequality of a certain opportunity.

Second, the graph illustrates the relationship between the D-Index and coverage. Given the definition of the D-Index (see chapter 2), it is easy to see that as coverage increases the share of misallocated opportunities out of the total number of available opportunities is likely to fall. While not a one-to-one relationship, it is likely to be true empirically, as demonstrated by figure 5.1. In all cases where the cross-country average coverage rate is high, the average D-Index is low and vice versa.

This discussion implies an important qualifier to the decomposition results that will follow. While the decomposition of the D-Index is useful in identifying the *relative* importance of each circumstance for a particular opportunity, comparisons *between* different opportunities can be misleading without taking into account the total inequality of opportunities for an opportunity. In the case of opportunities with a low D-Index, a circumstance which may significantly contribute to the D-Index may be responsible for a very small amount of inequality in terms of magnitude. The decomposition results for nutrition, in particular, need to be interpreted through the lens of this qualifier.

A second qualifier to the results of decompositions relates to the definitions of specific circumstances. As shown in chapter 2 (see table 2.2), a few of the circumstances used to estimate the D-Index for health opportunities are similar but not identical to those used for other opportunities. More specifically, circumstances related to education and household composition used for health opportunities refer to the mother of the child, whereas those used for other opportunities refer to the household head; and birth order is a circumstance for health opportunities but not for the others. Since these differences in the definition of circumstances do not have much impact on the D-Index and the HOI, they matter little for the results presented earlier in chapters 3 and 4. The inequality decomposition results may, however, be more sensitive to the definition of circumstances, and differences in these definitions could explain some of the differences in decomposition results between health and other opportunities.[4]

Figure 5.2a shows the average contribution of each group of circumstance(s) for every opportunity, when all countries are included. Figure 5.2b shows the same for the 10 most unequal countries, when they are sorted by the D-Index, for each opportunity.

Education Opportunities

Wealth, household head's education, and location (urban/rural) are the circumstances that are the main contributors toward inequality of opportunity in education as measured by the D-Index (see figure 5.2a). The only exception is the case of school attendance for 12- to 15-year-olds, where household composition contributes slightly more than location to inequality, on average. To keep the larger picture in mind: inequality of opportunity is significantly higher for timely start to school than for the attendance-related opportunities; and it is particularly low for attendance among 12- to 15-year-olds since the coverage rate of school attendance in this age group is high in most countries (figure 5.1).

The total contribution of wealth, household head's education, and location to the D-Index ranges between 70 percent and 85 percent for the four education opportunities. The first two circumstances represent the socioeconomic background of the child, and their importance indicates lack of social mobility in education, which can in turn be a serious obstacle to mobility in income status across generations. The difference between rural and urban locations is another way through which the parental background of a child affects his/her chances of accessing education opportunities. The gender of the child, and gender and age of the household head contribute little to inequality and seem to matter less than household composition, on average. Comparing across education opportunities, household composition, gender of the child, and gender and age of the head matter more for school attendance among 12- to 15-year-olds (and the top three circumstances less) than for the other three opportunities.

The results are not very different for the 10 most unequal countries, ranked by the D-Index for each education opportunity (figure 5.2b). Wealth, household head's education, and location together contribute between 78 percent and 87 percent of inequality in education opportunities among high-inequality countries. Location tends to matter a little more and education of the household head matter a little less for high-inequality countries than for all countries. Unlike what is seen for all countries, for high-inequality countries, location is among the top three circumstances for school attendance among 12- to 15-year-olds as well, exceeding the contribution of household composition to inequality by a sizable margin.

Figure 5.2 Contribution of Each Circumstance to Inequality of Opportunity

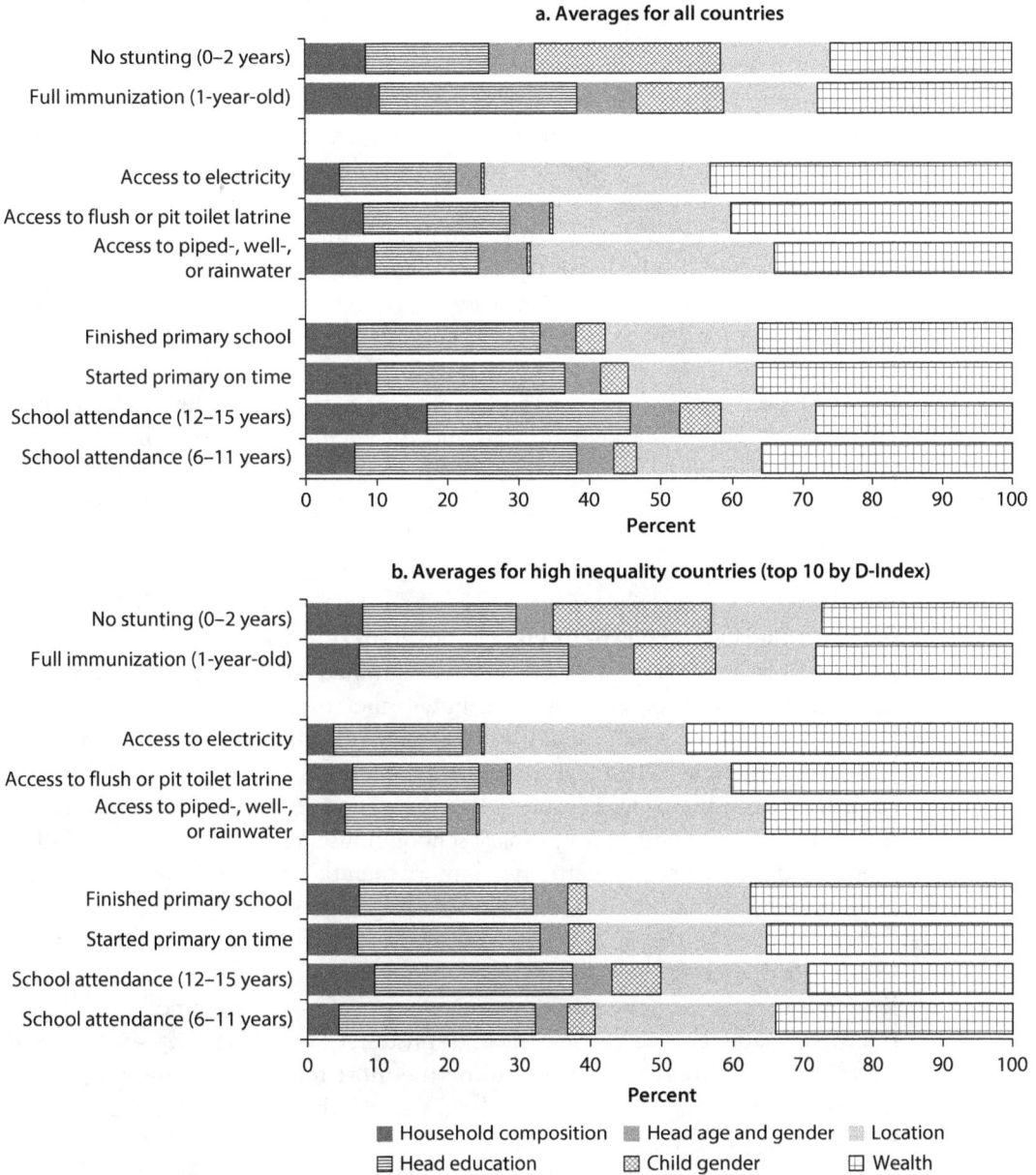

a. Averages for all countries

b. Averages for high inequality countries (top 10 by D-Index)

Legend: Household composition · Head age and gender · Location · Head education · Child gender · Wealth

Source: Authors' calculations using Demographic and Health Surveys data, various years.
Note: (1) High Inequality for each opportunity refers to top 10 countries by the dissimilarity index (D-Index) for that opportunity. (2) The average contribution of a circumstance to inequality of opportunity for a group of countries is calculated as the unweighted or simple average (across all countries) of Shapley decompositions of the D-index for that opportunity. (3) The list of circumstances is slightly different for immunization and not being stunted from that for the other opportunities (see table 2.2 for details).

There is considerable overlap in the group of high-inequality countries across education opportunities, with six countries (Cameroon, the Democratic Republic of Congo, Liberia, Mali, Mozambique, and Niger) being among the top 10 unequal countries for all four of the education opportunities, while 2 more (Senegal and Nigeria) are among the top 10 unequal countries for three of the four opportunities. It turns out that countries with relatively low inequality in education also present, on average, more equitable outcomes in the other dimensions analyzed such as access to infrastructure and health opportunities.

Underlying the averages, more variations emerge among high-inequality countries, some of which are worth highlighting as examples. Gender of the child accounts for an average of 4 and 7 percent of the D-Index for school attendance among 6- to 11-year-olds and 12- to 15-year-olds, respectively, in high-inequality countries. But it accounts for 14 percent and 20 percent among 6- to 11-year-olds and 12- to 15-year-olds, respectively, in Niger; and 11 percent for 12- to 15-year-olds in Mali and the Democratic Republic of Congo. Gender also accounts for 13 percent of the inequality in timely start to primary school in Tanzania, far above the average of 4 percent for high-inequality countries.

Similar examples are found for other circumstances as well. Education of the household head contributes 42 percent and 44 percent of the inequality in school attendance among 6- to 11-year-olds and 12- to 15-year-olds in Cameroon, compared to an average of 28 percent for high-inequality countries for both age groups. Household composition contributes much more than the average contribution for high-inequality countries in the Democratic Republic of Congo and Madagascar among 6- to 11-year-olds; and the same is true for household wealth in Ethiopia among 6- to 11-year-olds and location in Senegal among both age groups. For timely entry into primary school, household composition and other household characteristics matter much more than the average for high-inequality countries in Liberia.

Basic Infrastructure

For infrastructure opportunities—access to safe water (piped-, well-, or rainwater), adequate sanitation (flush or pit toilet), and electricity—wealth and location of the household appear to be the most relevant circumstances, with education of the head of the household being a distant third (figure 5.2a). In terms of the larger picture, inequality of opportunities, on average, is much higher for electricity than for water or sanitation and very low for water in particular (see figure 5.1).

Wealth and location together explain between 65 percent and 75 percent of the total inequality of opportunities, on average. Location is more important and education of household head less important for access to opportunities in infrastructure than education. If one were to speculate about the reasons for this difference, there are a few plausible explanations. *First*, it may be that the household head's own educational attainment is more likely to influence the household's preferences and attitudes toward education than those toward basic infrastructure.

Second (and related to the above), education of the household head can provide the knowledge to help the child improve his/her school performance, which may lead to more timely entry into school and completion of primary school. *Third,* the difference in the cost of providing basic infrastructure in rural and urban areas may be higher than the difference in the cost of providing educational services in rural versus urban areas, with the result that location matters more for access to infrastructure than education services.

Other circumstances such as gender and age of the household head and household composition play a much smaller role, while gender of the child has almost no contribution to inequality in access to water, sanitation, or electricity. *That gender of the child plays no role comes as no surprise, since the access to these services is measured at the household level, which implies that all children in a household regardless of gender have access to the same infrastructure.* Comparisons among the three opportunities indicate that location plays a larger role in explaining inequality in access to safe water than in the other two opportunities, and in fact contributes the most to inequality in the case of water. Wealth, on the other hand, is more important for access to electricity than for the other two opportunities and the most important among all circumstances in the case of electricity and sanitation. The contributions of circumstances are quite similar when averages for 10 countries with high inequality are considered (figure 5.2b). Wealth and location matter even more for access to electricity and safe water, respectively, for the 10 high-inequality countries than for all countries.

There are variations at the level of individual countries underlying the averages (for country-specific results, see figure 5A.1). For example, in some countries, wealth, location, or household education contribute to inequality to a much higher extent than suggested by cross-country averages. Wealth accounts for 47 percent of the inequality in access to safe water in Kenya, compared to an average of 35 percent for high-inequality countries. The contribution of household education to inequality is at least 10 percentage points higher in Madagascar (water, sanitation) and Ghana (sanitation) than the corresponding averages for high-inequality countries. And the contribution of location to inequality is higher by 12 percentage points or more in Cameroon, the Democratic Republic of Congo (water), and Niger (sanitation and electricity) than the corresponding averages for high-inequality countries.

Health Opportunities

The story of how circumstances contribute to inequality in health opportunities has some important differences with that for other opportunities (figure 5.2a). Wealth and education of the mother (which replaces education of the household head for health opportunities) are the most important contributors to inequality in immunization, explaining 56 percent of the D-Index; followed by location and gender of the child whose contributions are almost equal. Together, these four circumstances account for a little more than 80 percent of the inequality in full immunization. Also, wealth and location matter more and gender of the child matters less for the high-inequality countries than for all countries taken together (figure 5.2b). The discussion of health opportunities, however, must take into account the relatively low inequality of opportunity in nutrition (as shown in figure 5.1). The D-Index for the opportunity of not being stunted is low enough that even when a circumstance contributes significantly to inequality, the actual amount of inequality produced by that circumstance would be quite low.

In the case of the opportunity of not being stunted, wealth and gender of the child are the two most important contributors (with almost the same magnitude of contribution), followed by mother's education and location. Wealth, location, and mother's education together explain an average of about 60 percent of the D-Index in nutrition, which is, however, the lowest share of these three circumstances among all opportunities. As with immunization, the story changes when only high-inequality countries are considered. The contributions of these three circumstances are larger for high-inequality countries than for all countries, while gender of the child is the second most important contributor.

It turns out that the *gender difference in nutrition is in the form of an advantage for girls:* in all countries where gender matters, being a boy increases the probability of being stunted. On average, across all countries, boys make up 28 percent of the top quintile in terms of probability of not being stunted but 91 percent of those in the bottom quintile. The nutritional disadvantage for boys in SSA (and more generally for many low-income countries) is consistent with what other studies have found, including the *World Development Report* (2012).[5] The differences are, however, small, and their importance should not be overstated. Inequality in not being stunted is very low in these countries, as discussed earlier (see figure 5.1); and even among these countries, gender is less important when countries with relatively high inequality are considered.

Some countries stand out as outliers in terms of what circumstances matter the most for inequality in immunization or nutrition. Among countries ranked in the top 10 in inequality for immunization, a few merit special mention. For Sierra Leone, household composition and other household characteristics contribute 21 percent and 19 percent of the D-Index, respectively, compared to averages of 7 percent and 9 percent for the high-inequality (top 10) countries. Mother's education contributes 43 percent of the inequality in immunization in Ethiopia, compared to an average of 30 percent for high-inequality countries. Gender of the child (with an advantage for girls) contributes 31 percent of the inequality in Uganda, compared to an average contribution of 11 percent for high-inequality countries. In nutrition, the contribution of gender of the child to the D-Index in Malawi is more than twice the average contribution of gender in the top 10 countries by inequality; and the contribution of location in Niger is almost double that of the average for high-inequality countries.

Contribution of Circumstances to the Composite D-Index

How do circumstances contribute to inequality of opportunity, when the opportunity refers to a composite *bundle* of basic goods and services that every child

Figure 5.3 Contribution of Circumstances to Composite Index of Inequality of Opportunity

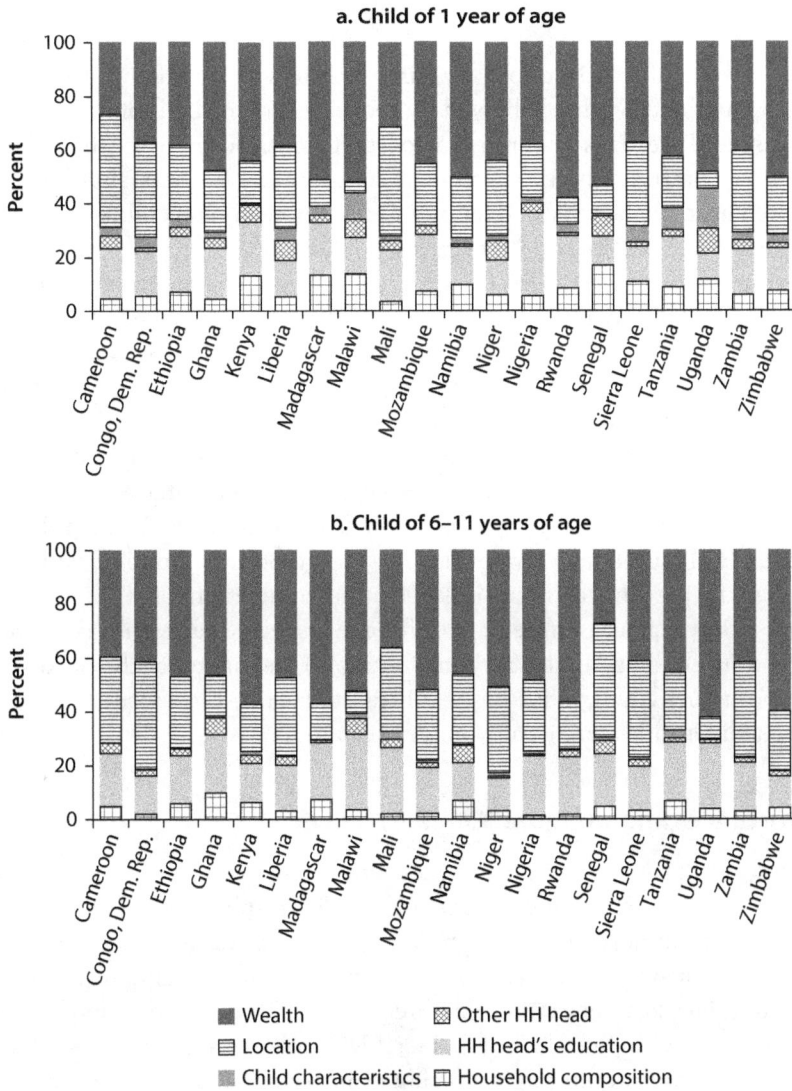

a. Child of 1 year of age

b. Child of 6–11 years of age

Legend:
- ■ Wealth
- ▦ Location
- ▨ Child characteristics
- ▨ Other HH head
- ▨ HH head's education
- ⊞ Household composition

Source: Authors' calculations using Demographic and Health Surveys data, various years.
Note: Composite index of inequality of opportunity refers to the D-Index for access to a bundle of opportunities for a certain age group. Children 1 year: opportunities included are access to water (piped-, well-, or rainwater), access to sanitation (pit/flush toilet), full immunization, and no stunting. Children 6–11 years: opportunities included are school attendance, access to water (as above), and access to sanitation (as above). A child has access to a bundle of opportunities if covered by all the opportunities in the bundle. HH = household.

should have access to? To address this question, figure 5.3 shows the contribution of circumstances to the composite D-Index (see earlier chapters), considered separately for children of age 1 year and 6–11 years. To recall from previous discussions, the composite D-Index measures inequality in the coverage of a bundle of goods and services relevant for an age group, among children of different circumstances. For children 1 year of age, the bundle comprises access to water and sanitation, full immunization, and not being stunted. For children of 6–11 years, the bundle includes school attendance, and access to water and sanitation.

The pattern of contributions by circumstances is similar for the two age groups. Household wealth, followed by location (urban/rural) and education of the household head, is the most important contributor to both D-Indexes. Household composition has a smaller contribution to inequality, and other household head characteristics (age and gender of head) and child characteristics (gender of the child) contribute even less in most cases.

There are significant variations across countries and opportunities. Location (and not household wealth) is the most important circumstance in terms of contribution to the D-Index for younger children in Cameroon and Mali. And household head's education (not wealth or location) is the second most important contributor to the D-Index in 4 out of 20 countries, with the largest contribution seen for Nigeria. For children of age 6–11 years, location contributes the most to inequality of opportunity in Senegal, while parental education is the second most important factor in Ghana, Madagascar, Malawi, Rwanda, Tanzania, and Uganda. Household composition is less important but still contributes more than 10 percent to the D-Index for the younger children in 7 out of 20 countries. Other circumstances matter for a few specific cases only. For example, gender of the child has almost no contribution to inequality for the 6- to 11-year age group in any country, but has a contribution of 8–15 percent for Tanzania, Malawi, and Uganda among the younger age group.[6]

Circumstances and Unequal "Chances" in Life

Until now, we have presented the results of decompositions in terms of "contributions" of each circumstance to inequality. The results imply that certain circumstances are important in differentiating groups in terms of their access to a particular opportunity and the relative contribution of each circumstance essentially determines how sharp these differences are. The decomposition results are also consistent with "profiles" of vulnerable (underserved) and nonvulnerable groups, where the profiles are constructed in terms of the circumstances that characterize each group. Such profiles can be useful for the design of programs as they communicate the characteristics that can be used to identify a vulnerable or underserved group.

The information from these *vulnerability profiles* can be potentially used to assess how current programs (and spending on these programs) are distributed across the population, and how future programs can be designed to reach underserved groups better. That said, since these profiles do not include some of the key circumstances (like ethnicity or tribe affiliation and detailed information on location) that can characterize vulnerable children, they are best seen as *examples*, rather than the complete set of information a policy maker may want to take into account in designing targeted programs in a country.

Unequal Chances in Life: Two Children with Contrasting Profiles

To illustrate how vast the gaps in opportunity are between the vulnerable and nonvulnerable groups, we consider an example of two (hypothetical) children whose circumstances situate them at opposite ends of the socioeconomic spectrum. These are two children of contrasting profiles: (a) a girl child in the lowest quintile (20 percent) of household wealth, living in a rural area and in a household headed by a woman with no education (child A); and (b) a boy child in the highest quintile of household wealth, living in an urban area and in a household headed by a man with 10 years or more of education (child B). For all countries, child A's and child B's profiles are associated with low and high probability, respectively, of being covered by a particular good or service.[7] In other words, regardless of which country she is born in, child A would have less access to all opportunities than child B, with the size of the gaps illustrating the substantial disadvantage in opportunities child A has to overcome in comparison with child B.

Figure 5.4 shows the "opportunity gap" between child A and child B for selected opportunities in all countries (see annex, figure 5A.2 for more). The largest opportunity gaps, among the six opportunities shown here, are associated with access to electricity—child A in most countries has zero probability of access, while child B has a more than 60 percent chance of access in 16 out of 20 countries. Even in Ghana, where access to electricity for child A is the highest among all countries, the probability of access for child A is only 3 percent compared to 98 percent for child B. The gap is uneven across countries for access to adequate sanitation and significant in most countries for school attendance and immunization. The gaps are also particularly large in access to the composite bundle of opportunities for both age groups, and vary widely across countries (box 5.2).

Profiles of "Most" and "Least" Vulnerable Groups—Some Examples

Given the large number of countries and opportunities, presenting all possible vulnerability profiles in this chapter is not practical. Instead, we illustrate these profiles through a few examples, which are selected by identifying the country with the *highest* inequality of opportunity (measured by the D-Index) in a particular opportunity and then contrasting the circumstances of two groups in that country: the bottom and top quintiles (20 percent) defined in terms of the (predicted) probability of accessing a particular opportunity.[8] The examples for a selected set of opportunities are presented in figure 5.5, while those for other opportunities are included in the annex (figure 5A.3). While these profiles are but snapshots for certain countries and opportunities, they illustrate the differences that exist between children who have the highest and lowest access to a particular opportunity in a country where the gap between these two groups is large.[9] The examples also illustrate the kind of insights that can be drawn from the HOI analytical framework, given that such profiles can be created for any country and opportunity in our sample.

Figure 5.4　Probability of Accessing Basic Goods or Services: Two Children of Different Profiles

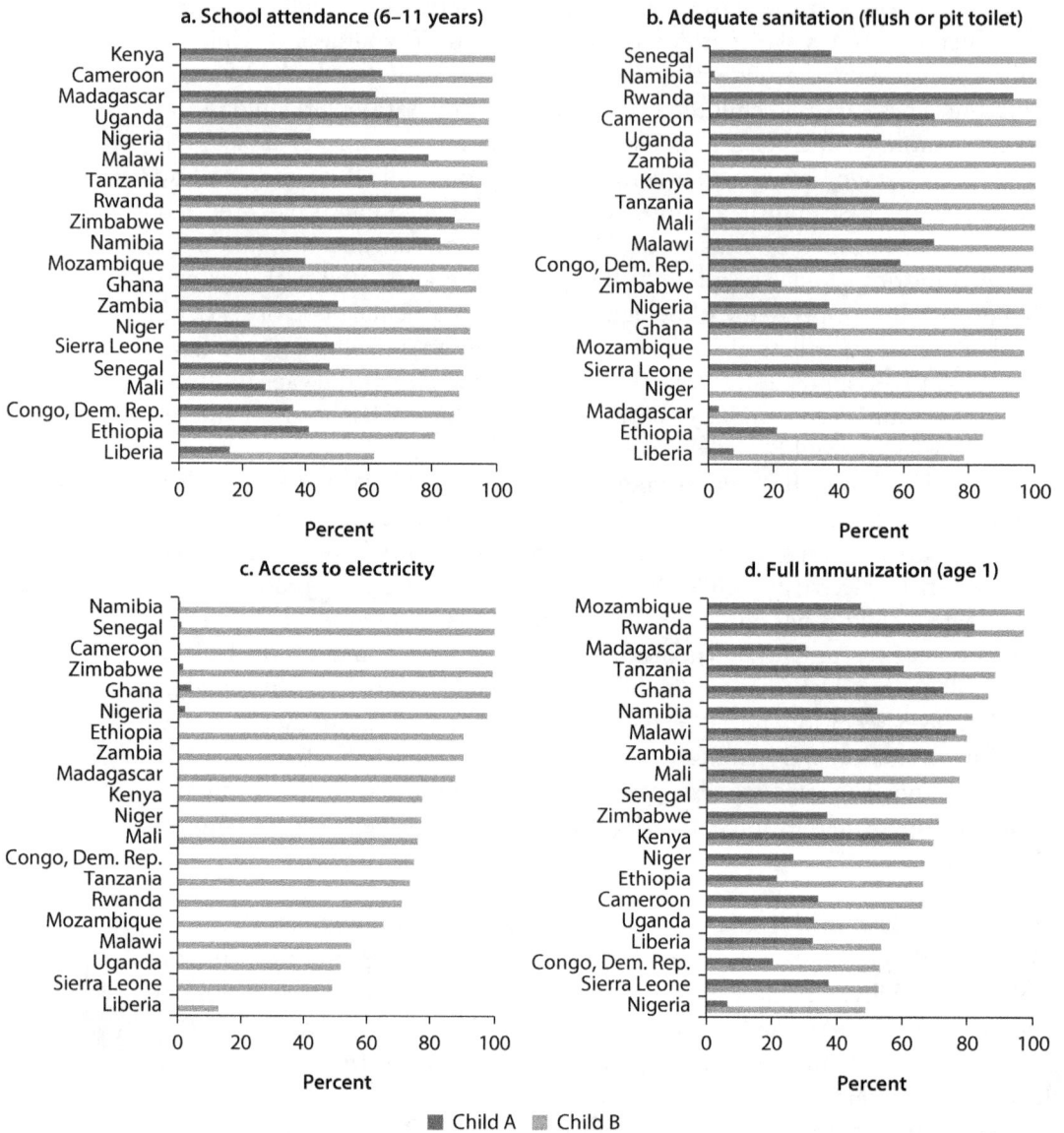

a. School attendance (6–11 years)

Kenya
Cameroon
Madagascar
Uganda
Nigeria
Malawi
Tanzania
Rwanda
Zimbabwe
Namibia
Mozambique
Ghana
Zambia
Niger
Sierra Leone
Senegal
Mali
Congo, Dem. Rep.
Ethiopia
Liberia

Percent

b. Adequate sanitation (flush or pit toilet)

Senegal
Namibia
Rwanda
Cameroon
Uganda
Zambia
Kenya
Tanzania
Mali
Malawi
Congo, Dem. Rep.
Zimbabwe
Nigeria
Ghana
Mozambique
Sierra Leone
Niger
Madagascar
Ethiopia
Liberia

Percent

c. Access to electricity

Namibia
Senegal
Cameroon
Zimbabwe
Ghana
Nigeria
Ethiopia
Zambia
Madagascar
Kenya
Niger
Mali
Congo, Dem. Rep.
Tanzania
Rwanda
Mozambique
Malawi
Uganda
Sierra Leone
Liberia

Percent

d. Full immunization (age 1)

Mozambique
Rwanda
Madagascar
Tanzania
Ghana
Namibia
Malawi
Zambia
Mali
Senegal
Zimbabwe
Kenya
Niger
Ethiopia
Cameroon
Uganda
Liberia
Congo, Dem. Rep.
Sierra Leone
Nigeria

Percent

■ Child A　■ Child B

figure continues next page

Figure 5.4 **Probability of Accessing Basic Goods or Services: Two Children of Different Profiles** *(continued)*

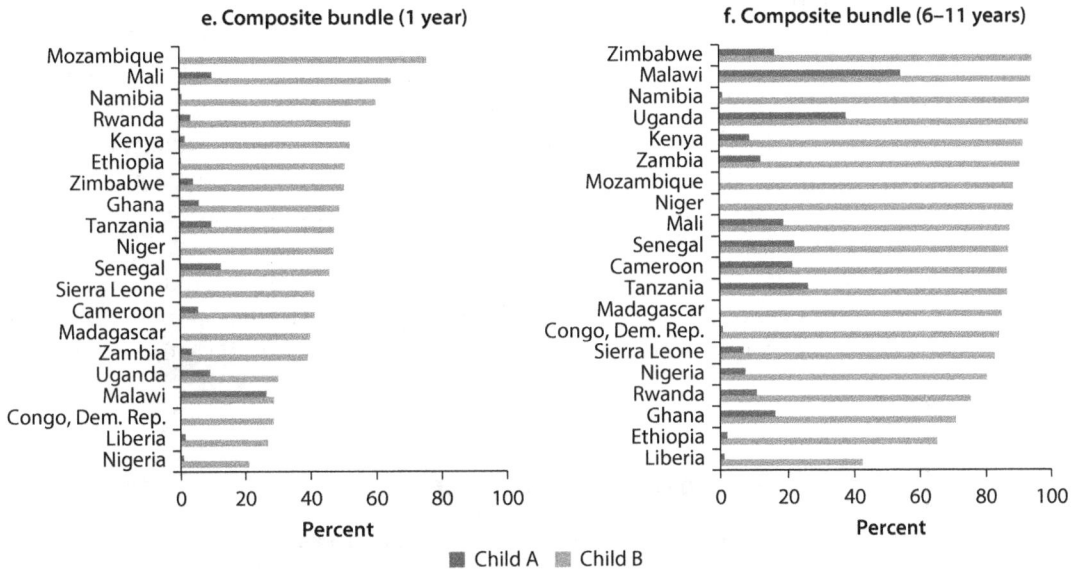

e. Composite bundle (1 year)

f. Composite bundle (6–11 years)

■ Child A ■ Child B

Source: Authors' calculations using Demographic and Health Surveys data, various years.
Note: (1) **Child A:** a girl, living in a rural household belonging to the bottom quintile of wealth and headed by a woman with zero years of education. **Child B:** a boy, living in an urban household belonging to the top quintile of wealth and headed by a man with 10 or more years of education. (2) Composite bundle (1 year): includes access to *water* (piped-, well-, or rainwater), access to *sanitation* (pit or flush toilet), full immunization, and no stunting. Composite bundle (6–11 years): includes school *attendance*, access to *water,* and *sanitation.*

Box 5.2 Access to a Bundle of Opportunities: The Story of Two Children

How different are the gaps between child A and child B across countries? To see an example, consider the countries with the *highest* probabilities for child A or child B having a composite bundle of opportunities. These are Malawi (child A) and Mozambique (child B) for the age group of 1-year-olds; and Malawi (child A) and Zimbabwe (child B) for the 6- to 11-year-olds (refer to figure 5.4). Child A in Malawi, if she is 1 year old, would have a 26 percent probability of accessing the bundle of basic services relevant for her age, compared to a probability of 29 percent for child B—the smallest gap among all countries for this age group. But the same 1-year-old child, if she were living in Mozambique, will have nearly zero probability of having the basic bundle of services, compared to a probability of 76 percent for child B—the largest gap for this age group. Now if child A was of age 6–11 years in Malawi, the probability of accessing the bundle of basic services for this age group would be 54 percent, compared to 94 percent for child B. The corresponding probabilities in Zimbabwe will be 16 percent and 94 percent.

Thus, even in Malawi, where child A has more opportunity in terms of the composite bundle than in any other country, she suffers from a large opportunity-deficit between ages 6 and 11 years when compared to child B. And the gap between child A and child B is enormous in countries where child B enjoys the most opportunities—such as Mozambique and Zimbabwe for 1-year-olds and 6- to 11-year-olds, respectively.

Figure 5.5 presents the profiles for the most unequal country in four of the nine opportunities in this study: Liberia for school attendance (6- to 11-year-olds), Niger for finishing primary school (12- to 15-year-olds), Tanzania for access to electricity, and Nigeria for full immunization (1-year-olds). These opportunities have been selected to achieve a balance across the type of opportunity, country, and level of overall inequality. For each country/opportunity, the graph contrasts the share of each circumstance among children belonging to the top quintile of probability of access with the corresponding shares in the bottom quintile.[10]

For school attendance (6–11 years) in Liberia, as one would expect from the decomposition results presented earlier, position in the wealth distribution and education of the head of the household differentiate consistently the most

Figure 5.5 Profiles of Top and Bottom Quintiles by Probability of Access

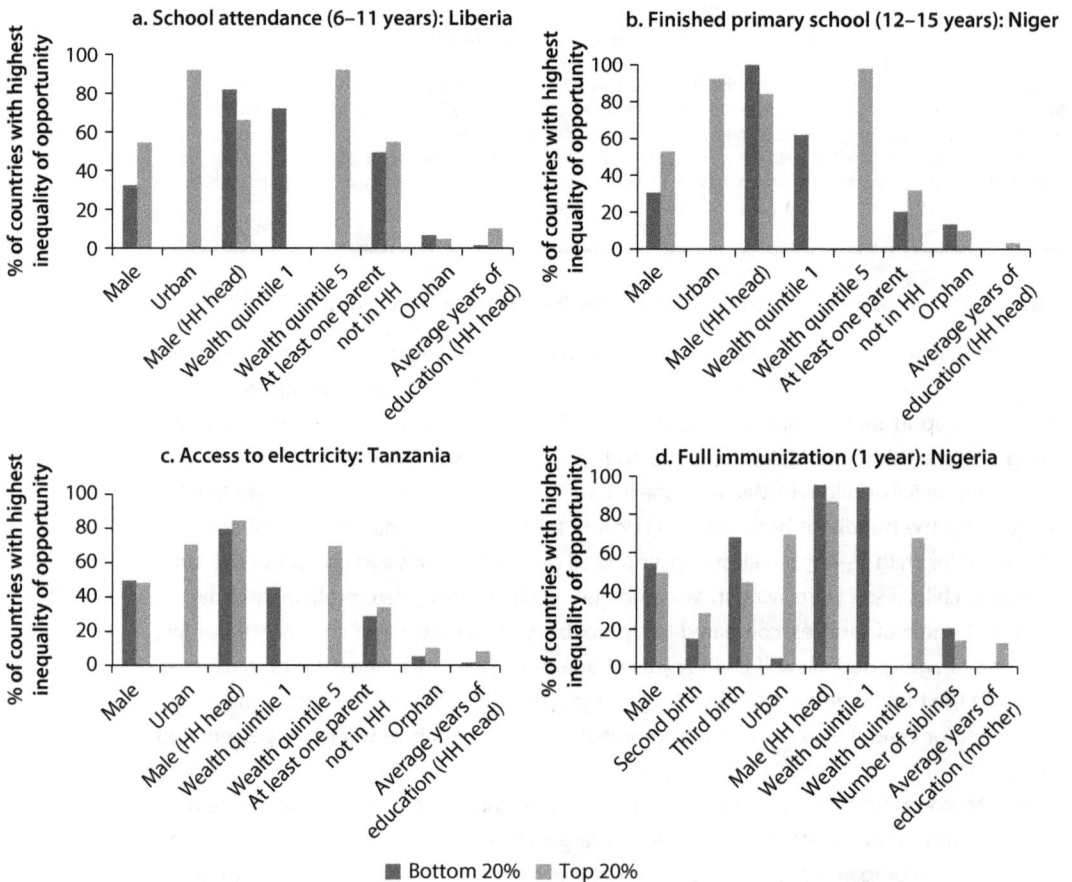

Source: Authors' calculations using Demographic and Health Surveys data, various years.
Note: HH = household.

and least vulnerable children (figure 5.5). Compared to children in the top quintile, those in the bottom quintile are also overwhelmingly more likely to be rural and female. Ninety-two percent of children in the top quintile of opportunity are in the top quintile of wealth, compared to zero percent of those in the bottom quintile; 54 percent of the top quintile are male and 92 percent are urban compared to 33 percent and 0 percent, respectively, of the bottom quintile; and the average education of the household head is 10 years for the top quintile compared to 1 year for the bottom quintile. As seen above, gender is not an important contributor to inequality of education opportunities in most cases and the case of Liberia is more of an exception, albeit an important one given the vast gulf between boys and girls.

In Niger, the bottom quintile of the opportunity of finishing primary school (age cohort of 12–15 years) is disproportionately composed of girls, rural children, children in the poorest quintile, and children living in households headed by someone with no education, compared to the top quintile. For access to electricity in Tanzania, household wealth status, average years of education of the household head, and whether the household is urban or rural are the most important differences between the top and bottom quintiles; and the same circumstances are important in differentiating between the top and bottom quintiles in full immunization in Nigeria as well. Interestingly, education of the household head (or mother in the case of immunization) continues to be an important difference between the top and bottom 20 percent for electricity and immunization. In the case of immunization in Nigeria, the average difference in mother's education between the two groups is a staggering 13 years.

Some of the differences between the least and most vulnerable children hint at deeper social issues. The absence of a parent differentiates high and low opportunity groups in education in both examples: the bottom quintiles in Liberia and Niger have a significantly higher share of children with at least one parent not alive than those in the top quintiles. And while gender of the child has a small correlation with vulnerability in immunization in Nigeria, the child's birth order has a stronger correlation. Children in the bottom quintile of opportunity are much more likely to be late (third or later) in order of birth and have more siblings than those in the top quintile. These are interesting patterns that illustrate a broader point: intra-household factors and decisions matter for health opportunities, even if how each factor matters for the probability of being immunized is not generalizable across countries.

Finally, the vulnerability profiles constructed above can also be useful for other types of analysis that is often used to guide policy. For example, the construction of a vulnerability profile allows us to expand the traditional benefit incidence analysis, which typically examines how the benefits of spending are distributed along the income distribution, into an incidence analysis of public spending along the distribution of *opportunities* (see box 5.3 for an example).

Box 5.3 Linking Equality of Opportunity with Fiscal Analysis: The Case of Liberia

The construction of a vulnerability profile allows for an "Opportunity Benefit Impact Analysis (Opp-BIA)"—an incidence analysis of public educational spending along the distribution of *opportunities* as opposed to the "traditional" Benefit Impact Analysis (BIA) that looks at how the spending is allocated along the income distribution. The Opp-BIA provides a sharper picture of the distribution of resources and opportunities directly associated with such resources; for instance, one can identify the statistical relationship between government benefit per pupil and probability of attending school. Moreover, patterns of public spending can be evaluated in terms of their "progressiveness" in equalizing opportunities, depending on whether the opportunity-vulnerable socioeconomic groups, as defined by circumstances, receive a significant share of the available public resources or not. Employing the Opp-BIA approach on data from the Core Welfare Indicator Questionnaire (CWIQ) survey and some fiscal data, Abras and Cuesta (2011) study the distributional consequences of reassigning public expenditures across different circumstance groups for school attendance in Liberia. Ex-ante simulation results show that even substantial redistributive interventions may lead to only modest improvements in the probability of attending school (less than three percentage points) and affect the average vulnerability status of children very little.

Source: Abras and Cuesta (2011).

Conclusion

This chapter has presented decompositions of the inequality of opportunity in education, infrastructure, and health among children in all 20 SSA countries included in our study. The decompositions allow us to quantify the role of each circumstance in explaining inequality, in terms of its marginal contribution to the inequality of opportunity index or D-Index. The results of this exercise are instructive, and some of the key messages emerging from the results are summarized below.

- *A child's socioeconomic background is crucial in explaining her/his chances of accessing basic services and goods.* Wealth and education of the head of the household that the child belongs to (or mother's education in the case of health opportunities) have the largest contributions to inequality across most countries and opportunities, followed by the location (rural or urban) of the household. Belonging to a household that is richer and with more education, and being located in an urban area are favorable circumstances for access to almost all opportunities. When "opportunity" refers to a *bundle* of basic goods and services appropriate for a child of a certain age, the same three circumstances are again the most important contributors.

- *Underlying the averages are important variations across countries and type of opportunities.* The average contribution of location is more pronounced for infrastructure opportunities than for education and health opportunities; and education of the head of the household has, on average, a higher contribution to inequality of education opportunities than that of other opportunities.[11] Mother's education matters significantly in explaining inequality of opportunities in health (being fully immunized and not being stunted).[12]

- *Access to opportunities is influenced by circumstances that go beyond poverty, remoteness, or lack of awareness* (proxied by education of the household head or mother), depending on the country and type of opportunity. In such cases, inequality of opportunities is partly attributable to factors such as gender and household composition, which may be symptomatic of social barriers that are more resistant to policy initiatives.

- *While circumstances traditionally associated with discrimination (such as gender of the child or the household head) appear to be less prominent, on average, there are important exceptions.* These are primarily in health opportunities, as well as in education opportunities in a few countries. In the case of education, for example, gender differences between the most and least vulnerable groups are stark in Liberia and Niger for the very same opportunities in which these countries rank as the most unequal among all countries. The gender difference in nutrition (not being stunted) seen in some countries takes the form of a disadvantage for boys, consistent with some of the literature on this issue.

- *Like gender, household demographics play a small role in the decomposition, on average, but again with a few exceptions.* For example, being an earlier-born child of the family and having fewer siblings improve the opportunity of being immunized and not being stunted in a few countries; and parents being alive and present in the household are associated with better education opportunities in a few countries.

- *To illustrate how circumstances matter for opportunities, we consider two hypothetical children with starkly different profiles:* child A (or B), a girl (boy) child in the lowest (highest) quintile of household wealth, living in a rural (urban) area and in a household headed by a woman (man) with no (10 years or more of) education. If child A is between 6 and 11 years old and living in Malawi, her likelihood of being covered by the bundle of basic services relevant for her age (school attendance, safe water, and sanitation) would be higher than that of a similar child in any other country but 40 percentage points lower than that of child B of the same age in Malawi. Thus, even in a country where child A has better access to certain opportunities than in any other country, she suffers from a huge disadvantage when compared to child B.

In concluding, it is useful to highlight two important issues that are important caveats to the results in this chapter. *First*, comparisons across opportunities can be misleading without taking into account the total inequality of a particular opportunity. Among the nine opportunities considered in this study, one opportunity in particular (nutrition, indicated by not being stunted) exhibits relatively low inequality of opportunity, as measured by the D-Index. This implies that the circumstances that account for a significant share of inequality in this opportunity can be much less "unequalizing" than one that contributes a smaller share of the inequality in, say, access to electricity, for which the D-Index tends to be much higher.

Second, the issue of "missing" circumstances (see chapter 2) has implications for how the results of this chapter should be interpreted. Recall that the estimated D-Index is in effect an "upper bound" that can only increase if more, hitherto unavailable, circumstances were to be added. One set of circumstances missing in our analysis but likely to be relevant in many countries would be some measure of ethnicity, including religious, tribal, or linguistic differences. Our results do not take into account inequalities due to such social and discriminatory factors.[13] While these sources of inequality are important to consider, the exact form they take is country-specific and therefore better suited for in-depth country studies rather than in a multicountry setting, where the need for cross-country comparison compels us to use identical circumstances across all countries. On this issue, our results can suggest only the following: if inequalities exist due to any of these social factors, our measures of inequality (D-Index) and inequality-adjusted coverage of an opportunity (HOI) can only go in one direction, namely that of a higher D-Index that in turn implies a lower HOI.[14]

Annex 5A

Shapley Decomposition of D-Index: An Example

In country A we want to calculate the contribution of income to the inequality in access to a basic opportunity. The circumstances considered are the gender of the head of the household, the gender of the child, and the household income, and the opportunity is defined as having electricity in the household. The total D-Index is obtained using all circumstance variables and equals 3.48 percent. The D-Index using only income as a circumstance equals 3.24 percent and the index without circumstances (only a constant in the logistic regression) equals 0 percent. In order to obtain the marginal addition to the D-Index of income or D_I, we estimate the D-Index with all possible sequences of circumstance variables where income can be added. In each situation we calculate the marginal contribution of income as the difference in the D-Index before and after income is added. Finally, we average the marginal contributions over all combinations. In a set with three circumstances (Income or I, Gender of child or G, and Gender of head or H), there are six different sequences in which income can enter {(C,H,I) (H,C,I)

(C,I,H) (H,I,C) (I,C,H) (I,H,C)}. Nevertheless, since in the regression model two sets of covariates with the same circumstances and different order generate the same result, there are only four different values for the marginal contribution of income. In the example below, income contributes to 63 percent of the D-Index.

$$D_I = \frac{2}{6}[D(I, C, H) - D(C, H)] + \frac{1}{6}[(D(I, C) - D(C)]$$

$$+ \frac{1}{6}[D(I, H) - D(H)] + \frac{2}{6}[D(I) - 0]$$

Circumstance set	Contribution to the D-Index	
gender head U gender child U income	D(gender head U gender child U income)	= 3.48
income	D(income)	= 3.24
Combinations of circumstance sets where income is added		
income U gender child	D(income) − D(constant)	= 3.24
income U gender head	D(income) − D(constant)	= 3.24
gender child U income	D(gender head U income) − D(gender child)	= 2.40
gender head U income	D(gender head U income) − D(gender head)	= 1.29
gender child U gender head U income	D(gender child U gender head U income) − D(gender child U gender head)	= 1.50
gender head U gender child U income	D(gender head U gender child U income) − D(gender head U gender child)	= 1.50
	Average contribution of income	**= 2.20**
	% contribution of income	**= 63%**

Figure 5A.1 Shapley Decompositions of D-Index by Opportunity for Each Country and Opportunity

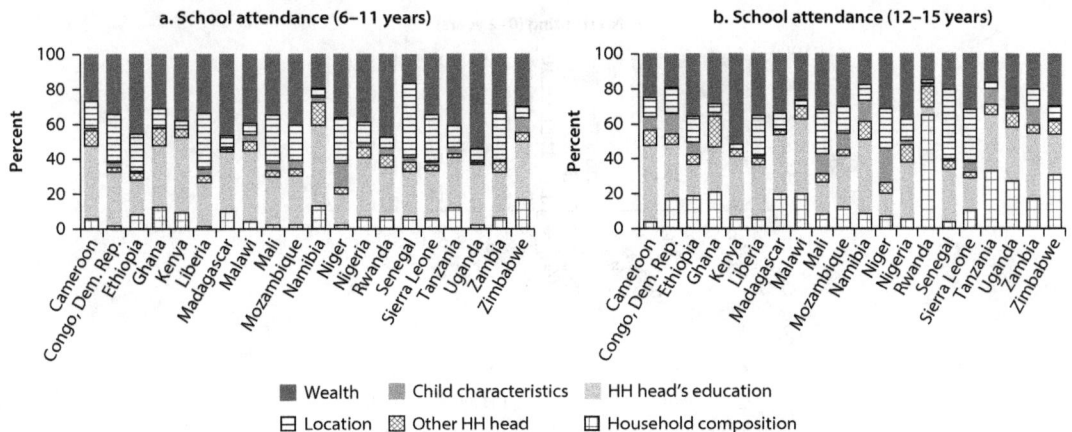

a. School attendance (6–11 years)

b. School attendance (12–15 years)

■ Wealth   ▦ Child characteristics   ▨ HH head's education
⊟ Location   ⊠ Other HH head   ▤ Household composition

figure continues next page

Figure 5A.1 **Shapley Decompositions of D-Index by Opportunity for Each Country and Opportunity** *(continued)*

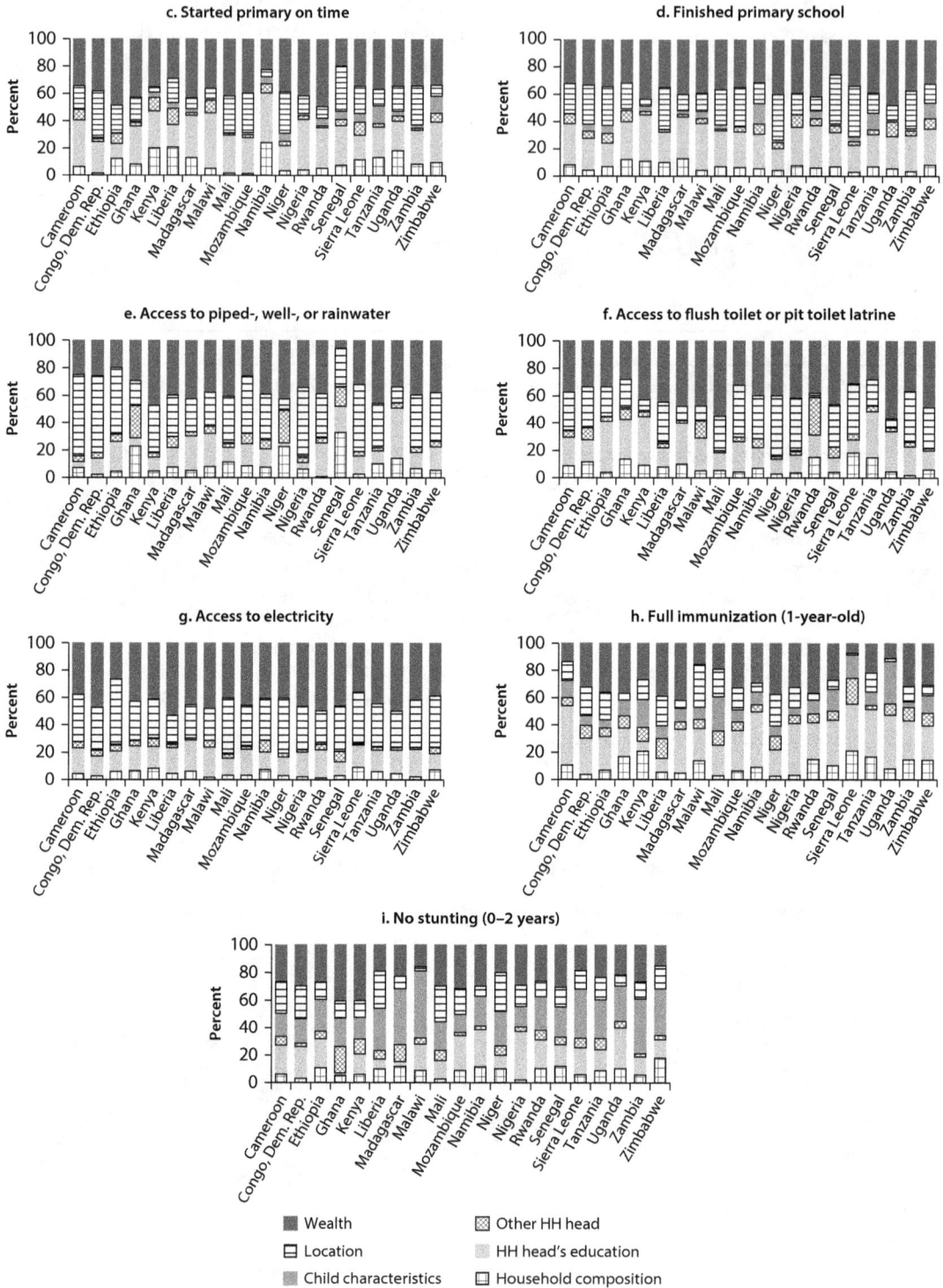

c. Started primary on time

d. Finished primary school

e. Access to piped-, well-, or rainwater

f. Access to flush toilet or pit toilet latrine

g. Access to electricity

h. Full immunization (1-year-old)

i. No stunting (0–2 years)

Wealth

Location

Child characteristics

Other HH head

HH head's education

Household composition

Source: Authors' calculations using Demographic and Health Surveys data, various years.
Note: D-Index = dissimilarity index; HH = household.

Figure 5A.2 Probability of Accessing a Good or Service: Two Children of Different Profiles

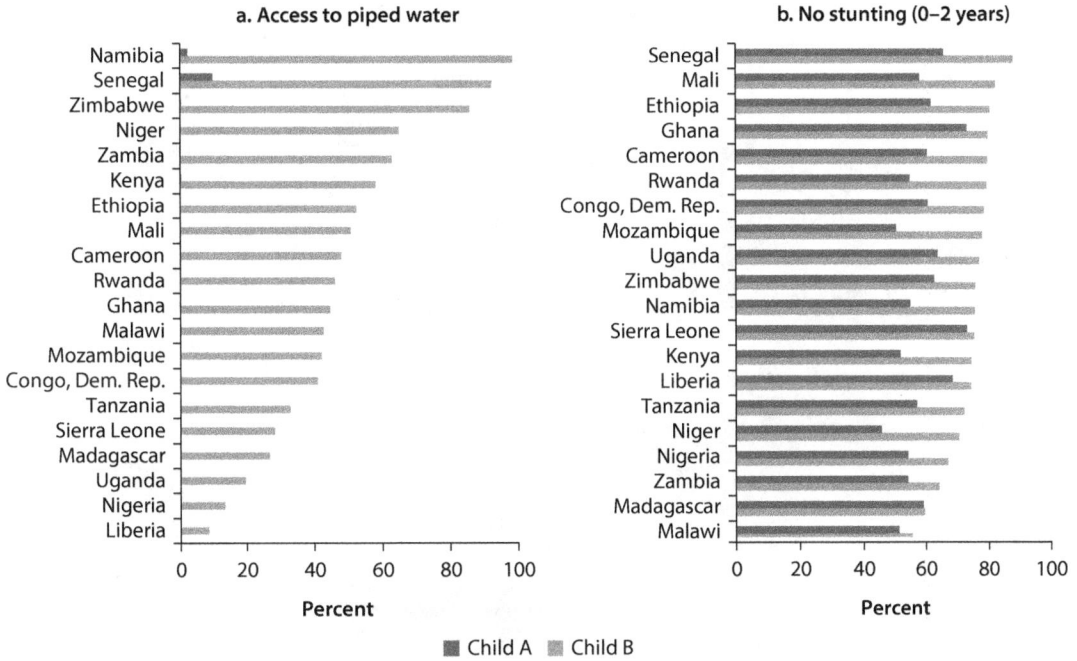

a. Access to piped water

b. No stunting (0–2 years)

■ Child A ■ Child B

Figure 5A.3 Vulnerable Profiles for the Most Unequal Countries

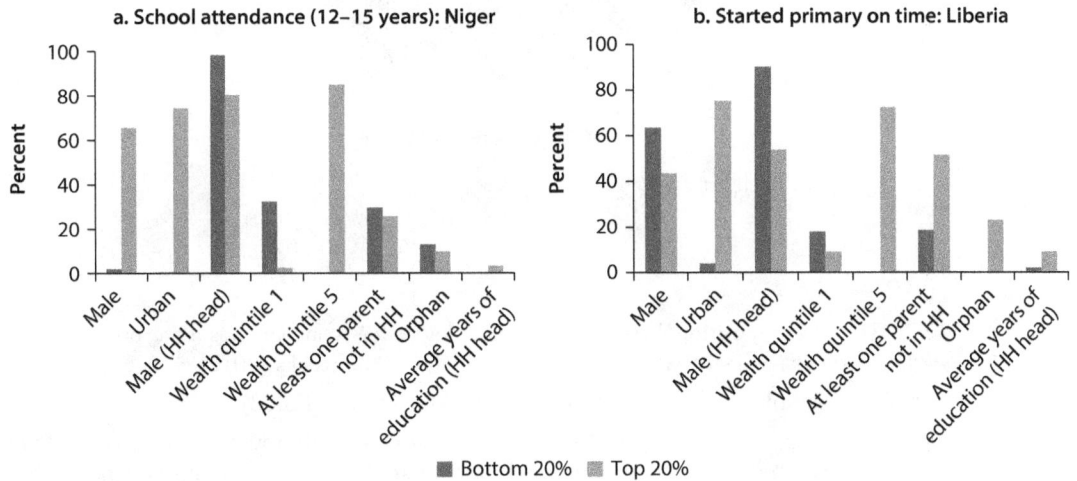

a. School attendance (12–15 years): Niger

b. Started primary on time: Liberia

■ Bottom 20% ■ Top 20%

figure continues next page

Figure 5A.3 Vulnerable Profiles for the Most Unequal Countries *(continued)*

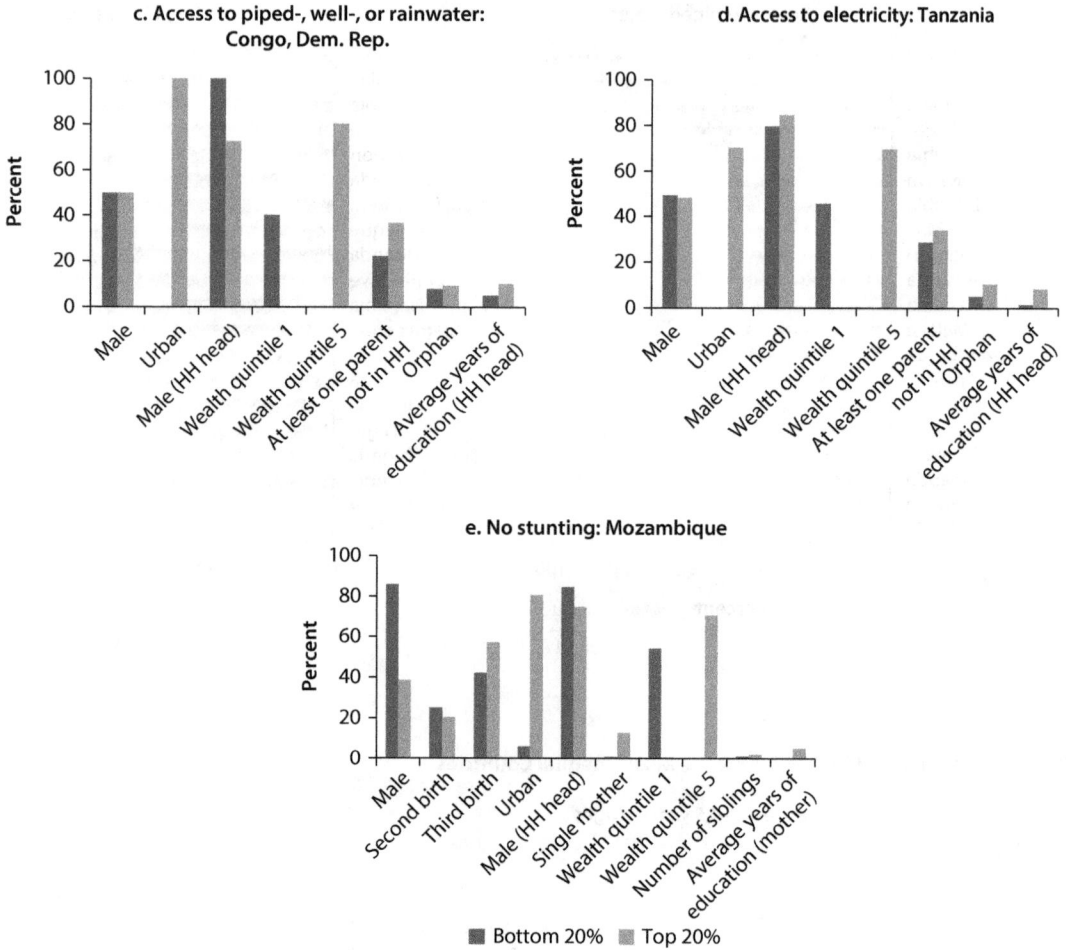

c. Access to piped-, well-, or rainwater: Congo, Dem. Rep.

d. Access to electricity: Tanzania

e. No stunting: Mozambique

■ Bottom 20%   ■ Top 20%

Source: Authors' calculations using Demographic and Health Surveys data, various years.
Note: HH = household.

Notes

1. The decomposition based on the Shapley value concept was first proposed by Shorrocks in 1999, which was published later as Shorrocks (2012).

2. For example, see Israeli (2007) and Sastre and Trannoy (2002).

3. A certain circumstance X, for example, may contribute much more in percentage terms to the D-Index of immunization than that of electricity. But this does not necessarily mean that inequality on account of X is higher in immunization than in access to electricity, given the considerable difference in the level of inequality between the two opportunities.

4. An additional caveat relates to the omission of interaction between circumstances in our regression model to estimate the D-Index. The interaction terms (e.g., between education of parents and parental wealth) are omitted from the model for simplicity. Including such terms would lead to a higher D-Index (and a lower HOI), just as

would happen if more circumstances were added, which in turn implies that the estimated D-Index is the lower bound of inequality of opportunities for a given set of circumstances. Not including the interaction terms, however, has implications for the contribution of each circumstance to the D-Index; these contributions could be different if the interaction terms were included. Including the interaction terms, however, leads to another problem: measuring the contribution of each circumstance becomes an arbitrary exercise.

5. "In sub-Saharan Africa, for instance, it is the boys who suffer nutritional deprivation"—WDR (2012), page 125. "In many low-income countries, the proportion of children stunted, wasted, or underweight remains high, but girls are no worse off than boys. In fact, data from the Demographic and Health Surveys show that boys are at a slight disadvantage"—WDR (2012), page 63. United Nations Statistics (2010) suggests similar findings for "several African countries including Central African Republic and Comoros."

6. It is important to note that the marginal contributions of circumstances to inequality for a bundle of opportunities (the composite D-Index, combining, say, k individual opportunities) is not related in a simple way to the marginal contributions of the same circumstances to inequality of k opportunities taken one at a time. This is because the composite D-Index is derived from a joint distribution of k opportunities, which implies that the marginal contribution of a circumstance to the composite D-Index depends on how adding that circumstance (in all possible sequences in accordance with the Shapley principle) affects that joint distribution.

7. Given that the same profiles are used for all countries and opportunities, the groups defined by profiles need not necessarily have the lowest and highest probabilities of being covered by a particular good or service. Also note that the profiles, as they are defined here, are incomplete and omit any characterization of some of the circumstances considered for the D-Index, such as whether parents are living or not and household composition.

8. It is important to recall that these probabilities are "predicted" probabilities from the logit model, which estimates the probability of a child, with his/her given set of circumstances, to access the opportunity.

9. However, inferences about the relative importance of different types of circumstances from these profiles can be misleading, since the profiles characterize only the top and bottom ends of the full distribution of probabilities.

10. Annex (figure 5A.3) shows similar profiles for Niger (school attendance among 12- to 15-year-olds), Liberia (starting primary school on time), the Democratic Republic of Congo for access to safe water, Tanzania for access to electricity, and Mozambique for nutrition.

11. The average contribution of education of household head to inequality of education, infrastructure, and health opportunities is 28 percent, 17 percent, and 23 percent, respectively. The average contribution of location to inequality of these opportunities is 18 percent, 30 percent, and 14 percent, in that order.

12. When information on mother's education is not available, which is for all education and infrastructure opportunities, information of the education of the household head is used instead.

13. Inequality due to ethnic, tribal, or linguistic differences does contribute to the D-Index we measure, to the extent that these differences are correlated with one or more of

the circumstances we do measure (e.g., household wealth, parental education, location). What our estimates of inequality fail to capture is the effect of ethnic/tribal differences, once the contribution of the socioeconomic circumstances we include are netted out.

14. Note that if additional circumstances are added, while the D-Index will increase, the "contribution" of all existing circumstances will remain unchanged—not in terms of their percentage share of the D-Index but in terms of their marginal absolute contribution to the D-Index.

References

Abras, A., and J. Cuesta. 2011. "Equality of Opportunities, Redistribution and Fiscal Policies: The Case of Liberia." Policy Research Working Paper 5801, World Bank, Washington, DC.

Demographic and Health Surveys. Various years. USAID. http://www.dhsprogram.com.

Hoyos, A., and A. Narayan. 2011. "Inequality of Opportunities among Children: How Much Does Gender Matter?" Background paper for the *World Development Report 2012: Gender Equality and Development*, World Bank, Washington, DC.

Israeli, O. 2007. "A Shapley-Based Decomposition of the R-Squared of a Linear Regression." *Journal of Economic Inequality* 5 (2): 199–212.

Sastre, M., and A. Trannoy. 2002. "Shapley Inequality Decomposition by Factor Components: Some Methodological Issues." *Journal of Economics Supplements* 9: 51–90.

Shapley, L. 1953. "A Value for n-Person Games." In *Contributions to the Theory of Games, Vol. 2*, edited by H. Kuhn and A. Tucker, 307–18. Princeton, NJ: Princeton University Press.

Shorrocks, A. 2012. "Decomposition Procedures for Distributional Analysis: A Unified Framework Based on the Shapley Value." *The Journal of Economic Inequality*, 11 (1): 99–126.

United Nations Statistics. 2010. *The World's Women: Trends and Statistics*. Department of Economic and Social Affairs. New York. http://unstats.un.org/unsd/demographic/products/Worldswomen/WW2010pub.htm.

World Bank. 2012. *World Development Report 2012: Gender Equality and Development*. Washington, DC: World Bank.

CHAPTER 6

Comparing Opportunities across Countries and Regions

While the earlier chapters have focused on analyzing access to opportunities among children and the factors that matter for access, this chapter will take an aggregated approach that relies on cross-country correlations and comparisons. *First*, the chapter will compare access to opportunities with indicators of economic development, such as gross domestic product (GDP) per capita and Gini coefficient, to see how strong the correlations are between equality of opportunities and the level and inequality of income, and between improvements in opportunities and economic growth. Such cross-country correlations are also useful for creating benchmarks to identify countries that are doing well (or poorly) in providing opportunities relative to their level of economic development. That said, our results must *not* be interpreted as causal relationships between access to opportunities and economic development, but rather as descriptive facts that set the stage for further exploration in future research.

Second, the chapter will compare access to opportunities between children in Francophone and Anglophone countries included in our sample, recognizing that countries in each of these groups share some common historical and institutional characteristics that may be important for human development. Systematic differences between the two groups, if they were to exist, can indicate how the history and evolution of institutions could matter for equitable access of opportunities in a country. But these aggregate comparisons are at best indicative, given the high variation that exists across countries within each group. The third comparison will be between our sample of 20 sub-Saharan African (SSA) countries and countries in the Latin America and the Caribbean (LAC) region. Limited as such comparisons are in scope, they can indicate the areas of relative success and challenges for SSA countries against the benchmark of countries in a different region.

Equality of Opportunities and Economic Development

Intuitively, one would expect the cross-country correlation of GDP per capita and the national Human Opportunity Index (HOI) to be positive. We find a positive relationship between GDP per capita (at 2005 PPP, or purchasing power parity) and the HOI for school attendance (6–11 years), finishing primary school, and full immunization in both periods (figure 6.1). The correlations are much stronger for the two education opportunities than for immunization. For the two education opportunities, the correlation is smaller in the second period (circa 2008) than in the first (circa 1998).

Is the apparent weakening of the link between economic development and education opportunities for children over time a positive development? It appears to be so, given earlier results (in chapter 4) that out of 16 countries for which data are available for both periods, statistically significant (at the 5 percent level) annual average improvement in the HOI is seen in all countries for school attendance (6–11 years) and in 13 countries for finishing primary school. These results, along with the weakening correlation between per capita GDP and the HOI, suggest that poorer countries have made progress toward catching up with their better-off neighbors in access to education opportunities for children. This inference also appears to be supported by the finding in chapter 4 that cross-country variation in these HOIs, as measured by coefficient of variation (CV) and standard deviation for each HOI, has declined between the late-1990s and late-2000s (see figure 4.7).

The low correlations between the HOI for immunization and per capita GDP suggest that immunization gaps were not closely associated with economic gaps between countries. While the correlations with GDP are not informative, the fact that 12 out of 16 countries showed a statistically significant improvement in the HOI for full immunization, resulting in a decline in cross-country variation (see chapter 4), suggests that gaps in access to immunization between leading and lagging countries narrowed over the period.

Figure 6.1 also shows the somewhat uneven relationship between (annual average) *growth* rates in GDP per capita and the HOI between the two periods. Countries with higher economic growth tend to have higher growth in the HOI for school attendance, finishing primary school, and full immunization. While more information will be needed to understand why this occurs, we can offer plausible hypotheses. As countries achieve economic growth, rising demand for education from parents (as returns to education rises) can combine with greater availability of resources for the government to invest in schooling, resulting in a rise in enrollments and completion rates of primary schooling. Similar forces are also likely to be at work for immunization of children. There are a few exceptions to these correlations. Nigeria and Zambia show a decline in the HOI for finishing primary school and full immunization, respectively, along with average annual per capita GDP growth of nearly 4 percent and 1.5 percent in the intervening period. Conversely, Zimbabwe

Figure 6.1 GDP, Economic Growth, and Opportunities

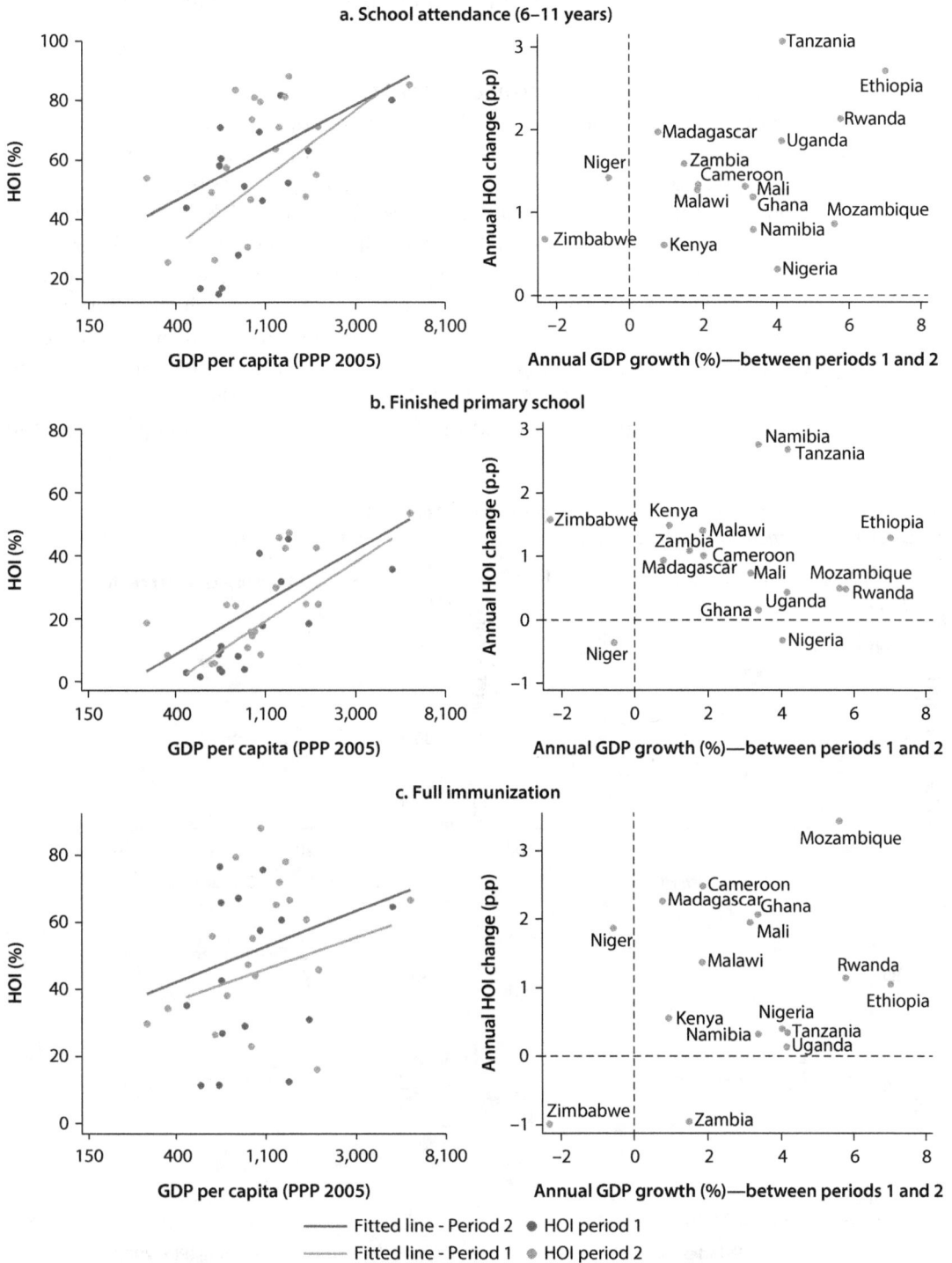

a. School attendance (6–11 years)

b. Finished primary school

c. Full immunization

Fitted line - Period 2 ● HOI period 1
Fitted line - Period 1 ● HOI period 2

Source: Authors' calculations using *World Development Indicators* (World Bank 2011) and Demographic and Health Surveys data, various years.
Note: Gross domestic product (GDP) growth in annual per capita terms. HOI = Human Opportunity Index; PPP = purchasing power parity.

and Niger show improvements in the HOI for finishing primary school and full immunization, respectively, even though their per capita GDP fell during this period.

Opportunities, GDP, and Income Inequality

A more aggregated view is offered by the correlations shown in figure 6.2. The positive relationship between the composite HOI (age one year) and GDP per capita (at 2005 PPP) for the late-2000s (circa 2008) is consistent with the results seen for HOIs of individual opportunities (figure 6.2a). The cross-country correlation between the composite HOI for children of age one year and per capita GDP is as high as 31 percent for the period selected and a similar correlation is seen if the other composite HOI were used. The D-Index, which is the component of the HOI measuring inequality of opportunity, has a similar (but negative) correlation with per capita GDP (figure 6.2b), with a coefficient of −0.3 (for all correlations, see appendix A, table A.23). Importantly, there is no correlation between the composite HOI and the Gini coefficient of consumption; and the

Figure 6.2 GDP, Income Inequality, and Composite HOI (1-Year-Old)
Cross-country correlations in period 2 (circa 2008)

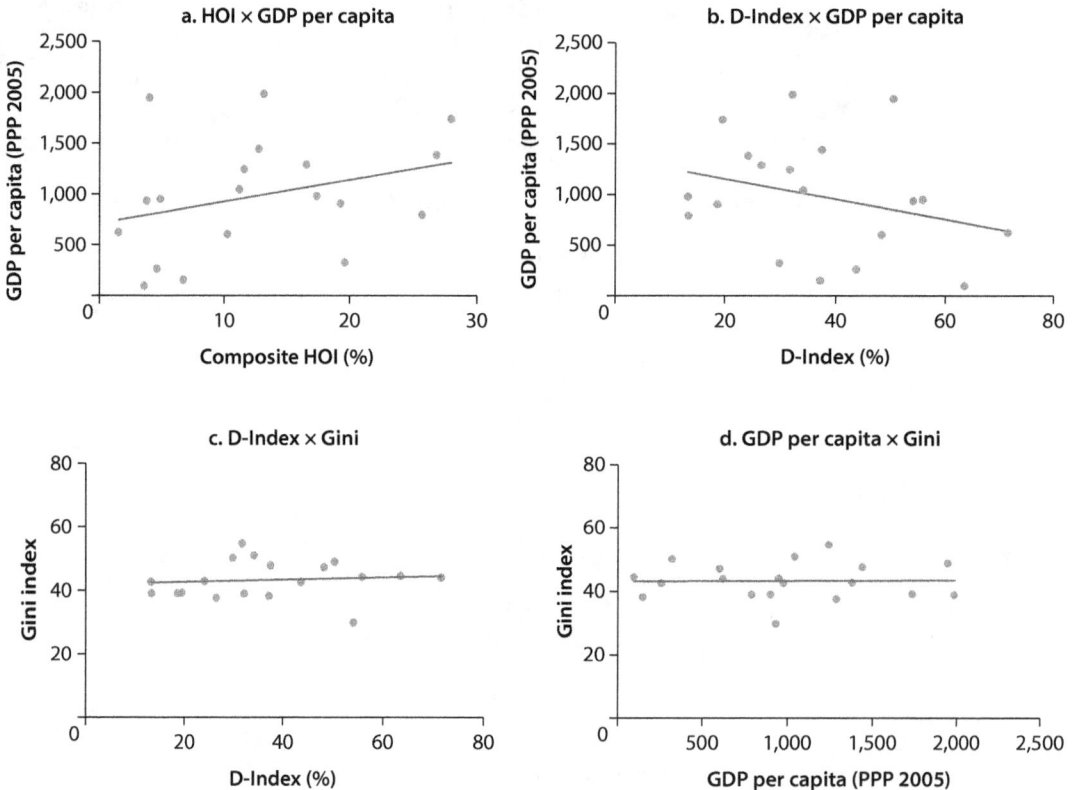

Source: Authors' calculations using *World Development Indicators* (World Bank 2011) and Demographic and Health Surveys data, various years.
Note: D-Index = dissimilarity index; GDP = gross domestic product; HOI = Human Opportunity Index; PPP = purchasing power parity.

correlation does not improve when the direct measure of inequality of opportunities (D-Index) is used instead of the HOI (figure 6.2c).[1]

Finally, there is no correlation between GDP per capita and consumption inequality (Gini) for the 20 SSA countries (figure 6.2d). The correlation coefficient is as low as 0.01, which is consistent with what is generally found about the relationship between average income and income inequality in the economic literature. While the well-known Kuznets Hypothesis posits that relative income inequality increases in the early stages of growth in a developing country but begins to fall after some point,[2] the evidence for such a relationship in a large cross-country data set has been found to be weak.[3] Moreover, time-series evidence suggests that not many developing countries have followed the prediction of the Kuznets Hypothesis of inequality rising with growth first and then falling.

In summary, average GDP for SSA countries is uncorrelated with consumption inequality, but positively correlated with the composite HOI (for 1-year-olds) and negatively correlated with the component of the HOI that measures inequality of opportunities. Similar results hold if the composite HOI for 6- to 11-year-olds was considered. These are important correlation patterns that merit attention.

How we should interpret these correlations is not clear based on the evidence we have, and we can only be speculative at this stage. On the one hand, the correlation between GDP and the HOI and GDP and inequality of opportunities could reflect the fact that better-off countries can invest more in improving access to and equity in opportunities for children; in contrast, policies to reduce inequality of income are more complex and often politically difficult. On the other hand, the correlations are also consistent with the hypothesis of a causal link in reverse: inequality of opportunities persisting for long in a country leads to inefficiencies in investment and utilization of physical and human capital that impose an economic cost, which leads to a lower trajectory of economic growth. Testing these competing hypotheses is no easy task due to the fundamentally difficult problem of separating cause from effect, and is a subject of ongoing research using different methods and measures of inequality of opportunities, some of which have produced evidence in favor of the second hypothesis (see the discussion in chapter 2). Molina, Narayan, and Saavedra (2013) and Marrero and Rodriguez (2013) have found evidence that inequality of opportunity has a negative effect on average income levels of countries (see box 2.2 in chapter 2).[4]

The correlations shown here are subject to three important caveats. First, the sample of countries and the time periods we use are too limited to yield robust conclusions about correlations. *Second,* the measures of inequality being used here are not strictly comparable. The Gini and D-Index are different in how they measure "inequality," and it is conceivable that the lack of correlation is an artifact of this mismatch. Calculating identical indexes for inequality of income and opportunities is not straightforward for theoretical and empirical reasons.[5] More work needs to be done to find the appropriate measures of inequality that are amenable to a "like-for-like" comparison, which is beyond the scope of this study. *Third,* we recall the discussions in chapters 2 and 5 about the HOI (D-Index) being likely to increase (decrease) with coverage. This would imply that the correlation between the HOI (and the D-Index) and GDP per capita partly reflects a relationship between average income and *coverage* rate of an opportunity, rather than strictly between average income and *inequality* of the opportunity. In other words, the relationship is best interpreted as one between the level of *and* equity in human development on the one hand and economic development on the other.

Inequality of Opportunity and Poverty

As one would expect from the observed correlation between per capita GDP and the composite HOI, monetary poverty and the composite HOI are negatively correlated, with poorer countries lagging behind better-off countries in access to opportunities. Map 6.1 shows maps with the poverty rate (using the international $1.25/day at 2005 PPP poverty line, from the WDI 2011 database) and the composite HOI for both age groups for countries included in this study, with the caveat that the poverty rate is not available for all countries.[6] Countries shaded a darker color in the top panel (indicating a higher poverty rate) are more likely to be shaded a lighter color (indicating a lower composite HOI) in the two lower panels. That said, for a few countries the ranking by poverty rate is quite different from the ranking by one or both of the composite HOI. Kenya, for example, has one of the lowest poverty rates in both periods, relative to other countries, but composite HOIs that are somewhere in the middle of the group. Malawi, on the other hand, has a poverty rate *and* composite HOI that are in the high range for SSA countries in both periods.

Map 6.1 Poverty Headcount Rate and HOI in SSA Countries

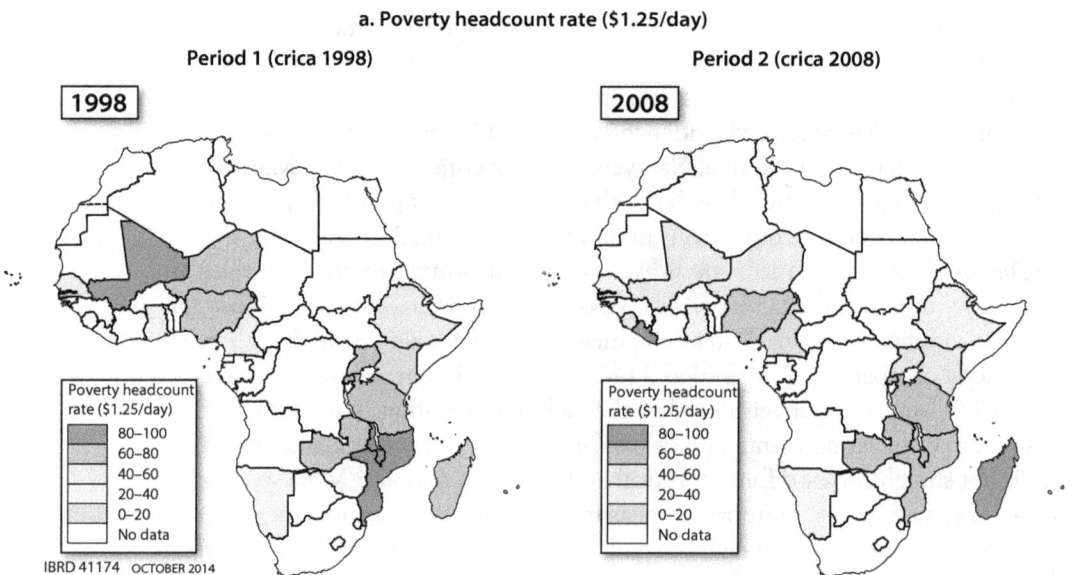

a. Poverty headcount rate ($1.25/day)

Period 1 (crica 1998)   Period 2 (crica 2008)

1998   2008

Poverty headcount rate ($1.25/day)
80–100
60–80
40–60
20–40
0–20
No data

IBRD 41174   OCTOBER 2014

map continues next page

Map 6.1 Poverty Headcount Rate and HOI in SSA Countries *(continued)*

b. Composite HOI (age 1 year)

Period 1 (crica 1998)	Period 2 (crica 2008)

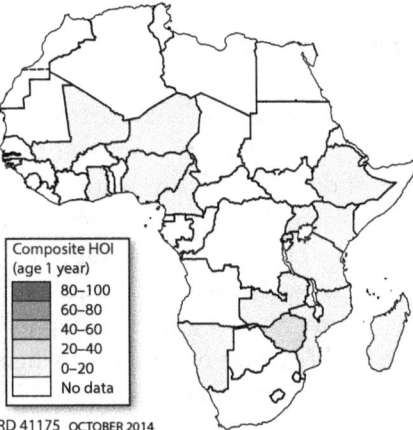
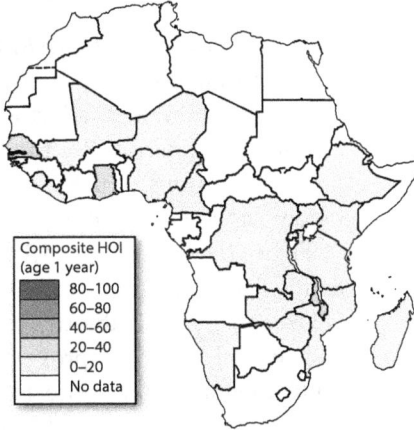

c. Composite HOI (age 6–11 years)

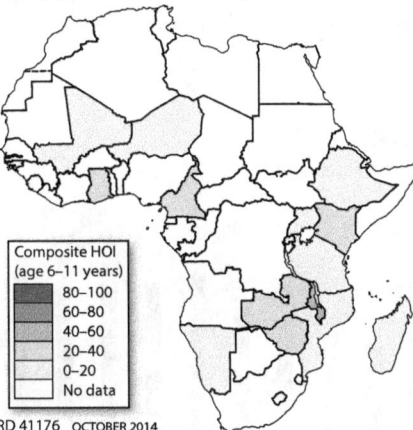
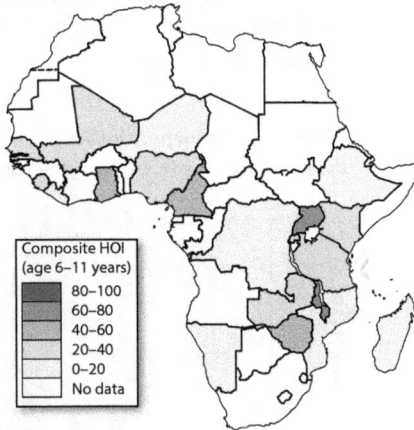

Source: Authors' illustrations using *World Development Indicators* (World Bank 2011) and Demographic and Health Surveys data, various years.
Note: HOI = Human Opportunity Index; SSA = Sub-Saharan Africa.

The maps also show the geographic pattern of a reduction in poverty and composite HOI for both age groups between the two periods. Improvements in the composite HOI for the older age group are seen pretty much across the board for the SSA countries included in our study, consistent with what was described earlier in chapter 4. Map 6.1 suggests that the positive trend in opportunities occurred in conjunction with poverty reduction across the board. While we have no evidence to draw causal links between one trend and the other, it seems clear that during the roughly 10-year period under study, reduction in monetary poverty and improvements in human opportunities for children of age 6–11 years occurred side by side for most countries.

How Do Countries Fare Relative to Their Income Levels?

In comparing countries by the opportunities they provide to their children, an important question to address is: what will the comparison look like if, instead of a straight comparison by the HOI, one were also to take into account the economic conditions of the country. One way of doing so is by weighting the HOI by per capita GDP (constant 2005 PPP) and using that to compare countries.

Figure 6.3 shows how 19 countries are ranked by composite HOI (one year) and weighted composite HOI, circa 2008. It is easy to see that some countries (Zimbabwe, Mozambique, Liberia, Sierra Leone, the Democratic Republic of Congo, and Niger) improve their ranking in this group of countries when the GDP-weighted composite HOI, instead of the unweighted composite HOI, is used for cross-country comparison.

Conversely, a number of countries fare worse in terms of their GDP-weighted composite HOI. Senegal, Cameroon, and Kenya drop by nine, seven, and five places, respectively, when countries are sorted by composite HOI weighted by per capita GDP. Ghana, Malawi, Uganda, Tanzania, Kenya, Zambia, Rwanda, Madagascar, and Nigeria are other countries that rank lower when the weighted HOI measure is used. The ranks of Mali and Ethiopia remain unchanged with the weighted measure.

Figure 6.3 Opportunities Relative to Income Levels
Rank by composite HOI, unweighted and weighted by GDP per capita

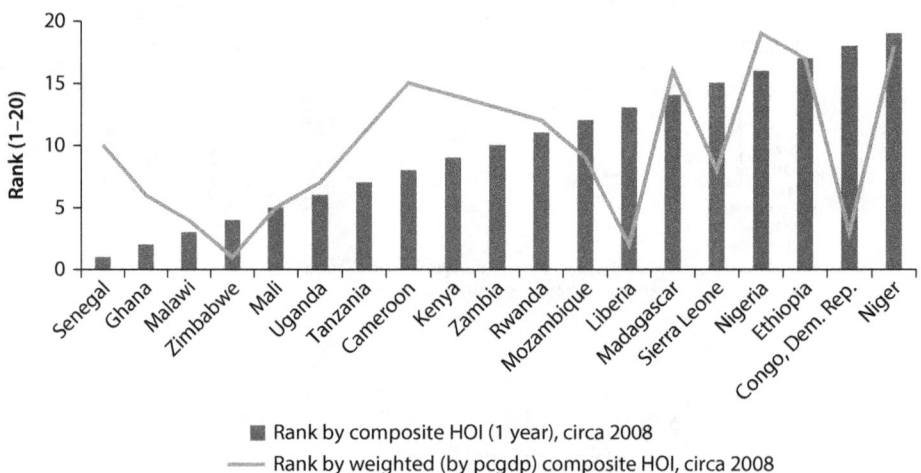

■ Rank by composite HOI (1 year), circa 2008
——— Rank by weighted (by pcgdp) composite HOI, circa 2008

Source: Authors' calculations using Demographic and Health Surveys data, various years.
Note: Lower number denotes higher rank. Countries are sorted by descending order of rank by composite HOI. GDP = gross domestic product; HOI = Human Opportunity Index; pcgdp = per capita gross domestic product.

While these comparisons suggest some interesting insights into how countries perform in terms of providing opportunities relative to their economic status, they have key limitations. First of all, the naïve comparison attempted here implicitly assumes a straightforward correlation between GDP and the HOI, ignoring other factors such as institutions, history, and preferences that may or may not be related to the income level of a country. Second, the GDP-weighted index used for these comparisons is an arbitrary way of taking into account the economic conditions that may matter for access to opportunities for children. Changes to the weighting scheme with the same (or a different) indicator of economic status can produce different rankings among the same group of countries. The comparisons here are thus best seen as *illustrating* how taking the economic status of countries into account can affect the cross-country comparison of opportunities for children, rather a robust, meaningful sorting.

Comparisons across Countries, Regions, and Continents

Comparing Anglophone and Francophone SSA Countries

As mentioned earlier, looking at differences between Anglophone and Francophone countries in our sample of countries can be instructive, as the two types of countries share some common characteristics in terms of institutions and historical background. Figure 6.4 shows such a comparison, as simple (unweighted) average HOI and coverage rates of each group of countries, for all nine opportunities included in this study. The comparisons are rough and indicative at best, due to two main caveats. *First*, HOIs for both periods are available for a partial list of countries, consisting of 11 Anglophone and 7 Francophone countries (see notes to figure 6.4 for the list of countries of each type). *Second*, the measures used—*unweighted cross-country averages*—have the benefit of simplicity but suffer from the drawback of not taking into account the population of children in each country.[7]

On average, Anglophone countries seem to do better in terms of the HOI in a majority of opportunities in both periods. Most of the gaps are attributable to differences in coverage rate, since the gap between coverage and the HOI (a rough measure of the average "penalty" due to inequality) is quite similar for the two groups of countries in most cases. Figure 6.4 also shows that over time the Anglo-Francophone gaps in the HOI have narrowed, particularly for school attendance for both age groups, starting primary school on time, and full immunization. The gap has not narrowed for finishing primary school (12- to 15-year-olds) and is almost non-existent for stunting and access to electricity in both periods.

Explaining the difference between Anglophone and Francophone averages in access to opportunities is beyond the scope of this study. The findings appear to be consistent with other pieces of evidence. *First*, Anglophone countries in our sample are better off, on average, with a per capita GDP of around US$1,405 compared to $1,048 for the Francophone sample, which may explain in part the difference in opportunities among children. Moreover, there is some evidence in the literature that gender and rural-urban gaps in school attendance are common among children in many Francophone SSA countries but not in most Anglophone countries (Lewin and Sabates 2011). Finally, the trend of narrowing of Anglo-Francophone gaps between the late-1990s (circa 1998) and late-2000s (circa 2008) is consistent with other pieces of cross-country evidence discussed earlier, which suggest that the gap between the leading and lagging countries in providing education opportunities for children has narrowed during this period.

Underlying the simple averages in figure 6.4 are wide variations among Anglophone and Francophone countries alike. This is illustrated in the annex (figure 6A.1), which graphs the HOI and coverage rates for all opportunities for each country in the late-2000s, differentiating between Anglo and Francophone countries. Clearly, while Anglophone countries do better, on average, for all opportunities, the top performing Francophone countries do much better than most of the Anglophone countries for the same opportunity. Largely, variation *within* each group of countries is larger than differences *between* groups, indicating that comparisons between groups of countries have limited value in explaining the cross-country story of opportunities in SSA.

Finally, to consider the possibility that "geography" plays some role in explaining differences across countries, we compare across SSA countries classified into regions: Central (2 countries), Eastern (10 countries), Southern (1 country) and Western (7 countries). The only meaningful comparison would be between the East and West, given the small number of countries in the other two regions. The comparisons for education opportunities, shown in the annex (figure 6A.2), indicate that eastern countries fare better, on average, but cross-country variation in the HOI *within* regions is extremely high. Looking at the opportunity of attending school, inequality among children of different circumstances—shown by the gap between the HOI and coverage—tends to be higher in the western SSA countries, particularly for the 12- to 15-year age group.

Comparing SSA and LAC Countries

International comparisons, besides being interesting in their own right, can also be helpful in contextualizing the performance of countries and identifying their most important challenges going forward. Access to opportunities for children in SSA countries is compared here with that in LAC countries, using the HOI figures provided in earlier publications by the LAC region of the World Bank.[8] The choice of the LAC region as the comparator for SSA countries is primarily because HOIs are available, for a comparable set of opportunities, for most LAC countries. The high variation among LAC countries in terms of their income and level of development also makes for a rich set of comparators. That said, such a comparison has limited value due to a number of factors, as is true for any such cross-regional comparison, even after accounting for differences in income level. The most important factor is that LAC countries, including those that are comparable to some of the SSA countries in income level, have attributes vastly different from those of SSA countries, which have much more to do with history, and policy, institutional, and economic environment, than geographic location.

Figure 6.4 Anglophone and Francophone Countries: Average HOI and Coverage

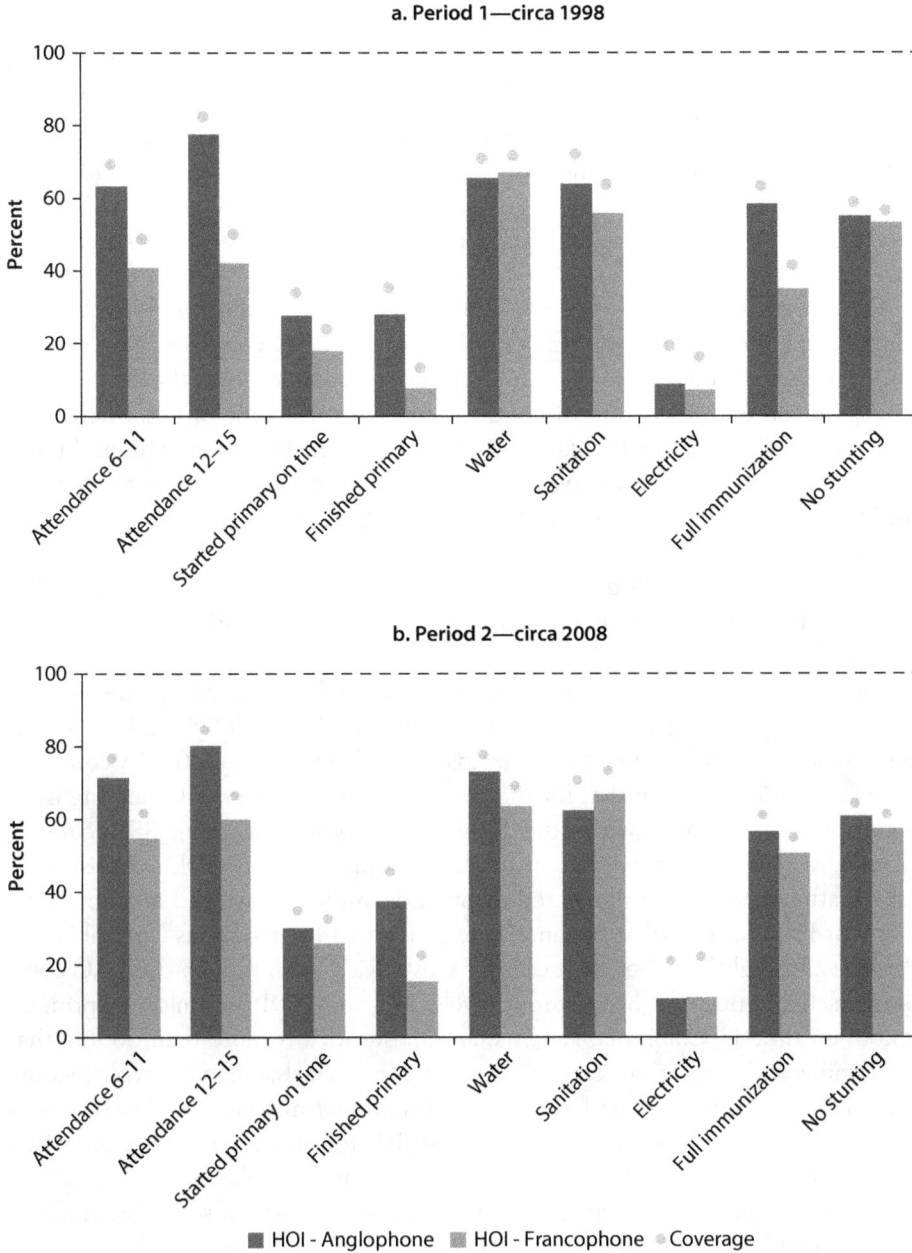

a. Period 1—circa 1998

b. Period 2—circa 2008

■ HOI - Anglophone ▨ HOI - Francophone ● Coverage

Source: Authors' calculations using Demographic and Health Surveys data, various years.
Note: (1) **Anglophone**: Ghana, Kenya, Liberia, Malawi, Namibia, Nigeria, Sierra Leone, Tanzania, Uganda, Zambia, and Zimbabwe. **Francophone**: Cameroon, the Democratic Republic of Congo, Madagascar, Mali, Niger, Rwanda, and Senegal. (2) The Human Opportunity Index (HOI) and coverage for Anglophone (Francophone) are computed as simple averages of HOI and coverage, respectively, for all countries belonging to the Anglophone (Francophone) group.

Figure 6.5 shows the HOI for two education opportunities—school attendance among children of age 10–14 years and finishing sixth grade (primary
school) "on time" for children of 13–15 years—for 20 SSA and 19 LAC countries,
corresponding to the late-2000s (approximately 2008) of this study. It also
includes graphs showing the annual average rate of change of the HOI and coverage for these two opportunities for 16 each of SSA and LAC countries. Notably,
the choice and definition of these opportunities, which are similar but *not identical* to the education opportunities analyzed so far in this study, are guided by the
fact that the exact same definitions across all countries need to be used for a
meaningful comparison.

For school attendance among 10- to 14-year-olds, coverage and the HOI in
most SSA countries are not far behind those for LAC countries. The average
HOI for SSA countries is lower, which is understandable, given the much lower
average income in SSA countries and the presence of fragile or extremely poor
countries in SSA—countries like Niger, Mali, Ethiopia, Liberia, and Sierra Leone,
for which there are no reasonable comparators in the LAC region (except
for Haiti, which is not in our sample). Even so, there are a number of SSA countries (e.g., Kenya, Namibia, Rwanda, Uganda, and Zimbabwe) with an HOI for
school attendance for 10- to 14-year-olds on par with or better than that for the
poorer LAC countries (such as Nicaragua, Ecuador, El Salvador, Honduras, and
Guatemala).

The story is very different for the opportunity of finishing sixth grade on time,
among children of age 13–15 years.[9] SSA countries lag much behind LAC countries, on average and in one-to-one comparisons. Only 3 out of 20 SSA countries
have an HOI higher than that for the country with the lowest HOI among LAC
countries (Guatemala); while the HOI of the best-performing SSA country
(Zimbabwe) is topped by that of 16 LAC countries. The stark contrast with
school attendance is best illustrated through examples. Kenya and Namibia have
a similar HOI for school attendance among 10- to 14-year-olds as Colombia and
Panama and slightly higher than that for Costa Rica, even though the LAC comparators have much higher income levels. But the HOI for finishing primary
school on time in Colombia, Panama, and Costa Rica is more than double that
of Namibia and three times that of Kenya. In other words, while the wide income
gaps between many SSA and LAC countries are *not* matched by differences in
the opportunity of attending school among 10- to 14-year-olds, they are often
exceeded by the gap in timely completion of primary school.

A trend of rapid improvements in an HOI and coverage of school attendance
is seen in all but three countries (Nigeria in SSA, and Paraguay and Jamaica in
LAC) between the two periods under study (circa 1998 and 2008). The average
improvement in SSA countries is higher than that for LAC countries over the
same period, which may be related to the fact that most of these countries had
much lower school attendance to start with, in period one. It also means that the
gaps between SSA and LAC countries have narrowed over the period, with the
rate of convergence being especially high for SSA countries that had an extremely
low HOI in school attendance to start with.

Figure 6.5 Comparing the HOI in Education in LAC and SSA Countries

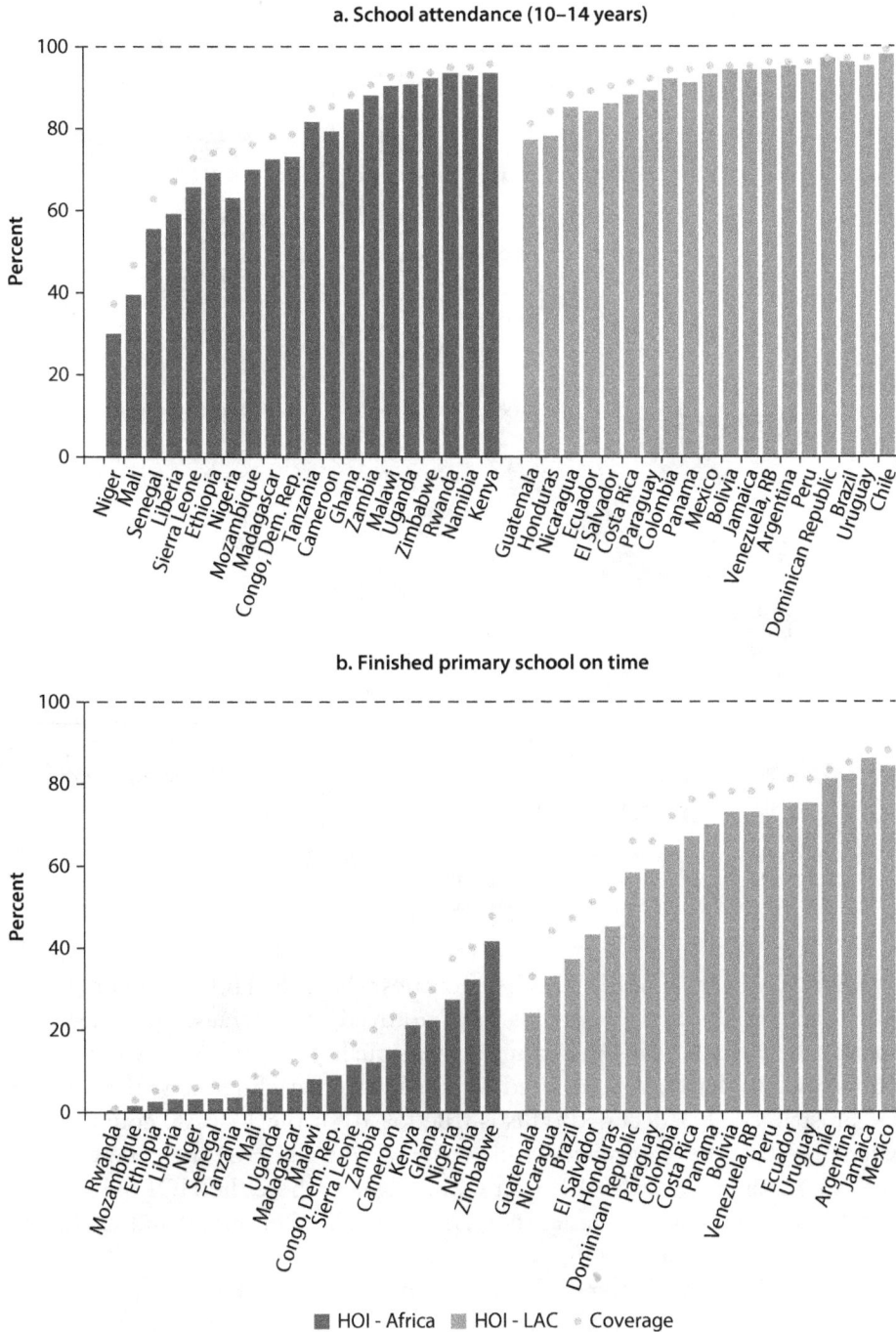

a. School attendance (10–14 years)

b. Finished primary school on time

■ HOI - Africa   ■ HOI - LAC   • Coverage

figure continues next page

Figure 6.5 Comparing the HOI in Education in LAC and SSA Countries *(continued)*

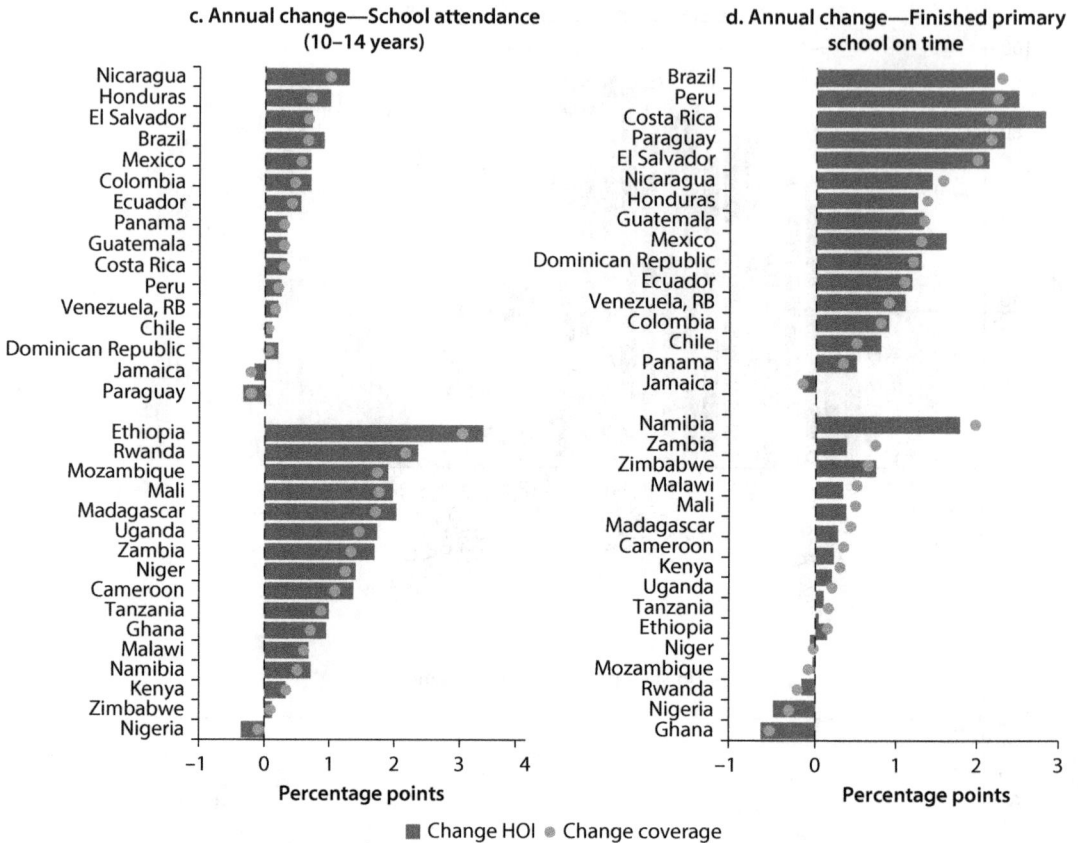

c. Annual change—School attendance (10–14 years)

d. Annual change—Finished primary school on time

Percentage points

■ Change HOI ● Change coverage

Sources: Barros et al. (2009, 2012); and authors' calculations using Demographic and Health Surveys data, various years.
Note: (1) Finishing primary school *on time* refers to completing sixth grade by age 12. (2) Percentage point change refers to *annual average* change in the HOI and coverage. HOI = Human Opportunity Index; LAC = Latin America and the Caribbean; SSA = Sub-Saharan Africa.

Interestingly, in all of the 15 SSA countries where the HOI for school attendance among 10- to 14-year-olds has improved, the increase is higher than that of the coverage rate, indicating that inequality of opportunity—available opportunities that are distributed unequally among children with different circumstances—has declined. This is true for 10 of the 14 LAC countries for which the HOI has improved, while coverage and the HOI have increased at the same rate in the other 4 countries. In Nigeria where the HOI fell slightly, the decline is attributable more to a rise in inequality of opportunities than to a fall in average coverage rate.

In contrast to school attendance, improvement in an HOI for on time completion of sixth grade is highly uneven for SSA countries and, in most cases, smaller than for most LAC countries. For 5 out of 16 SSA countries, the HOI for timely completion of sixth grade has fallen and for 9 others, the annual average improvement in the HOI amounts to less than 0.5 percentage point. In comparison, among LAC countries, the HOI has fallen for only 1 country (Jamaica), improved at a rate of less than 0.5 percentage point per year for 1 more (Panama), and improved at the rate of at least 1 point annually for 12 countries. Gaps between LAC and SSA countries in the HOI have actually widened between the two periods.

For 10 of the 11 African countries that show some improvement in the HOI for timely completion of sixth grade, the increase in the HOI is less than that in coverage, indicating that inequality of opportunity has actually increased. In contrast, for 11 out of 15 LAC countries showing an improvement in the HOI, inequality of opportunities has fallen. Another way of seeing this is that the gap in the HOI between SSA and LAC countries in period two would have been narrower in most cases if inequality of opportunity—that relates to the gap between vulnerable and nonvulnerable groups of children *within* each country— had not increased as coverage rates improved in SSA countries.

All told, the comparative story of SSA and LAC countries in education opportunities is one of opposite trends: SSA countries improving rapidly and catching up with (mostly better-off) LAC countries in the opportunity of attending school, while falling behind in timely completion of primary school. In the absence of more direct measures like student achievement scores, timely completion can be considered as an indicator of education quality, albeit a highly imperfect one. And with that assumption, the story is one of convergence between the two regions on school attendance but divergence on the quality of education received. A combination of delayed start to schooling and grade repetition is a likely explanation for why SSA countries lag behind on finishing primary school at the right age, even as school attendance improves rapidly for the 10- to 14-year age group.

How do SSA and LAC countries compare in the opportunity of children to have access to basic infrastructure? Figure 6.6 (a) and (b) graphs the HOI for safe water—limiting the definition to only piped water to be consistent with what is measured for LAC countries in earlier publications—and electricity. SSA countries fare much worse than LAC countries in comparison, which is illustrated by two telling statistics. The highest HOI in access to electricity (for Ghana) among 20 SSA countries is eight points lower than the lowest HOI (for Honduras) among LAC countries; and the highest HOI in access to piped water in SSA (for Senegal) is eight points lower than the lowest HOI (for Nicaragua) in LAC countries. Similar results are seen for sanitation (defined by access to a flush toilet) as well (see annex, figure 6A.3).

Two qualifications are important here. *First*, the gaps in some instances are even wider *among* SSA countries—between Ghana and Liberia, for instance, in access to electricity and between Senegal and Uganda in access to piped water— than between average SSA and LAC countries. *Second*, the LAC-SSA gaps would be smaller if more liberal and perhaps more appropriate (for countries of the income level as they are in SSA) definitions of safe water and sanitation were to be used for all countries, as they have been for the most part in this study.

How will the same comparison look if one were to take into account the difference in income levels between countries? To illustrate, we use the same weighted (by per capita GDP) HOI measure as was used earlier and compare the

Figure 6.6 Comparing SSA and LAC Countries by the HOI for Basic Infrastructure

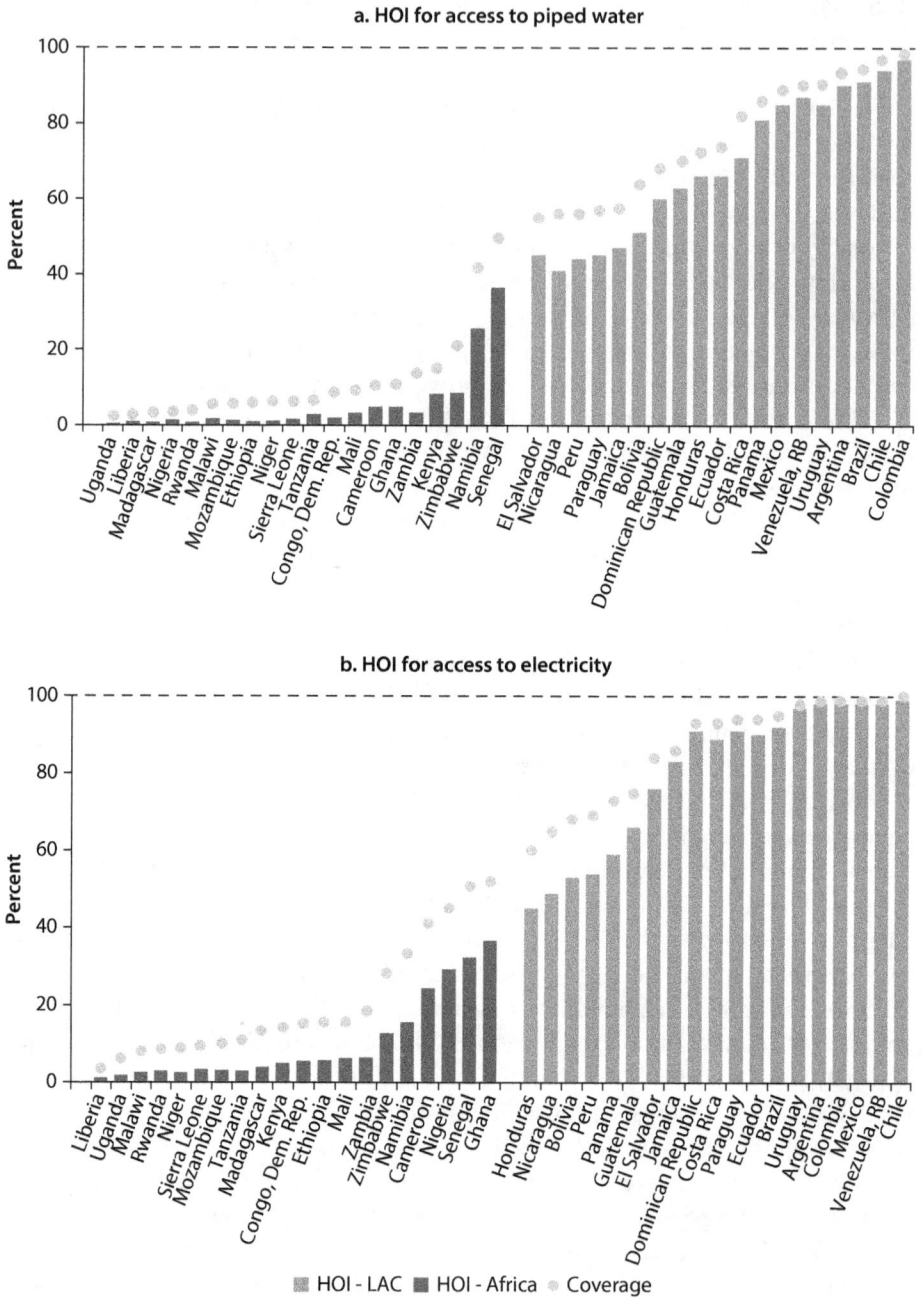

a. HOI for access to piped water

b. HOI for access to electricity

HOI - LAC   ▓ HOI - Africa   ● Coverage

figure continues next page

Figure 6.6 Comparing SSA and LAC Countries by the HOI for Basic Infrastructure *(continued)*

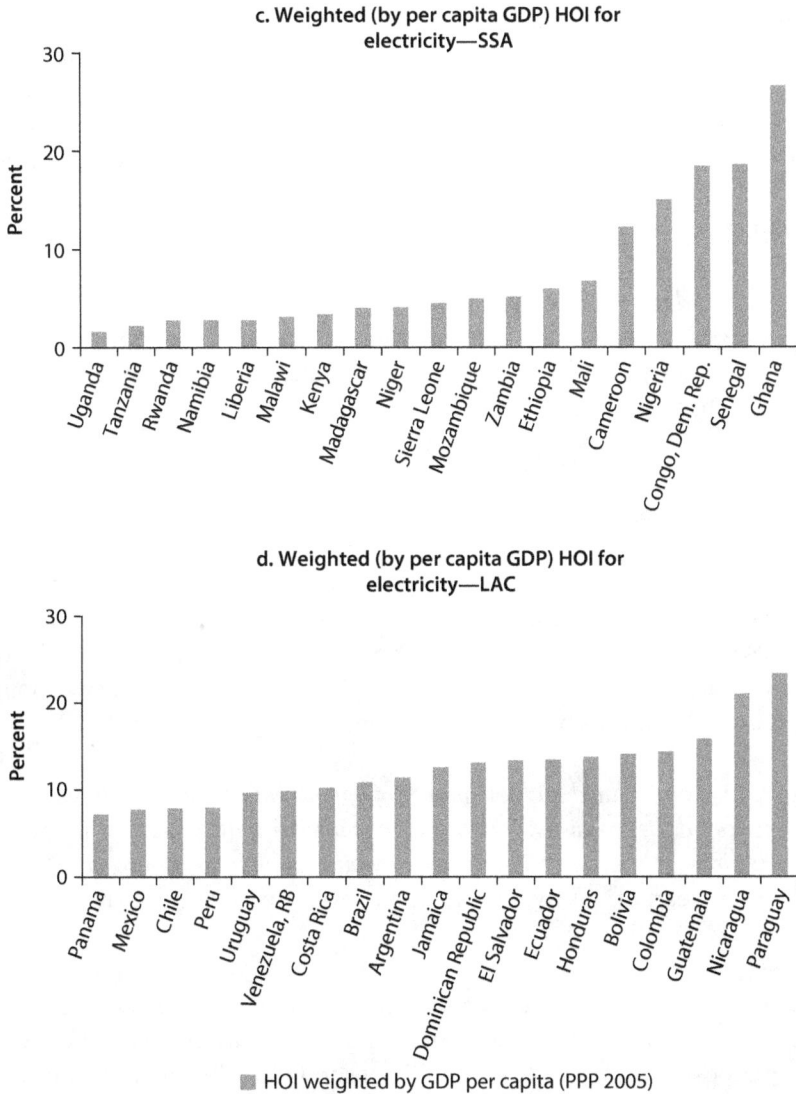

c. Weighted (by per capita GDP) HOI for electricity—SSA

d. Weighted (by per capita GDP) HOI for electricity—LAC

▨ HOI weighted by GDP per capita (PPP 2005)

Sources: Barros et al. (2009, 2012); and authors' calculations using Demographic and Health Surveys data, various years.
Note: GDP = gross domestic product; HOI = Human Opportunity Index; LAC = Latin America and the Caribbean; PPP = purchasing power parity; SSA = Sub-Saharan Africa.

results with a weighted and unweighted HOI for access to electricity. As expected, the use of the per capita GDP-weighted HOI narrows the difference between the two regions (figure 6.6c, d), and some countries like Ghana, Senegal, and the Democratic Republic of Congo do better than most others in SSA and LAC relative to their income level. Even then, the cross-country average for the weighted HOI is higher for LAC countries. And the cross-country variation is much higher for SSA than for LAC, as some of the SSA countries score very low, even in terms of the weighted HOI.

Do African Children Have an Equal Chance? • http://dx.doi.org/10.1596/978-1-4648-0332-1

Conclusion

The cross-country comparisons presented in this chapter take a number of different forms: comparisons between access to (and inequality of) opportunities and economic indicators of well-being and poverty; comparisons between countries grouped by language, historical, and institutional features (Francophone and Anglophone); and comparisons between SSA countries and LAC countries, to put the SSA experience in a global context. The highlights of these comparisons are summarized below.

- *The HOI and the index of inequality of opportunities are correlated with GDP per capita across SSA countries.* The correlation is stronger for some opportunities (e.g., education) than for others (e.g., immunization), and significant for composite HOIs that combine multiple opportunities. At the same time, inequality of opportunities is uncorrelated with inequality of income.

- *Correlations between HOIs in education and GDP tend to be lower in the late-2000s (circa 2008) than in the first (circa 1998),* confirming what was suggested by earlier evidence: gaps in key opportunities such as school attendance between countries have narrowed over time as poorer countries have made progress in catching up with the leaders. For immunization, where the cross-country gaps have low correlation with differences in GDP, evidence points to the narrowing of gaps between leading and lagging performers.

- *That GDP is correlated with inequality of opportunities but not with inequality of income could be consistent with the hypothesis that persistent inequality of opportunities in a country imposes a cost on economic development.* The causal link at the heart of this hypothesis is, however, a tricky issue that merits much deeper examination.

- *Consumption poverty and a composite HOI are negatively correlated, with poorer countries lagging behind less poor countries in access to opportunities.* Between the two periods, improvements in the composite HOI—for the 6- to 11-year age group in particular—are seen for most SSA countries, along with a reduction in consumption poverty.

- *Factoring in the level of economic development can be important for a cross-country comparison of opportunities.* An easy, albeit imperfect, way of doing this is by sorting countries by the composite HOI *weighted* by per capita GDP, based on which some countries (e.g., Zimbabwe, Mozambique, Liberia, Sierra Leone, and the Democratic Republic of Congo) improve their cross-country ranking significantly, relative to their rank by an (unweighted) composite HOI. And for some countries, like Senegal, Cameroon, and Kenya, it is the opposite, indicating that they underperform relative to their income levels.

- *As a group, Anglophone countries do better, on average, than Francophone countries in terms of the HOI in both periods.* Most of the gaps between the two groups are attributable to differences in coverage rate. The gap has narrowed over time for immunization, starting primary school on time, and school attendance of both age groups. Wide variation within each group implies that country-specific factors matter much more for access to opportunities than systematic institutional or historical differences between the two groups.

- *SSA countries lag far behind LAC countries in access to basic infrastructure,* with the gaps being narrower but still present if per capita GDP of countries is taken into account. In education, SSA countries compare quite well with LAC countries for the HOI in school attendance among 10- to 14-year-olds, after the gaps have narrowed considerably between the late-1990s and late-2000s. SSA countries, however, lag far behind LAC countries in completing sixth grade on time, with the gaps in many cases having increased over time.

These findings have a few key implications. *First*, the evidence suggests an important trend: gaps between better-performing and lagging SSA countries in terms of a few key opportunities for children (particularly in education and health) have narrowed over time. Thus, improving access to some basic services among children is possible, even for the poorest countries. Moreover, the rapid strides they have made in improving these opportunities support the view that policy initiatives can make a difference, even in resource-constrained environments.

Second, most SSA countries have achieved impressive progress in school attendance but less so in "second-generation" education opportunities like completing and starting primary school on time, which are likely to influence the *quality* of education a child receives. Available evidence on student learning achievements from seven countries also seems to support this hypothesis. There is wide variation—across countries and among groups within countries—in the share of students who achieved (in 2007) basic skills in reading and numeracy in tests administered by the SACMEQ-III project (see chapter 2). And the average test scores for five out of these seven countries have shown marginal or no improvement between 2000 and 2007 (see chapter 3).

On the one hand, it is understandable that an improvement in school attendance precedes improvements in opportunities that are influenced by a complex combination of factors, from quality of (and returns to) education to opportunity cost of schooling. But for the very same reason, it is by no means inevitable that improvements in attendance will lead to eventual improvements in the second-generation opportunities. Rather, achieving gains in these would depend on the extent to which countries can invest in improving the quality of education, and preschool and early childhood learning, as well as promote policies that benefit broader economic conditions that affect the differential between cost of and returns to education for a household.

Third, the rapid improvements in some dimensions should not distract policy makers from the challenges posed by the relative lack of progress in others. In addition to the second-generation education opportunities mentioned above, considerable challenges remain in access to critical services such as safe water, adequate sanitation, and electricity. For these opportunities, even the best performers among SSA countries lag behind the lowest performer among LAC countries. Even using more liberal definitions for water and sanitation, the progress in SSA countries has been uneven and with the exception of a few countries, lagging behind the gains in school attendance. Answering this challenge, as well as that of improving opportunities in immunization and nutrition (as seen in earlier chapters), will require as concerted an effort as has been seen in many of these countries for improving access to education.

Annex 6A

Figure 6A.1 Comparing HOIs for Anglophone and Francophone Countries (circa 2008)

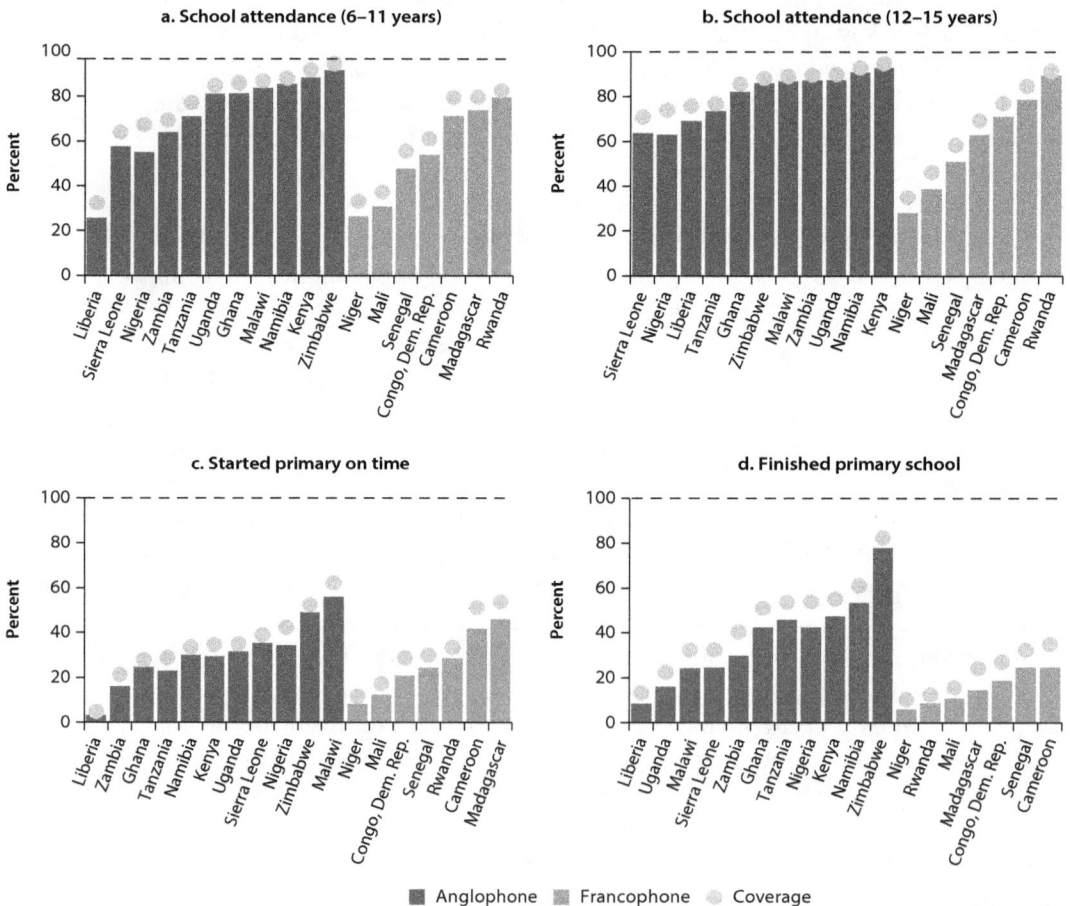

figure continues next page

Figure 6A.1 Comparing HOIs for Anglophone and Francophone Countries (circa 2008) *(continued)*

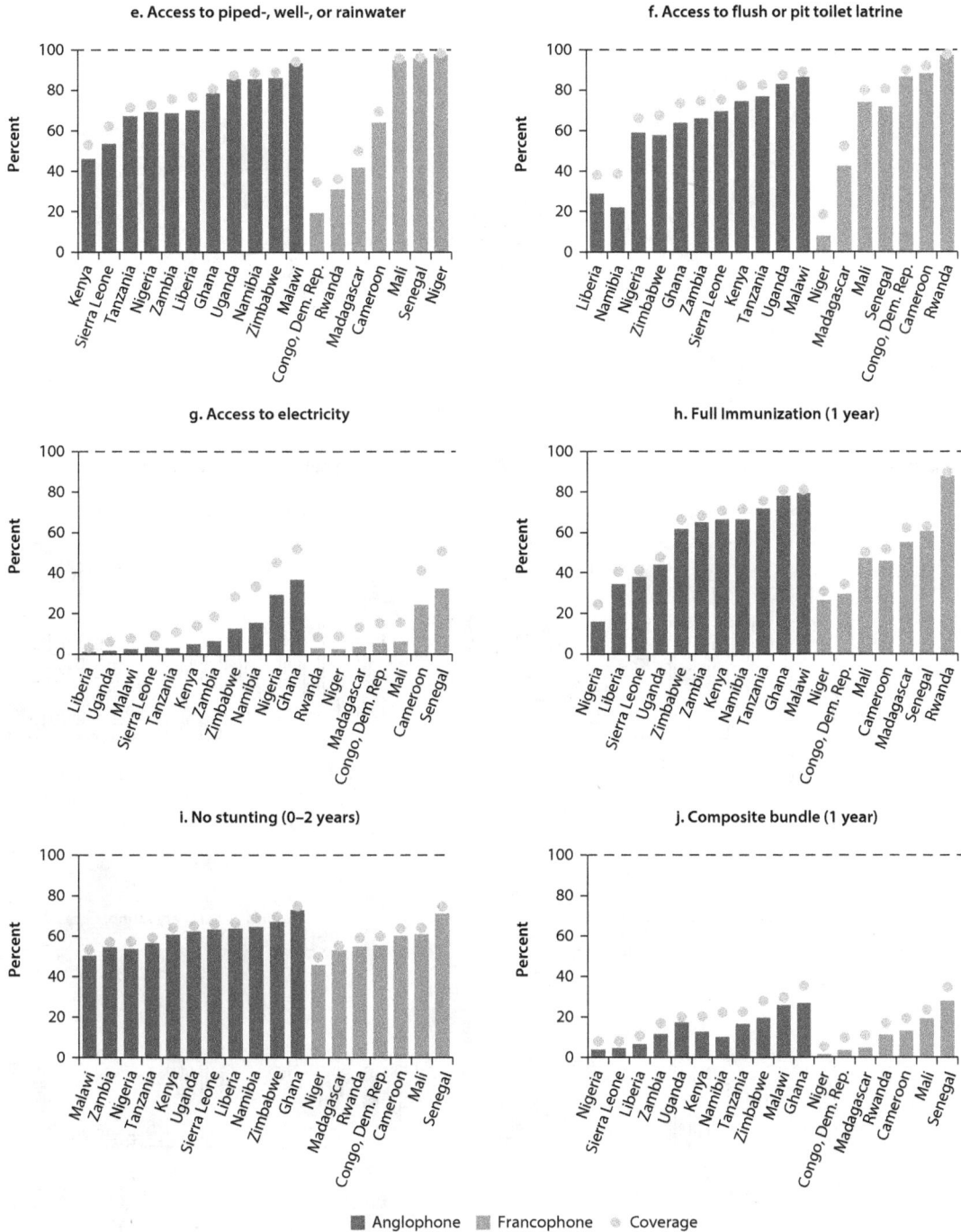

e. Access to piped-, well-, or rainwater

f. Access to flush or pit toilet latrine

g. Access to electricity

h. Full immunization (1 year)

i. No stunting (0–2 years)

j. Composite bundle (1 year)

■ Anglophone ■ Francophone ○ Coverage

Do African Children Have an Equal Chance? • http://dx.doi.org/10.1596/978-1-4648-0332-1

Figure 6A.1 Comparing HOIs for Anglophone and Francophone Countries (circa 2008) *(continued)*

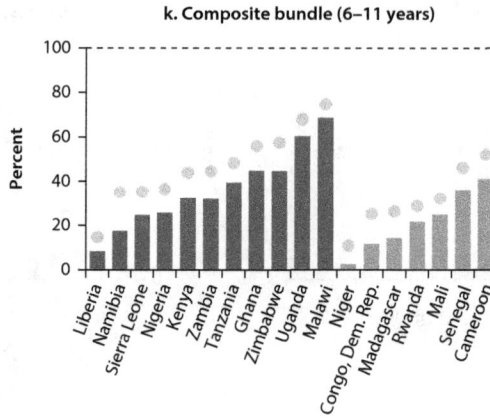

k. Composite bundle (6–11 years)

Source: Authors' calculations using Demographic and Health Surveys data, various years.
Note: HOI = Human Opportunity Index.

Figure 6A.2 Comparing HOIs for SSA Countries in Different Geographical Regions (circa 2008)

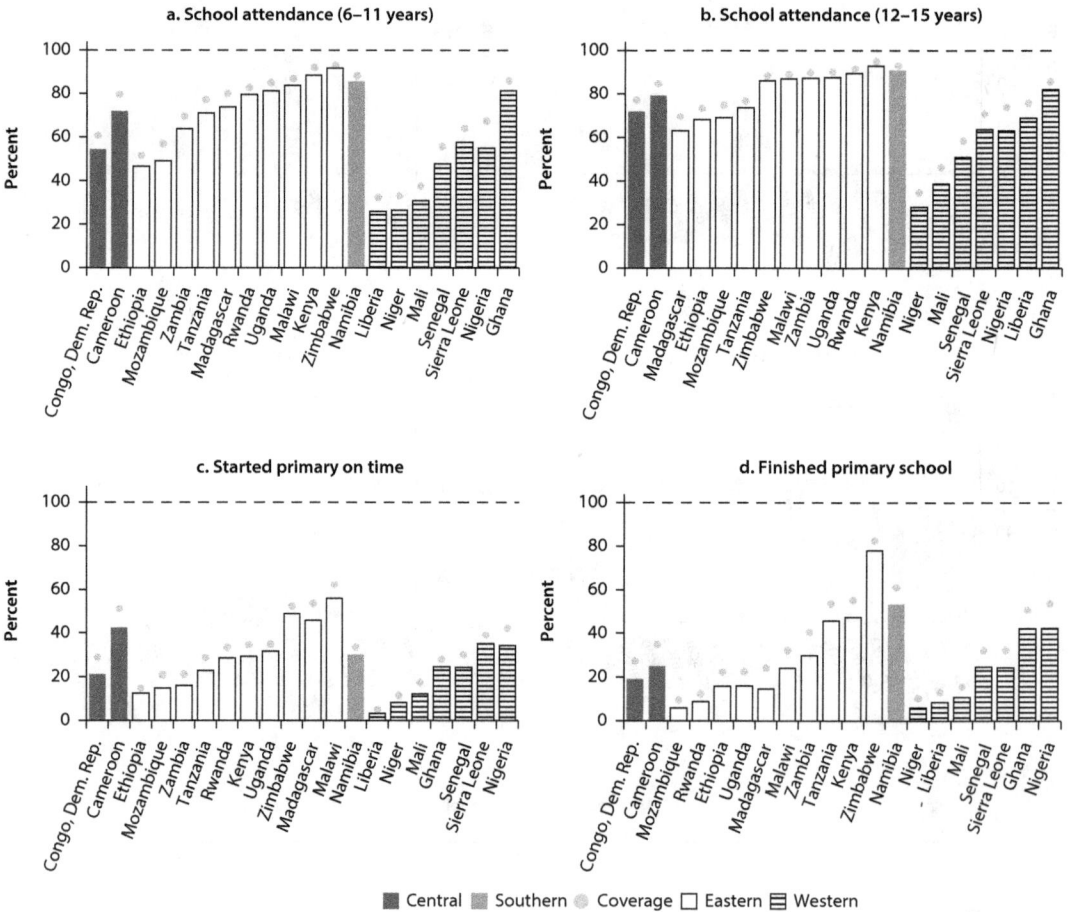

a. School attendance (6–11 years)

b. School attendance (12–15 years)

c. Started primary on time

d. Finished primary school

■ Central ■ Southern ● Coverage □ Eastern ▤ Western

figure continues next page

Figure 6A.2 Comparing HOIs for SSA Countries in Different Geographical Regions (circa 2008) *(continued)*

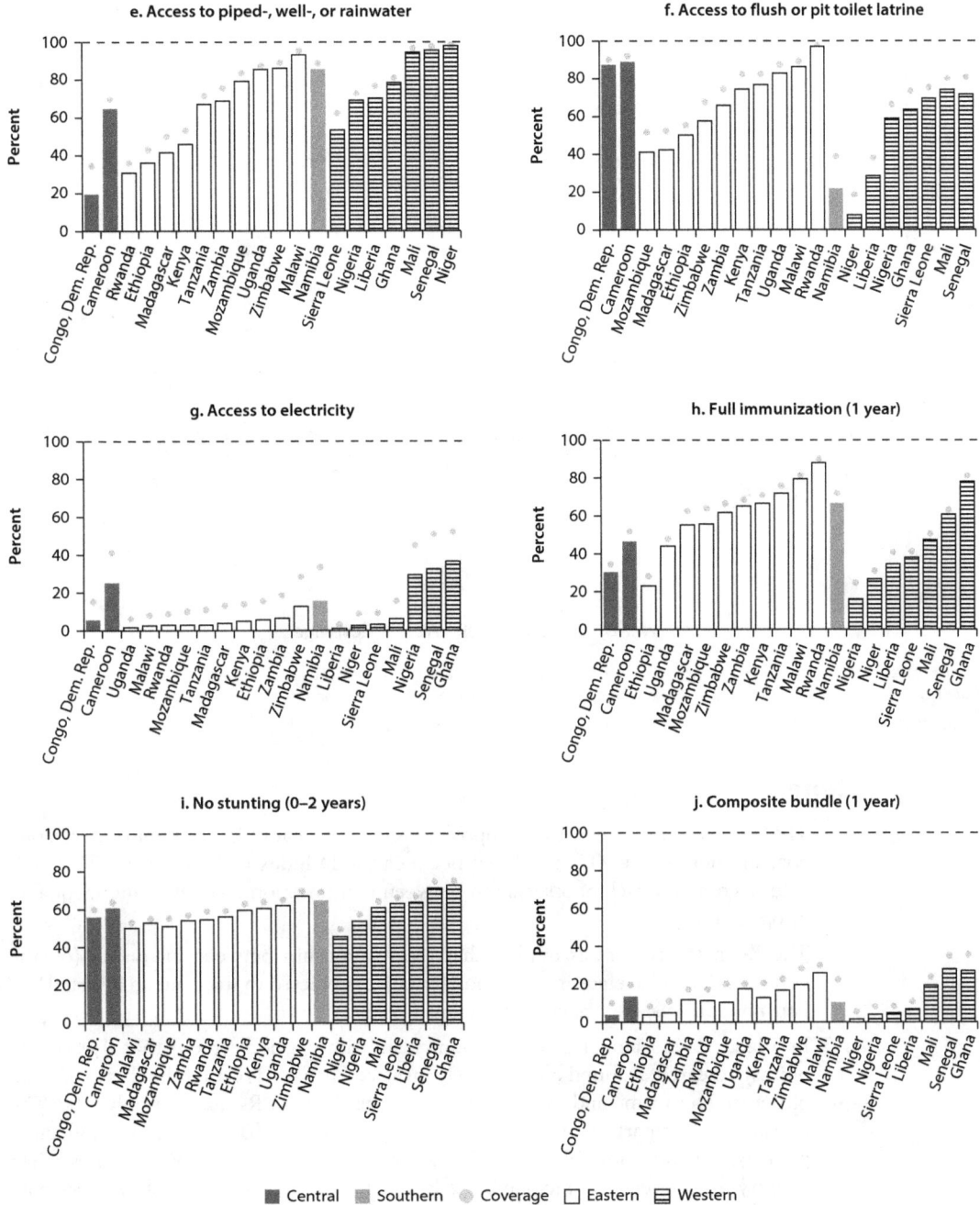

e. Access to piped-, well-, or rainwater

f. Access to flush or pit toilet latrine

g. Access to electricity

h. Full immunization (1 year)

i. No stunting (0–2 years)

j. Composite bundle (1 year)

■ Central   ▨ Southern   ◉ Coverage   ☐ Eastern   ▤ Western

Source: Authors' calculations using Demographic and Health Surveys data, various years.
Note: HOI = Human Opportunity Index; SSA = Sub-Saharan Africa.

Figure 6A.3 Comparing HOIs for LAC and SSA Countries

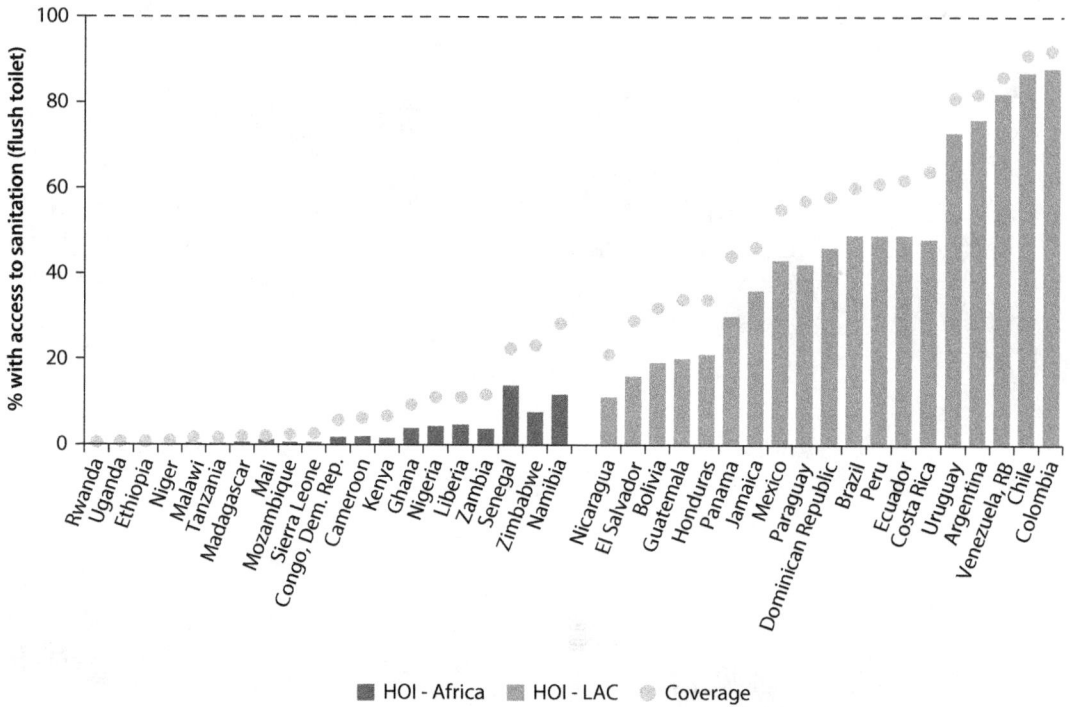

Sources: Barros et al. (2009, 2012); and authors' calculations using Demographic and Health Surveys data, various years.
Note: HOI = Human Opportunity Index; LAC = Latin America and the Caribbean; SSA = Sub-Saharan Africa.

Notes

1. The correlation between the composite HOI for 1-year-olds and Gini of per capita consumption is just −0.09; and that between the D-Index and Gini is 0.1. This indicates a complete lack of association between consumption inequality and inequality of opportunity.

2. The Kuznets Hypothesis implies that the relationship between inequality (on the vertical axis) and average income (horizontal) is predicted to trace out an inverted "U." For more on this, see Anand and Kanbur (1993).

3. In a large data set pooling many country and time periods (more than 1,000 data points), researchers found only a weakly inverted U-shaped relationship between Gini of per capita income and log of GDP per capita, with an R-square of only 0.08. The upward sloping part of the curve is particularly hard to discern, with the inflection point being quite unstable. Even this weak inverted U relationship vanishes when country fixed effects are included. See Bruno, Ravallion, and Squire (1998) for more on this.

4. While the correlations for 20 SSA countries in our study can by no means test the validity of the hypothesis, they are consistent with what one would expect to find if inequality of opportunities were indeed an important determinant of a country's level of economic development and if such inequality were to persist over time in a country.

5. One cannot, for example, compute the Gini index for access to opportunity as defined here (a 0–1 variable); nor can one compute a D-Index for income, without defining an "opportunity" in terms of income. The latter would in turn lead to a notion of income inequality (based on "smoothed distributions") that is quite different from what is generally used. Measuring a D-Index for income would also be fraught with conceptual and empirical problems, since exogenous "circumstances" are not easily defined (or available from household data) for people who earn incomes, namely adults. For a recent example of how inequality of opportunities in income can be measured—in a framework different from the HOI but with some similarities—see a recent paper by Ferreira and Gignoux (2011).

6. The countries for which both the composite HOI and poverty rate are available are 15 in period one and 19 in period two.

7. This has the problematic implication that a country as populous as Nigeria has the same weight as a small country like Rwanda or Sierra Leone.

8. See Barros et al. (2009, 2012).

9. Finishing sixth grade *on time* refers to completing sixth grade by age 12 years, measured in the universe of children of ages 13–15.

References

Anand, S., and R. Kanbur. 1993. "Inequality and Development: A Critique." *Journal of Development Economics* 41: 19–43.

Barros, R., F. Ferreira, J. Molinas Vega, and J. Saavedra. 2009. *Measuring Inequality of Opportunities in Latin America and the Caribbean*. Washington, DC: World Bank.

Barros, R., J. Molinas Vega, J. Saavedra, and M. Giugale. 2012. *Do Our Children Have a Chance? A Human Opportunity Report for Latin America and the Caribbean*. Washington, DC: World Bank.

Bruno, M., M. Ravallion, and L. Squire. 1998. "Equity and Growth in Developing Countries: Old and New Perspectives on the Policy Issues." In *Income Distribution and High-Quality Growth*, edited by V. Tanzi and K-Y. Chu, 117–46. Cambridge, MA: MIT Press.

Demographic and Health Surveys. Various years. USAID. http://www.dhsprogram.com.

Ferreira, F., and J. Gignoux. 2011. "The Measurement of Inequality of Opportunity: Theory and an Application to Latin America." *Review of Income and Wealth* 57 (4): 622–57.

Lewin, K., and R. Sabates. 2011. "Who Gets What? Is Improved Access to Basic Education Pro-Poor in SSA?" *International Journal of Educational Development* 32 (4): 517–28.

Marrero, G., and J. Rodríguez. 2013. "Inequality of Opportunity and Growth." *Journal of Development Economics* 104 (C): 107–22.

Molina, E., A. Narayan, and J. Saavedra. 2013. "Outcomes, Opportunity and Development: Why Unequal Opportunities and Not Outcomes Hinder Economic Development." Policy Research Working Paper 6735, World Bank, Washington, DC.

World Bank. 2011. *World Development Indicators*. http://data.worldbank.org/data-catalog /world-development-indicators/wdi-2011.

Additional Tables with All Results

Table A.1 Levels and Decomposition over Time: School Attendance (6–11 Years)

Country	Period 1 (circa 1998)				Period 2 (circa 2008)				Annual change HOI (p.p)	Composition effect (p.p)	Scale effect (p.p)	Equalization effect (p.p)
	Coverage (%)	D-Index (%)	HOI (%)	SD HOI (%)	Coverage (%)	D-Index (%)	HOI (%)	SD HOI (%)				
Cameroon	73.4	13.8	63.2	0.8	79.8	10.7	71.2	0.6	1.3	0.1	0.8	0.4
Congo, Dem. Rep.					61.2	11.9	53.9	0.9				
Ethiopia	23.3	27.4	16.9	0.5	51.5	9.4	46.7	0.6	2.7	0.1	1.8	0.9
Ghana	76.3	8.9	69.5	0.8	86.1	5.5	81.4	0.5	1.2	-0.1	0.9	0.4
Kenya	85.7	4.4	81.9	0.6	91.9	3.9	88.3	0.5	0.6	0.0	0.5	0.1
Liberia					32.3	20.4	25.7	0.7				
Madagascar	60.9	16.0	51.1	0.7	79.9	7.6	73.8	0.4	2.0	0.0	1.4	0.6
Malawi	75.9	6.5	70.9	0.6	86.9	3.8	83.7	0.4	1.3	0.1	0.9	0.2
Mali	25.3	32.7	17.0	0.4	37.5	17.8	30.8	0.5	1.3	0.0	0.8	0.6
Mozambique	52.3	15.8	44.0	1.2	57.1	13.9	49.1	0.6	0.9	0.1	0.5	0.2
Namibia	84.1	4.6	80.3	0.8	88.2	3.2	85.4	0.5	0.8	0.0	0.6	0.2
Niger	22.1	31.8	15.1	0.5	33.1	20.1	26.4	0.5	1.4	-0.1	1.1	0.4
Nigeria	63.4	17.5	52.3	0.7	67.5	18.3	55.1	0.3	0.3	-0.1	0.4	0.0
Rwanda	61.1	4.6	58.3	0.6	82.6	3.7	79.6	0.5	2.1	0.1	2.0	0.1
Senegal					55.7	14.2	47.8	0.5				
Sierra Leone					64.1	10.0	57.7	0.7				
Tanzania	33.1	15.0	28.1	0.6	77.3	8.0	71.1	0.6	3.1	0.1	2.6	0.4
Uganda	66.2	8.4	60.6	0.8	84.9	4.4	81.1	0.5	1.9	0.1	1.5	0.3
Zambia	53.5	13.3	46.4	0.6	69.5	8.1	63.9	0.7	1.6	0.0	1.3	0.3
Zimbabwe	83.1	3.3	80.4	0.6	92.9	1.5	91.6	0.4	0.7	0.2	0.4	0.1

Source: Authors' calculations using Demographic and Health Surveys data, various years.
Note: HOI = Human Opportunity Index, p.p = percentage point, SD = standard deviation.

Table A.2 Levels and Decomposition over Time: School Attendance (12–15 Years)

Country	Period 1 (circa 1998)				Period 2 (circa 2008)				Annual change HOI (p.p)	Composition effect (p.p)	Scale effect (p.p)	Equalization effect (p.p)
	Coverage (%)	D-Index (%)	HOI (%)	SD HOI (%)	Coverage (%)	D-Index (%)	HOI (%)	SD HOI (%)				
Cameroon	77.8	9.7	70.2	1.2	84.8	7.2	78.7	0.8	1.4	0.2	0.9	0.3
Congo, Dem. Rep.					77.3	7.9	71.1	1.1				
Ethiopia	42.4	19.5	34.1	0.9	73.5	7.1	68.2	0.8	3.1	0.3	2.0	0.8
Ghana	80.1	7.5	74.1	1.1	85.8	4.3	82.1	0.6	0.8	-0.2	0.6	0.3
Kenya	91.0	2.7	88.6	0.7	94.9	2.3	92.7	0.6	0.6	0.0	0.5	0.0
Liberia					75.9	9.0	69.1	1.2				
Madagascar	52.3	18.6	42.6	1.1	69.6	9.5	63.0	0.7	1.8	0.2	1.1	0.5
Malawi	85.2	3.2	82.5	0.7	89.1	2.5	86.9	0.4	0.4	0.1	0.3	0.1
Mali	27.0	34.7	17.6	0.6	46.5	16.2	39.0	0.9	2.0	-0.1	1.3	0.9
Mozambique	64.5	10.1	58.0	1.7	75.1	7.9	69.2	0.9	1.9	0.4	1.2	0.3
Namibia	90.6	4.0	86.9	0.9	93.0	2.4	90.7	0.6	0.6	0.1	0.2	0.2
Niger	25.0	32.1	17.0	0.8	35.0	19.8	28.1	0.9	1.4	0.0	0.9	0.5
Nigeria	75.7	11.3	67.2	1.0	74.0	14.8	63.0	0.4	-0.5	-0.5	0.1	-0.1
Rwanda	67.3	5.6	63.6	0.9	91.5	2.2	89.5	0.5	2.6	0.2	2.1	0.3
Senegal					58.5	12.6	51.1	0.7				
Sierra Leone					70.9	10.2	63.7	0.9				
Tanzania	77.5	5.2	73.5	1.0	76.9	4.3	73.6	0.8	0.0	0.2	-0.2	0.0
Uganda	75.0	7.9	69.0	1.1	90.0	2.9	87.4	0.5	1.7	0.1	1.1	0.4
Zambia	75.1	8.1	69.0	0.9	89.8	2.9	87.2	0.7	1.7	0.1	1.2	0.4
Zimbabwe	89.4	2.4	87.3	0.8	88.3	2.6	86.0	0.7	-0.1	0.1	-0.2	0.0

Source: Authors' calculations using Demographic and Health Surveys data, various years.
Note: HOI = Human Opportunity Index; p.p = percentage point, SD = standard deviation.

Table A.3 Levels and Decomposition over Time: Started Primary School on Time

Country	Period 1 (circa 1998)				Period 2 (circa 2008)				Annual change HOI (p.p)	Composition effect (p.p)	Scale effect (p.p)	Equalization effect (p.p)
	Coverage (%)	D-Index (%)	HOI (%)	SD HOI (%)	Coverage (%)	D-Index (%)	HOI (%)	SD HOI (%)				
Cameroon	50.3	20.8	39.8	1.3	51.1	18.6	41.6	0.9	0.3	0.2	−0.1	0.2
Congo, Dem. Rep.					28.6	27.6	20.7	1.1				
Ethiopia	4.6	45.6	2.5	0.3	14.6	14.6	12.5	0.6	0.9	0.0	0.5	0.4
Ghana	51.2	14.7	43.7	1.4	27.8	11.9	24.5	0.9	−1.9	0.0	−2.0	0.1
Kenya	50.3	13.9	43.3	1.2	34.5	15.2	29.2	1.3	−1.4	0.0	−1.4	0.0
Liberia					4.8	33.5	3.2	0.4				
Madagascar	36.6	24.4	27.7	1.0	53.7	14.7	45.8	0.8	1.6	−0.1	1.2	0.5
Malawi	48.8	12.6	42.7	0.9	62.2	9.9	56.0	0.7	1.3	0.1	1.0	0.2
Mali	11.0	38.2	6.8	0.4	17.2	28.7	12.2	0.5	0.5	0.0	0.3	0.2
Mozambique	19.8	28.5	14.2	1.2	20.8	29.1	14.7	0.7	0.1	0.1	0.1	0.0
Namibia	20.4	12.4	17.9	1.2	33.4	10.6	29.9	1.1	1.9	0.0	1.7	0.1
Niger	5.4	46.7	2.9	0.3	11.4	28.3	8.2	0.5	0.7	0.0	0.4	0.2
Nigeria	48.9	22.9	37.7	1.0	42.2	19.1	34.1	0.5	−0.4	−0.1	−0.5	0.2
Rwanda	15.5	19.1	12.5	0.7	33.3	14.6	28.4	0.8	1.6	0.1	1.4	0.1
Senegal					29.9	18.8	24.3	0.6				
Sierra Leone					38.9	9.7	35.1	1.1				
Tanzania	3.3	36.3	2.1	0.3	28.7	20.6	22.8	0.9	1.5	0.0	1.2	0.3
Uganda	31.0	18.7	25.2	1.0	34.8	9.4	31.5	0.9	0.6	0.0	0.3	0.3
Zambia	13.5	36.6	8.5	0.5	21.1	24.7	15.9	0.8	0.7	−0.1	0.5	0.2
Zimbabwe	35.8	18.9	29.0	1.1	52.5	6.7	48.9	1.2	1.2	0.4	0.5	0.3

Source: Authors' calculations using Demographic and Health Surveys data, various years.
Note: HOI = Human Opportunity Index, p.p = percentage point, SD = standard deviation.

Table A.4 Levels and Decomposition over Time: Finished Primary School

Country	Period 1 (circa 1998)				Period 2 (circa 2008)				Annual change HOI (p.p)	Composition effect (p.p)	Scale effect (p.p)	Equalization effect (p.p)
	Coverage (%)	D-Index (%)	HOI (%)	SD HOI (%)	Coverage (%)	D-Index (%)	HOI (%)	SD HOI (%)				
Cameroon	27.9	33.8	18.4	1.1	34.8	29.7	24.5	0.8	1.0	0.3	0.6	0.1
Congo, Dem. Rep.					27.1	31.1	18.6	0.9				
Ethiopia	6.0	73.6	1.6	0.2	22.2	29.1	15.7	0.6	1.3	0.0	0.4	0.9
Ghana	49.4	17.5	40.8	1.6	51.0	17.1	42.3	0.9	0.2	-0.1	0.2	0.1
Kenya	39.1	19.0	31.7	1.1	55.3	14.4	47.3	1.3	0.9	0.1	0.7	0.1
Liberia					13.1	35.7	8.4	0.7				
Madagascar	10.2	61.8	3.9	0.4	24.1	39.5	14.6	0.5	0.9	0.1	0.5	0.4
Malawi	15.8	36.6	10.0	0.5	32.2	25.1	24.1	0.5	1.4	0.1	1.0	0.4
Mali	6.6	52.3	3.2	0.3	15.5	30.1	10.8	0.6	0.7	0.0	0.4	0.4
Mozambique	6.1	53.4	2.9	0.4	9.4	38.4	5.8	0.4	0.5	0.2	0.1	0.2
Namibia	44.9	20.8	35.5	1.6	61.1	12.6	53.5	1.0	2.8	0.4	1.7	0.7
Niger	14.4	39.0	8.8	0.7	10.4	43.6	5.9	0.5	-0.4	0.0	-0.3	-0.1
Nigeria	54.5	17.1	45.2	1.4	53.8	21.3	42.4	0.5	-0.3	-0.2	0.0	-0.1
Rwanda	6.2	36.3	3.9	0.4	12.4	29.5	8.7	0.4	0.5	0.0	0.4	0.1
Senegal					32.2	23.3	24.7	0.6				
Sierra Leone					32.2	24.3	24.4	0.9				
Tanzania	11.3	27.5	8.2	0.7	53.8	15.0	45.7	1.0	2.7	0.0	2.1	0.5
Uganda	16.3	31.4	11.2	0.8	22.3	28.6	16.0	0.7	0.4	0.1	0.2	0.1
Zambia	25.4	29.8	17.9	0.8	40.3	26.0	29.8	0.9	1.1	0.2	0.8	0.1
Zimbabwe	59.3	12.4	51.9	1.4	82.5	5.4	78.0	0.9	1.6	0.4	0.9	0.3

Source: Authors' calculations using Demographic and Health Surveys data, various years.

Note: HOI = Human Opportunity Index, p.p = percentage point, SD = standard deviation.

Table A.5 Levels and Decomposition over Time: Access to Piped-, Well-, or Rainwater

Country	Period 1 (circa 1998)				Period 2 (circa 2008)				Annual change HOI (p.p)	Composition effect (p.p)	Scale effect (p.p)	Equalization effect (p.p)
	Coverage (%)	D-Index (%)	HOI (%)	SD HOI (%)	Coverage (%)	D-Index (%)	HOI (%)	SD HOI (%)				
Cameroon	60.7	11.8	53.6	0.6	69.6	8.0	64.1	0.4	1.7	0.5	0.8	0.5
Congo, Dem. Rep.					34.6	44.3	19.3	0.3				
Ethiopia	67.2	4.2	64.4	0.4	43.1	16.0	36.3	0.4	-2.6	0.0	-2.2	-0.4
Ghana	69.5	10.6	62.2	0.6	80.7	2.8	78.5	0.3	1.6	0.2	0.7	0.7
Kenya	48.2	17.2	39.9	0.4	53.2	13.2	46.1	0.5	0.6	-0.1	0.5	0.2
Liberia					76.6	8.4	70.2	0.5				
Madagascar	38.3	23.6	29.3	0.4	50.0	16.5	41.7	0.3	1.1	-0.1	1.0	0.2
Malawi	89.4	2.2	87.4	0.2	94.2	0.9	93.3	0.1	0.6	0.0	0.4	0.1
Mali	96.1	1.3	94.9	0.2	95.8	1.3	94.6	0.1	0.0	0.0	0.0	0.0
Mozambique	69.0	10.2	62.0	0.8	83.4	5.1	79.2	0.3	2.9	0.3	1.6	0.9
Namibia	90.4	3.1	87.6	0.4	88.6	3.5	85.4	0.3	-0.3	0.1	-0.4	-0.1
Niger	91.4	2.6	89.1	0.2	98.3	0.3	98.0	0.1	1.1	0.1	0.8	0.2
Nigeria	58.2	10.5	52.1	0.5	72.7	4.8	69.2	0.2	1.9	0.0	1.4	0.5
Rwanda	44.6	12.7	38.9	0.4	36.1	14.4	30.9	0.3	-0.8	0.0	-0.7	-0.1
Senegal	97.0	0.7	96.3	0.2	96.4	0.7	95.7	0.2	0.0	0.0	0.0	0.0
Sierra Leone					62.2	14.0	53.4	0.4				
Tanzania	63.9	8.5	58.5	0.4	71.4	5.9	67.2	0.4	0.6	0.1	0.4	0.2
Uganda	45.9	10.1	41.3	0.5	87.4	2.2	85.4	0.3	4.0	0.0	3.3	0.6
Zambia	81.9	7.2	76.0	0.4	75.6	9.1	68.7	0.4	-0.7	-0.1	-0.4	-0.2
Zimbabwe	88.3	3.7	85.0	0.4	88.9	3.2	86.1	0.3	0.1	0.1	-0.1	0.0

Source: Authors' calculations using Demographic and Health Surveys data, various years.
Note: HOI = Human Opportunity Index, p.p = percentage point, SD = standard deviation.

Table A.6 Levels and Decomposition over Time: Access to Flush or Pit Toilet

Country	Period 1 (circa 1998)				Period 2 (circa 2008)				Annual change HOI (p.p)	Composition effect (p.p)	Scale effect (p.p)	Equalization effect (p.p)
	Coverage (%)	D-Index (%)	HOI (%)	SD HOI (%)	Coverage (%)	D-Index (%)	HOI (%)	SD HOI (%)				
Cameroon	89.2	5.4	84.4	0.4	91.9	4.1	88.1	0.3	0.6	0.3	0.2	0.1
Congo, Dem. Rep.					89.9	3.6	86.7	0.4				
Ethiopia	15.2	46.2	8.2	0.2	55.4	9.3	50.2	0.4	3.8	0.1	1.8	1.9
Ghana	74.0	11.1	65.8	0.5	73.4	13.3	63.6	0.3	-0.2	0.1	-0.2	-0.2
Kenya	82.4	6.9	76.7	0.4	82.3	9.4	74.5	0.4	-0.2	0.0	0.0	-0.2
Liberia					38.1	25.0	28.6	0.4				
Madagascar	36.2	27.6	26.2	0.4	52.3	18.9	42.4	0.3	1.4	0.0	1.0	0.4
Malawi	83.1	5.8	78.3	0.3	89.1	3.3	86.2	0.2	0.8	0.1	0.5	0.2
Mali	72.8	10.0	65.5	0.4	80.0	7.5	74.0	0.3	0.8	0.0	0.6	0.2
Mozambique	37.1	25.8	27.5	0.6	51.6	20.2	41.1	0.4	2.3	0.4	1.4	0.4
Namibia	36.0	44.0	20.2	0.4	38.8	44.2	21.7	0.3	0.2	0.5	-0.2	-0.1
Niger	19.4	59.0	7.9	0.2	18.4	57.6	7.8	0.2	0.0	0.0	0.0	0.0
Nigeria	73.2	7.7	67.5	0.4	66.3	11.2	58.9	0.2	-1.0	-0.1	-0.6	-0.2
Rwanda	97.0	1.1	95.9	0.2	97.8	0.7	97.2	0.1	0.1	0.0	0.1	0.0
Senegal	66.2	17.6	54.5	0.4	80.6	11.1	71.7	0.3	1.3	0.1	0.8	0.4
Sierra Leone					75.4	7.9	69.5	0.4				
Tanzania	85.9	4.6	82.0	0.4	82.3	6.8	76.7	0.4	-0.4	0.1	-0.3	-0.1
Uganda	82.5	4.8	78.6	0.4	87.4	5.2	82.8	0.3	0.4	0.1	0.4	-0.1
Zambia	72.6	13.8	62.5	0.4	74.5	11.5	65.9	0.4	0.3	0.0	0.2	0.1
Zimbabwe	56.7	21.5	44.5	0.5	67.6	14.7	57.6	0.4	0.8	0.2	0.4	0.2

Source: Authors' calculations using Demographic and Health Surveys data, various years.
Note: HOI = Human Opportunity Index, p.p = percentage point, SD = standard deviation.

Table A.7 Levels and Decomposition over Time: Access to Electricity

Country	Period 1 (circa 1998) Coverage (%)	D-Index (%)	HOI (%)	SD HOI (%)	Period 2 (circa 2008) Coverage (%)	D-Index (%)	HOI (%)	SD HOI (%)	Annual change HOI (p.p)	Composition effect (p.p)	Scale effect (p.p)	Equalization effect (p.p)
Cameroon	38.9	40.3	23.2	0.4	41.1	40.6	24.4	0.2	0.2	0.5	−0.1	−0.2
Congo, Dem. Rep.					15.2	65.1	5.3	0.1				
Ethiopia	8.7	85.5	1.3	0.0	15.3	63.3	5.6	0.1	0.4	0.0	0.1	0.3
Ghana	34.9	43.6	19.7	0.4	52.1	29.5	36.7	0.3	1.7	0.4	0.6	0.6
Kenya	9.0	70.2	2.7	0.1	13.9	64.8	4.9	0.2	0.3	0.0	0.1	0.2
Liberia					3.1	66.7	1.0	0.1				
Madagascar	8.7	74.0	2.3	0.1	13.2	71.0	3.8	0.1	0.1	0.0	0.1	0.1
Malawi	4.9	80.3	1.0	0.0	7.9	68.2	2.5	0.1	0.2	0.0	0.1	0.1
Mali	6.2	75.0	1.6	0.1	15.5	60.5	6.1	0.1	0.4	0.0	0.2	0.2
Mozambique	9.1	71.1	2.6	0.1	9.9	69.7	3.0	0.1	0.1	0.1	0.0	0.0
Namibia	26.0	57.5	11.1	0.2	33.4	53.6	15.5	0.2	0.7	0.3	0.3	0.1
Niger	7.1	80.1	1.4	0.1	8.8	71.1	2.5	0.1	0.1	0.0	0.1	0.1
Nigeria	44.0	35.9	28.2	0.3	45.1	35.0	29.3	0.2	0.1	−0.1	0.1	0.1
Rwanda	6.0	76.0	1.4	0.1	8.6	66.3	2.9	0.1	0.1	0.0	0.1	0.1
Senegal	29.2	55.8	12.9	0.2	50.8	36.5	32.3	0.2	1.5	0.0	0.8	0.7
Sierra Leone					9.2	64.9	3.2	0.1				
Tanzania	7.3	78.4	1.6	0.1	10.9	73.5	2.9	0.1	0.1	0.0	0.0	0.1
Uganda	5.9	72.7	1.6	0.1	6.0	73.2	1.6	0.1	0.0	0.0	0.0	0.0
Zambia	20.0	63.1	7.4	0.1	18.5	65.1	6.4	0.1	−0.1	−0.1	0.0	0.0
Zimbabwe	19.5	71.5	5.5	0.1	28.3	55.3	12.6	0.2	0.4	0.1	0.1	0.2

Source: Authors' calculations using Demographic and Health Surveys data, various years.
Note: HOI = Human Opportunity Index, p.p = percentage point, SD = standard deviation.

Table A.8 Levels and Decomposition over Time: Full Immunization (1 Year)

Country	Period 1 (circa 1998)				Period 2 (circa 2008)				Annual change HOI (p.p)	Composition effect (p.p)	Scale effect (p.p)	Equalization effect (p.p)
	Coverage (%)	D-Index (%)	HOI (%)	SD HOI (%)	Coverage (%)	D-Index (%)	HOI (%)	SD HOI (%)				
Cameroon	37.6	17.6	31.0	2.0	51.8	11.4	45.8	1.5	2.5	0.1	1.9	0.6
Congo, Dem. Rep.					34.4	13.7	29.7	1.7				
Ethiopia	15.4	26.1	11.4	0.9	27.9	18.1	22.9	1.4	1.0	0.1	0.6	0.3
Ghana	63.9	10.0	57.5	2.1	81.1	3.7	78.1	2.0	2.1	0.0	1.5	0.5
Kenya	64.9	6.5	60.7	1.8	70.9	6.1	66.6	2.3	0.6	0.0	0.5	0.0
Liberia					40.6	15.3	34.4	2.1				
Madagascar	37.8	23.0	29.1	1.5	62.4	11.7	55.2	1.3	2.3	0.0	1.7	0.6
Malawi	70.0	6.0	65.8	1.3	81.2	2.1	79.5	1.0	1.4	0.1	1.0	0.3
Mali	32.9	18.5	26.8	1.2	50.5	6.2	47.3	1.4	2.0	0.0	1.3	0.6
Mozambique	47.8	26.3	35.2	2.4	64.1	12.9	55.8	1.6	3.4	-0.3	2.2	1.5
Namibia	68.7	6.1	64.5	2.4	71.7	7.2	66.6	1.9	0.3	0.1	0.3	-0.1
Niger	18.8	38.9	11.5	0.8	30.8	14.2	26.5	1.4	1.9	0.0	0.9	0.9
Nigeria	19.7	37.2	12.4	0.9	24.5	34.8	16.0	0.5	0.4	0.2	0.1	0.1
Rwanda	79.1	3.1	76.6	1.4	89.9	2.0	88.0	0.9	1.1	-0.1	1.1	0.1
Senegal					63.1	3.7	60.8	1.3				
Sierra Leone					41.2	7.5	38.1	1.9				
Tanzania	72.1	6.7	67.2	1.6	75.8	5.1	71.9	1.5	0.3	0.0	0.2	0.1
Uganda	47.9	11.1	42.6	1.6	47.9	8.0	44.1	1.5	0.1	0.2	-0.2	0.1
Zambia	79.1	4.3	75.6	1.3	68.4	4.7	65.2	1.6	-1.0	0.0	-0.9	0.0
Zimbabwe	81.5	4.1	78.1	1.9	66.5	7.1	61.8	1.8	-1.0	0.3	-1.1	-0.2

Source: Authors' calculations using Demographic and Health Surveys data, various years.

Note: HOI = Human Opportunity Index, p.p = percentage point, SD = standard deviation.

Table A.9 Levels and Decomposition over Time: No Stunting (0–2 Years)

Country	Period 1 (circa 1998)				Period 2 (circa 2008)				Annual change HOI (p.p)	Composition effect (p.p)	Scale effect (p.p)	Equalization effect (p.p)
	Coverage (%)	D-Index (%)	HOI (%)	SD HOI (%)	Coverage (%)	D-Index (%)	HOI (%)	SD HOI (%)				
Cameroon	63.9	6.4	59.8	1.3	63.8	5.7	60.1	1.2	0.1	0.1	−0.1	0.1
Congo, Dem. Rep.					59.9	7.5	55.4	1.6				
Ethiopia	47.1	5.9	44.3	0.9	63.0	5.1	59.8	1.0	1.4	0.1	1.2	0.1
Ghana	73.4	3.9	70.5	1.2	75.0	2.9	72.8	1.3	0.2	0.1	0.0	0.1
Kenya	62.4	7.0	58.0	1.1	64.0	5.4	60.6	1.2	0.2	0.0	0.1	0.1
Liberia					66.9	4.6	63.8	1.2				
Madagascar	43.7	6.1	41.0	1.0	55.1	3.7	53.0	1.1	1.0	0.0	1.0	0.1
Malawi	48.9	7.1	45.4	0.8	53.2	5.5	50.2	1.2	0.5	0.3	0.2	0.1
Mali	63.2	4.9	60.1	0.8	64.2	5.1	61.0	0.7	0.1	0.0	0.0	0.0
Mozambique	53.8	8.9	49.0	1.8	55.5	7.7	51.3	1.0	0.4	−0.1	0.4	0.1
Namibia	73.1	3.8	70.2	1.4	69.3	6.6	64.7	1.1	−0.9	0.0	−0.6	−0.3
Niger	52.6	5.3	49.8	0.9	49.5	7.6	45.7	1.3	−0.5	0.0	−0.4	−0.1
Nigeria	34.1	11.9	30.0	0.9	57.4	6.2	53.8	0.5	2.6	0.1	2.2	0.4
Rwanda	58.1	5.0	55.2	0.9	59.1	7.3	54.8	1.1	0.0	−0.1	0.2	−0.2
Senegal					74.7	4.7	71.2	1.0				
Sierra Leone					66.3	4.6	63.2	1.5				
Tanzania	53.1	5.5	50.2	1.0	59.4	5.0	56.4	1.0	0.4	0.0	0.4	0.0
Uganda	56.9	5.5	53.7	1.0	65.1	4.5	62.2	1.4	0.8	0.1	0.7	0.0
Zambia	53.8	8.0	49.5	0.9	57.1	4.8	54.4	1.0	0.4	0.0	0.3	0.1
Zimbabwe	70.8	4.2	67.8	1.2	69.8	3.8	67.2	1.0	0.0	0.1	−0.2	0.0

Source: Authors' calculations using Demographic and Health Surveys data, various years.
Note: HOI = Human Opportunity Index, p.p = percentage point, SD = standard deviation.

Table A.10 Levels and Decomposition over Time: Composite Bundle (1 Year)

Country	Period 1 (circa 1998)				Period 2 (circa 2008)				Annual change HOI (p.p)	Composition effect (p.p)	Scale effect (p.p)	Equalization effect (p.p)
	Coverage (%)	D-Index (%)	HOI (%)	SD HOI (%)	Coverage (%)	D-Index (%)	HOI (%)	SD HOI (%)				
Cameroon	13.8	42.1	8.0	1.0	19.5	32.2	13.2	1.2	0.9	0.1	0.5	0.3
Congo, Dem. Rep.					9.9	63.6	3.6	0.6				
Ethiopia	2.6	78.9	0.6	0.1	8.2	54.2	3.8	0.5	0.3	0.0	0.1	0.2
Ghana	27.0	35.0	17.5	1.5	35.5	24.2	26.9	2.0	0.9	0.2	0.4	0.3
Kenya	18.2	35.3	11.8	1.0	20.5	37.5	12.8	1.2	0.1	0.2	0.0	-0.1
Liberia					10.7	37.3	6.7	0.9				
Madagascar	4.3	74.3	1.1	0.2	11.0	55.9	4.9	0.6	0.3	0.0	0.1	0.2
Malawi	22.4	22.9	17.2	0.9	29.7	13.4	25.8	1.6	0.9	0.2	0.4	0.2
Mali	17.4	31.4	11.9	0.8	23.8	18.7	19.3	1.0	0.7	0.0	0.4	0.3
Mozambique	15.9	51.2	7.8	0.9	20.0	48.4	10.3	0.6	0.4	-0.2	0.4	0.2
Namibia	22.0	47.0	11.6	1.1	22.3	54.5	10.2	0.8	-0.2	0.0	0.0	-0.2
Niger	4.2	78.0	0.9	0.1	5.4	71.6	1.5	0.3	0.1	0.0	0.0	0.0
Nigeria	3.4	59.2	1.4	0.3	8.1	50.5	4.0	0.2	0.3	0.1	0.1	0.1
Rwanda	18.2	33.3	12.1	0.9	17.1	34.2	11.2	1.1	-0.1	0.0	0.0	-0.1
Senegal					34.8	19.6	28.0	1.7				
Sierra Leone					8.2	43.8	4.6	0.9				
Tanzania	19.6	31.4	13.4	1.0	22.6	26.6	16.6	1.1	0.2	0.0	0.1	0.1
Uganda	11.3	35.7	7.3	0.7	20.1	13.3	17.4	1.9	0.9	0.1	0.5	0.4
Zambia	27.3	33.3	18.2	1.0	17.0	31.8	11.6	0.9	-0.6	-0.2	-0.4	0.0
Zimbabwe	32.7	33.3	21.8	1.5	28.0	29.9	19.6	1.2	-0.1	0.0	-0.2	0.0

Source: Authors' calculations using Demographic and Health Surveys data, various years.
Note: HOI = Human Opportunity Index, p.p = percentage point, SD = standard deviation.

Table A.11 Levels and Decomposition over Time: Composite Bundle (6–11 Years)

Country	Period 1 (circa 1998)				Period 2 (circa 2008)				Annual change HOI (p.p)	Composition effect (p.p)	Scale effect (p.p)	Equalization effect (p.p)
	Coverage (%)	D-Index (%)	HOI (%)	SD HOI (%)	Coverage (%)	D-Index (%)	HOI (%)	SD HOI (%)				
Cameroon	40.4	30.7	28.0	0.7	51.9	20.5	41.3	0.6	2.2	0.0	1.3	0.9
Congo, Dem. Rep.					25.1	53.5	11.7	0.4				
Ethiopia	7.1	74.7	1.8	0.1	16.0	41.3	9.4	0.3	0.7	0.0	0.2	0.5
Ghana	46.7	25.7	34.7	0.8	55.9	19.8	44.9	0.5	1.0	0.1	0.6	0.3
Kenya	37.4	28.8	26.6	0.6	43.8	25.8	32.5	0.7	0.6	0.0	0.4	0.1
Liberia					14.5	42.7	8.3	0.4				
Madagascar	19.1	64.7	6.7	0.2	26.3	45.6	14.3	0.3	0.7	-0.1	0.3	0.5
Malawi	60.4	16.3	50.6	0.5	74.6	7.8	68.8	0.4	1.8	0.0	1.1	0.7
Mali	22.2	40.0	13.3	0.3	32.3	22.5	25.0	0.5	1.1	0.0	0.6	0.6
Mozambique	23.2	48.0	12.1	0.6	32.1	41.4	18.8	0.3	1.1	0.1	0.7	0.3
Namibia	32.6	49.5	16.5	0.4	34.9	50.0	17.5	0.4	0.2	0.2	0.0	0.0
Niger	8.2	74.3	2.1	0.1	10.9	75.4	2.7	0.1	0.1	-0.1	0.1	0.0
Nigeria	26.4	33.9	17.5	0.5	36.4	29.3	25.7	0.3	0.9	0.0	0.7	0.3
Rwanda	26.8	34.2	17.6	0.4	28.8	24.1	21.9	0.4	0.4	0.2	0.0	0.2
Senegal					46.1	21.7	36.1	0.4				
Sierra Leone					35.2	29.4	24.8	0.5				
Tanzania	20.7	29.8	14.6	0.4	48.2	18.2	39.4	0.6	1.8	0.1	1.3	0.4
Uganda	26.3	27.2	19.1	0.5	67.8	10.7	60.6	0.6	3.8	0.0	2.7	1.1
Zambia	37.3	30.4	26.0	0.5	44.3	27.5	32.1	0.6	0.6	-0.1	0.5	0.1
Zimbabwe	45.1	28.7	32.1	0.6	57.5	22.3	44.7	0.6	0.8	0.1	0.4	0.2

Source: Authors' calculations using Demographic and Health Surveys data, various years.
Note: HOI = Human Opportunity Index, p.p = percentage point, SD = standard deviation.

Table A.12 Shapley Decomposition: School Attendance (6–11 Years)
Percent

	Marginal contribution to the total inequality of opportunities					
Country	Household composition	Household head's education	Other household head characteristics	Child characteristics	Location	Wealth
Cameroon	5.8	42.0	8.7	1.3	15.6	26.6
Congo, Dem. Rep.	1.9	30.8	2.5	2.8	27.9	34.2
Ethiopia	8.3	19.5	4.4	0.9	21.6	45.3
Ghana	12.4	35.5	9.9	0.4	11.1	30.7
Kenya	9.4	43.0	4.8	0.0	5.0	37.9
Liberia	1.6	24.9	4.1	3.8	32.0	33.6
Madagascar	10.1	34.3	1.5	1.1	6.7	46.3
Malawi	4.2	40.6	5.5	3.8	6.7	39.2
Mali	2.4	27.4	3.7	4.1	27.9	34.6
Mozambique	2.4	28.1	3.9	4.8	20.4	40.4
Namibia	13.2	46.2	13.3	2.6	5.5	19.3
Niger	2.2	17.7	3.9	13.8	26.3	36.2
Nigeria	6.5	34.1	6.3	2.2	12.2	38.8
Rwanda	7.1	28.0	7.1	4.3	6.2	47.3
Senegal	7.0	25.9	5.3	2.6	42.8	16.3
Sierra Leone	6.0	27.2	3.1	1.8	27.4	34.6
Tanzania	12.1	28.4	2.5	3.9	12.3	40.8
Uganda	2.2	34.5	1.3	0.9	7.2	53.9
Zambia	6.1	26.2	6.3	0.4	28.2	32.9
Zimbabwe	16.6	33.3	5.3	8.3	6.9	29.7

Source: Authors' calculations using Demographic and Health Surveys data, various years.

Table A.13 Shapley Decomposition: School Attendance (12–15 Years)
Percent

	Marginal contribution to the total inequality of opportunities					
Country	Household composition	Household head's education	Other household head characteristics	Child characteristics	Location	Wealth
Cameroon	3.8	44.0	8.7	7.3	11.4	24.8
Congo, Dem. Rep.	17.3	30.9	6.2	11.2	15.3	19.0
Ethiopia	18.7	17.7	6.0	7.0	15.0	35.6
Ghana	20.8	26.1	17.5	2.0	5.1	28.6
Kenya	6.5	34.7	4.2	0.2	2.9	51.5
Liberia	6.3	30.0	3.9	1.3	23.5	35.0
Madagascar	19.6	34.3	2.7	0.3	9.3	33.9
Malawi	19.8	42.9	7.5	0.3	3.3	26.3
Mali	8.4	17.8	5.3	11.3	25.6	31.6
Mozambique	12.4	29.2	3.5	9.5	15.4	30.0
Namibia	8.6	42.4	10.5	11.8	9.3	17.5
Niger	6.9	13.3	6.2	19.7	22.8	31.2

table continues next page

Table A.13 Shapley Decomposition: School Attendance (12–15 Years) *(continued)*
Percent

| Country | Marginal contribution to the total inequality of opportunities | | | | | |
	Household composition	Household head's education	Other household head characteristics	Child characteristics	Location	Wealth
Nigeria	5.2	32.7	10.2	2.1	12.6	37.2
Rwanda	65.1	4.7	11.6	1.5	2.3	14.9
Senegal	3.9	29.9	5.0	0.7	40.4	20.2
Sierra Leone	10.4	18.6	3.2	5.9	30.5	31.5
Tanzania	33.0	32.1	6.1	8.9	3.8	16.2
Uganda	27.1	31.1	8.1	2.5	1.0	30.1
Zambia	17.1	37.4	4.9	10.5	10.2	19.9
Zimbabwe	30.8	23.3	7.7	0.3	8.5	29.3

Source: Authors' calculations using Demographic and Health Surveys data, various years.

Table A.14 Shapley Decomposition: Started Primary School on Time
Percent

| Country | Marginal contribution to the total inequality of opportunities | | | | | |
	Household composition	Household head's education	Other household head characteristics	Child characteristics	Location	Wealth
Cameroon	6.5	34.1	7.8	0.5	17.0	34.1
Congo, Dem. Rep.	1.8	22.8	2.2	0.9	34.2	38.1
Ethiopia	12.6	10.7	7.5	0.5	20.3	48.6
Ghana	8.3	27.9	2.7	0.9	17.6	42.5
Kenya	20.1	27.4	9.6	4.0	3.9	35.0
Liberia	20.9	16.4	11.9	4.0	18.1	28.8
Madagascar	13.2	31.0	1.9	2.7	8.1	43.2
Malawi	5.3	40.8	9.1	1.3	7.5	36.0
Mali	1.7	28.1	1.1	0.5	26.9	41.7
Mozambique	1.6	26.1	2.4	1.5	28.8	39.6
Namibia	24.1	36.7	6.5	5.0	5.3	22.3
Niger	3.7	18.2	3.3	6.0	30.2	38.7
Nigeria	4.2	37.0	2.9	1.6	12.8	41.4
Rwanda	5.4	29.9	1.4	5.6	8.4	49.2
Senegal	7.8	28.9	4.7	6.1	32.9	19.7
Sierra Leone	11.7	18.2	9.5	6.2	20.0	34.4
Tanzania	13.4	22.2	2.7	13.0	12.1	36.4
Uganda	18.4	21.5	4.0	3.6	18.0	34.5
Zambia	8.7	24.7	1.5	2.4	28.6	34.0
Zimbabwe	9.7	29.7	6.6	12.3	8.2	33.6

Source: Authors' calculations using Demographic and Health Surveys data, various years.

Table A.15 Shapley Decomposition: Finished Primary School on Time

Percent

Country	Marginal contribution to the total inequality of opportunities					
	Household composition	Household head's education	Other household head characteristics	Child characteristics	Location	Wealth
Cameroon	8.4	30.0	7.4	0.2	22.0	32.1
Congo, Dem. Rep.	4.4	23.2	5.4	5.1	28.8	33.1
Ethiopia	7.1	17.2	7.1	5.8	28.4	34.4
Ghana	12.2	27.6	8.5	1.3	18.8	31.7
Kenya	11.0	34.0	2.6	3.7	5.2	43.5
Liberia	10.3	22.3	1.8	0.1	30.6	34.8
Madagascar	13.0	30.6	1.9	2.7	11.7	40.2
Malawi	4.3	34.3	3.7	5.4	13.3	38.9
Mali	7.2	26.3	1.1	3.2	25.7	36.5
Mozambique	6.5	26.2	3.7	0.4	28.4	34.8
Namibia	5.6	25.3	7.6	14.8	15.5	31.2
Niger	4.5	16.0	4.3	1.7	33.4	39.9
Nigeria	8.0	28.1	9.1	0.2	15.5	39.1
Rwanda	6.3	30.8	5.2	5.8	10.2	41.6
Senegal	7.3	25.0	4.8	1.3	36.1	25.6
Sierra Leone	3.3	19.6	2.9	3.3	37.2	33.8
Tanzania	7.2	23.6	3.6	12.1	14.9	38.6
Uganda	5.6	23.7	11.0	1.2	10.7	47.7
Zambia	3.7	26.4	3.3	1.6	27.9	37.2
Zimbabwe	8.3	26.3	7.8	11.2	14.1	32.2

Source: Authors' calculations using Demographic and Health Surveys data, various years.

Table A.16 Shapley Decomposition: Access to Piped-, Well-, or Rainwater

Percent

Country	Marginal contribution to the total inequality of opportunities					
	Household composition	Household head's education	Other household head characteristics	Child characteristics	Location	Wealth
Cameroon	7.2	4.1	4.6	0.1	59.2	24.8
Congo, Dem. Rep.	2.5	11.3	4.3	0.1	56.0	25.8
Ethiopia	4.8	21.2	5.5	0.7	48.1	19.6
Ghana	23.0	6.0	23.6	0.5	17.7	29.2
Kenya	4.9	10.0	3.1	0.5	34.2	47.3
Liberia	7.7	14.1	8.1	0.2	30.2	39.5
Madagascar	5.3	25.0	2.9	0.3	24.1	42.2
Malawi	8.1	24.0	5.3	0.8	24.2	37.6
Mali	11.4	10.5	2.9	0.5	34.3	40.5
Mozambique	8.9	15.8	7.4	0.2	41.9	25.9
Namibia	7.7	13.3	6.5	1.1	32.6	38.8
Niger	22.9	2.2	24.1	0.8	7.6	42.4

table continues next page

Table A.16 Shapley Decomposition: Access to Piped-, Well-, or Rainwater *(continued)*
Percent

Country	Household composition	Household head's education	Other household head characteristics	Child characteristics	Location	Wealth
			Marginal contribution to the total inequality of opportunities			
Nigeria	6.6	4.5	3.6	1.4	49.9	34.1
Rwanda	0.9	24.3	3.7	0.8	31.8	38.4
Senegal	33.0	19.2	14.1	0.3	28.0	5.5
Sierra Leone	2.7	13.4	2.9	0.2	49.0	31.8
Tanzania	10.4	9.3	2.3	1.1	31.2	45.6
Uganda	14.2	36.8	3.6	0.1	11.8	33.5
Zambia	6.9	11.7	3.7	0.3	38.3	39.1
Zimbabwe	5.6	16.8	4.2	0.0	35.9	37.4

Source: Authors' calculations using Demographic and Health Surveys data, various years.

Table A.17 Shapley Decomposition: Access to Flush or Pit Toilet
Percent

Country	Household composition	Household head's education	Other household head characteristics	Child characteristics	Location	Wealth
			Marginal contribution to the total inequality of opportunities			
Cameroon	8.9	20.8	4.6	0.3	28.4	37.0
Congo, Dem. Rep.	11.7	16.0	9.0	0.4	29.7	33.2
Ethiopia	4.2	37.1	3.4	0.5	21.6	33.2
Ghana	13.9	29.0	7.8	0.9	20.5	27.8
Kenya	9.4	35.6	3.4	0.9	8.1	42.5
Liberia	8.1	13.8	3.3	1.1	29.3	44.4
Madagascar	10.4	29.6	2.2	0.0	10.4	47.5
Malawi	5.4	23.9	12.5	0.4	10.5	47.4
Mali	5.6	12.9	1.3	0.4	25.2	54.5
Mozambique	4.6	21.9	3.5	0.1	38.0	32.0
Namibia	7.2	15.0	6.5	0.2	31.5	39.5
Niger	3.2	10.7	2.1	0.1	44.4	39.4
Nigeria	4.1	12.9	2.5	0.9	38.2	41.4
Rwanda	15.4	16.2	27.6	1.5	1.6	37.7
Senegal	4.3	10.9	7.6	0.0	31.3	45.9
Sierra Leone	18.7	9.2	4.6	0.1	36.6	30.8
Tanzania	15.1	33.5	4.1	0.6	18.9	27.8
Uganda	4.8	29.3	2.8	0.1	6.8	56.1
Zambia	2.0	20.9	3.3	0.2	37.1	36.4
Zimbabwe	6.2	13.8	1.8	0.1	30.0	48.0

Source: Authors' calculations using Demographic and Health Surveys data, various years.

Table A.18 Shapley Decomposition: Access to Electricity

Percent

	Marginal contribution to the total inequality of opportunities					
Country	Household composition	Household head's education	Other household head characteristics	Child characteristics	Location	Wealth
Cameroon	4.4	18.7	4.4	0.1	34.6	37.7
Congo, Dem. Rep.	2.7	14.6	4.1	0.1	31.2	47.2
Ethiopia	6.2	14.7	4.2	0.6	47.7	26.5
Ghana	6.7	17.7	4.0	0.5	28.4	42.8
Kenya	8.3	15.8	5.7	0.7	28.3	41.2
Liberia	4.6	18.6	2.5	0.9	20.4	53.0
Madagascar	6.4	22.6	1.2	0.3	24.2	45.3
Malawi	2.1	21.7	4.7	0.2	23.3	48.1
Mali	3.5	12.4	2.9	0.7	40.3	40.2
Mozambique	3.5	18.7	2.1	0.5	29.5	45.8
Namibia	7.6	12.8	8.4	0.1	30.6	40.4
Niger	3.4	13.5	2.5	0.3	40.1	40.3
Nigeria	2.4	17.9	1.6	0.2	31.7	46.2
Rwanda	1.5	20.3	4.1	0.3	24.2	49.6
Senegal	3.4	9.8	7.5	0.2	33.2	45.8
Sierra Leone	9.2	16.2	0.9	0.5	37.3	35.9
Tanzania	6.2	15.4	2.3	0.4	31.4	44.2
Uganda	4.8	16.8	2.1	0.3	26.3	49.7
Zambia	2.5	19.6	1.5	0.2	34.6	41.6
Zimbabwe	7.6	11.6	4.4	0.3	37.5	38.7

Source: Authors' calculations using Demographic and Health Surveys data, various years.

Table A.19 Shapley Decomposition: Full Immunization (1 Year)

Percent

	Marginal contribution to the total inequality of opportunities					
Country	Household composition	Household head's education	Other household head characteristics	Child characteristics	Location	Wealth
Cameroon	10.6	43.2	6.2	12.4	14.1	13.5
Congo, Dem. Rep.	3.9	26.5	9.1	7.3	20.9	32.3
Ethiopia	6.9	24.7	6.2	6.0	20.2	36.0
Ghana	16.7	20.9	9.0	11.5	5.1	36.7
Kenya	20.9	7.0	10.2	20.6	14.5	26.8
Liberia	5.5	10.2	14.5	8.9	21.9	39.0
Madagascar	4.9	31.8	5.5	9.8	6.0	42.0
Malawi	13.8	23.5	6.8	8.6	31.9	15.4
Mali	3.0	22.1	10.7	24.8	20.4	18.9
Mozambique	6.6	29.3	6.3	8.8	16.2	32.8
Namibia	9.3	40.2	5.4	9.2	6.7	29.2
Niger	2.8	19.1	10.1	7.2	23.5	37.4

table continues next page

Table A.19 Shapley Decomposition: Full Immunization (1 Year) (continued)
Percent

	Marginal contribution to the total inequality of opportunities					
Country	Household composition	Household head's education	Other household head characteristics	Child characteristics	Location	Wealth
Nigeria	3.4	37.8	6.0	5.4	15.1	32.3
Rwanda	15.0	26.8	6.5	10.2	4.8	36.6
Senegal	10.5	33.4	6.5	15.6	6.9	27.0
Sierra Leone	21.3	34.2	18.9	17.1	1.4	7.2
Tanzania	16.8	34.8	3.0	9.6	14.1	21.6
Uganda	8.1	39.3	8.5	31.1	2.3	10.7
Zambia	14.7	28.6	9.6	4.3	11.3	31.5
Zimbabwe	14.6	24.9	9.4	12.6	8.0	30.6

Source: Authors' calculations using Demographic and Health Surveys data, various years.

Table A.20 Shapley Decomposition: No Stunting (0–2 Years)
Percent

	Marginal contribution to the total inequality of opportunities					
Country	Household composition	Household head's education	Other household head characteristics	Child characteristics	Location	Wealth
Cameroon	6.4	20.6	6.6	16.9	23.0	26.4
Congo, Dem. Rep.	3.2	22.8	2.6	18.0	23.9	29.6
Ethiopia	10.8	21.2	5.6	23.1	12.5	26.8
Ghana	5.4	1.7	18.9	21.0	12.5	40.5
Kenya	6.0	14.8	11.0	16.0	12.0	40.2
Liberia	10.0	7.1	6.2	30.7	27.1	18.9
Madagascar	11.8	3.6	12.3	40.6	9.2	22.4
Malawi	9.0	19.0	4.5	48.6	3.2	15.7
Mali	2.8	13.5	7.2	21.1	26.0	29.4
Mozambique	8.8	25.6	2.3	13.0	18.8	31.4
Namibia	11.6	27.2	2.7	21.3	7.8	29.5
Niger	10.1	9.8	6.8	25.4	28.3	19.6
Nigeria	2.2	35.2	3.5	14.8	15.3	29.1
Rwanda	10.3	21.0	7.1	24.2	11.5	25.8
Senegal	12.0	15.6	5.9	22.0	14.1	30.4
Sierra Leone	6.1	19.3	7.1	35.8	13.4	18.2
Tanzania	9.1	14.8	8.5	28.2	16.1	23.4
Uganda	10.3	29.8	4.9	25.7	7.9	21.4
Zambia	5.8	13.1	2.4	39.9	12.5	26.3
Zimbabwe	18.1	13.4	3.1	33.9	16.7	14.7

Source: Authors' calculations using Demographic and Health Surveys data, various years.

Table A.21 Shapley Decomposition: Composite Bundle (1 Year)

Percent

Country		Marginal contribution to the total inequality of opportunities				
	Household composition	Household head's education	Other household head characteristics	Child characteristics	Location	Wealth
Cameroon	5.0	18.3	4.9	3.2	42.1	26.5
Congo, Dem. Rep.	5.9	16.4	1.4	3.9	35.5	36.9
Ethiopia	7.4	20.7	3.4	3.0	27.5	38.1
Ghana	4.7	18.7	4.0	2.1	23.1	47.4
Kenya	13.3	19.9	6.3	0.4	16.2	43.8
Liberia	5.7	13.4	7.4	4.6	30.5	38.4
Madagascar	13.6	19.5	2.6	3.4	10.0	51.0
Malawi	14.0	13.4	6.9	9.8	4.0	51.9
Mali	3.9	18.7	3.7	1.5	40.9	31.1
Mozambique	7.7	20.9	3.2	0.1	23.0	45.3
Namibia	10.0	13.9	1.2	2.0	22.9	49.9
Niger	6.1	13.0	7.1	1.7	28.3	43.7
Nigeria	5.9	30.5	3.9	1.9	20.2	37.6
Rwanda	8.7	19.3	1.1	3.2	10.0	57.7
Senegal	17.2	10.5	7.7	0.6	11.0	53.1
Sierra Leone	11.0	13.0	1.7	6.0	31.1	37.2
Tanzania	9.0	18.5	2.8	7.8	19.6	42.3
Uganda	11.9	9.4	9.5	14.6	6.3	48.3
Zambia	6.2	16.7	3.5	3.0	30.2	40.5
Zimbabwe	7.8	15.5	1.9	3.2	21.6	50.0

Source: Authors' calculations using Demographic and Health Surveys data, various years.

Table A.22 Shapley Decomposition: Composite Bundle (6–11 Years)

Percent

Country		Marginal contribution to the total inequality of opportunities				
	Household composition	Household head's education	Other household head characteristics	Child characteristics	Location	Wealth
Cameroon	5.0	19.4	4.0	0.1	31.9	39.5
Congo, Dem. Rep.	2.0	14.3	2.2	0.3	39.8	41.5
Ethiopia	6.0	17.6	2.6	0.3	26.8	46.7
Ghana	9.9	21.6	6.4	0.5	15.2	46.5
Kenya	6.3	14.5	3.2	1.2	17.7	57.1
Liberia	3.3	16.9	3.1	0.2	29.2	47.3
Madagascar	7.4	21.1	0.9	0.0	13.8	56.7
Malawi	3.6	28.0	6.0	1.7	8.4	52.4
Mali	2.0	24.5	3.2	3.0	31.1	36.2
Mozambique	2.3	16.9	1.9	0.6	26.6	51.8
Namibia	7.1	13.9	6.5	0.2	26.4	45.9
Niger	3.1	12.3	0.7	1.1	32.1	50.6

table continues next page

Table A.22 **Shapley Decomposition: Composite Bundle (6–11 Years)** *(continued)*
Percent

Country	Household composition	Household head's education	Other household head characteristics	Child characteristics	Location	Wealth
			Marginal contribution to the total inequality of opportunities			
Nigeria	1.5	21.9	0.7	1.0	26.6	48.3
Rwanda	1.9	21.1	2.5	0.4	17.7	56.4
Senegal	4.7	19.4	5.1	1.2	42.2	27.4
Sierra Leone	3.4	16.2	2.5	0.7	36.0	41.1
Tanzania	6.8	21.8	1.5	2.7	21.7	45.4
Uganda	3.8	24.5	1.2	0.4	8.0	62.0
Zambia	2.9	18.2	1.5	0.3	35.5	41.6
Zimbabwe	4.2	11.7	1.9	0.3	22.2	59.6

Source: Authors' calculations using Demographic and Health Surveys data, various years.

Table A.23 **Cross-Country Correlations between GDP, Income Inequality, and Inequality of Opportunity (circa 2008)**
Percent

	D-Index (composite HOI: 1-yr)	GDP per capita	Gini of consumption	HOI (composite for 1-yr-olds)
D-Index (composite HOI: 1-yr-olds)	1.00	−0.30	0.10	−0.87
GDP per capita	−0.30	1.00	0.01	0.31
Gini of consumption	0.10	0.01	1.00	−0.09
HOI (composite for 1-yr-olds)	−0.87	0.31	−0.09	1.00

Source: Authors' calculations using World Development Indicators (World Bank 2011) and Demographic and Health Surveys data, various years.

References

Demographic and Health Surveys. Various years. USAID. http://www. dhsprogram.com.

World Bank. 2011. *World Development Indicators.* http://data.worldbank.org/data-catalog/world-development-indicators/wdi-2011.

Environmental Benefits Statement

The World Bank Group is committed to reducing its environmental footprint. In support of this commitment, the Publishing and Knowledge Division leverages electronic publishing options and print-on-demand technology, which is located in regional hubs worldwide. Together, these initiatives enable print runs to be lowered and shipping distances decreased, resulting in reduced paper consumption, chemical use, greenhouse gas emissions, and waste.

The Publishing and Knowledge Division follows the recommended standards for paper use set by the Green Press Initiative. Whenever possible, books are printed on 50 percent to 100 percent postconsumer recycled paper, and at least 50 percent of the fiber in our book paper is either unbleached or bleached using Totally Chlorine Free (TCF), Processed Chlorine Free (PCF), or Enhanced Elemental Chlorine Free (EECF) processes.

More information about the Bank's environmental philosophy can be found at http://crinfo.worldbank.org/wbcrinfo/node/4.

www.ingramcontent.com/pod-product-compliance
Lightning Source LLC
Chambersburg PA
CBHW080422270326
41929CB00018B/3120